The
Common
Core
Lesson
Book
K–5

Working with Increasingly Complex Literature, Informational Text, and Foundational Reading Skills

Gretchen Owocki

Heinemann
Portsmouth, NH

Heinemann
361 Hanover Street
Portsmouth, NH 03801–3912
www.heinemann.com

Offices and agents throughout the world

The author and publisher wish to thank those who have generously given permission to reprint borrowed material:

Excerpts from the *Common Core State Standards* © Copyright 2010. National Governors Association Center for Best Practices and Council of Chief State School Officers. All rights reserved.

Figure RFS 2.2: 37 Most Common Rimes from "Teaching Vowels Through Phonograms" by Richard E. Wylie and Donald D. Durrell. Originally appeared in *Elementary English*, Vol. 47, pp. 787–791. Copyright © 1970 by the National Council of Teachers of English. Reprinted with permission of the publisher.

Library of Congress Cataloging-in-Publication Data
Owocki, Gretchen.
  The common core lesson book, K–5 : working with increasingly complex literature, informational text, and foundational reading skills / Gretchen Owocki.
      p.   cm.
  Includes bibliographical references.
  ISBN 978-0-325-04293-0
  ISBN 0-325-04293-4
  1. Language arts (Elementary). 2. Reading comprehension—Study and teaching (Elementary).   I. Title.

  LB1576.O95 2012
  372.6—dc23   2011047788

Editors: Kate Montgomery *and* Tobey Antao
Production: Vicki Kasabian
Cover design: Night & Day Design
Typesetter: Kim Arney
Manufacturing: Steve Bernier

Printed in the United States of America on acid-free paper
16 15 14 13   ML   5

CONTENTS

Reading : Literature

Instructional Strategies for

Reading : Literature

Reading : Literature

Reading : Informational Text

Reading : Informational Text

Instructional Strategies for

Reading : Informational Text

Reading : Foundational Skills

Reading : Foundational Skills

Instructional Strategies for

Phonics and Word Recognition   340

DEMONSTRATION

COLLABORATIVE ENGAGEMENT

INDEPENDENT APPLICATION

Fluency   356

Reading : Foundational Skills

Instructional Strategies for

For David and our little Emilia

• • •

And for four teachers:

Kae Hartford,
for eyes that merrily twinkled in response to anything from
students giving their best to a request for the meaning of a colorful
term. You took time to enjoy the phenomenon of childhood in
your classroom. I believe your magic had every one of your
students believing he or she was your favorite.

Wayne Salow,
for guiding students to see that The Odyssey and Death Be Not Proud
could actually be understood and enjoyed. You gave your students a reading
confidence that opened doors to lifelong learning.

Allen Roberts,
for tackling content that would be challenging to teach, but that would
endure. The ideas you brought to Albion changed my worldview forever.

Yetta Goodman,
for helping me find a lasting lens for viewing
children and their learning.

ACKNOWLEDGMENTS

I wish to express my gratitude to the people who have most influenced the writing of this book:

The graduate students at Saginaw Valley State University for providing so many outstanding examples of teaching at its best.

Melissa Kaczmarek for sending teaching strategies and writing mojo.

Emilia Owocki, Lucia Rumery, and Reagan Wood for the many instances of inspiration.

Kate Montgomery for the always-magnificent eye.

OVERVIEW

Everywhere we turn, conversations about the Common Core State Standards (CCSS) are at hand. National conferences are providing sessions; state departments are holding meetings; books and journal articles are being published; blogs are buzzing; websites are popping up; and teachers are sharing ideas. For the first time ever, schools across the United States are expected to use a common set of literacy standards to guide assessment and instruction—and educators and school leaders are grappling with the implications.

Many are examining their existing practices in light of the new standards and are beginning to make curricular and instructional overhauls. They have analyzed how the new standards align with the existing standards, and are working with the new elements they feel need their attention first. Others are wondering whether it is enough to simply be aware of the new standards—and for the most part to continue with or gently tweak existing practices. Others, admittedly, have never paid much attention to standards and are wondering if there is a reason to pay attention now. Some educators are concerned that new standards—regardless of how they're used—may not have much positive impact on student learning; after all, good teaching is good teaching regardless of the standards we have. And there are others who fear that because standards are quite often linked with standardized testing, teachers will feel compelled to place an emphasis on test preparation rather than on fostering broadly meaningful literacy. Clearly, the issues are complex.

Some Options

Within such complexity, we could approach the adoption of the standards in a number of ways. We could sit tight until we have more information regarding how the new standardized assessments will play out, or until we know exactly what our state offices will be recommending regarding curriculum development. But this might leave our kids out of something that is potentially important. After all, there are many educators across the country fervently discussing how to use the standards to make our instruction better: more engaging, more connected to students' lives, and more in touch with their needs as learners. And watching from the sidelines would imply that we have nothing to contribute.

So another possible response is to get focused and assess and teach what we think the standards developers must have intended. Schools could quickly scramble to provide professional development opportunities and teachers could look for ideas to develop instruction in areas they deem not strong enough. But such efforts don't necessarily involve a system for nurturing a balanced or manageable approach that's based on solid evidence, planning, and discussion.

Yet another option is for educators to come together and start looking for curricular programs that advertise "comprehensive" and "research-based" ways to meet the Common Core standards. But we are teaching in an era in which research evidence has confirmed that the teacher—not the program— is the most important variable in student achievement (Brown 2010–2011; Cunningham and Allington 2011; Wong and Wong 2010).

The Places We Could Go

At the crossroads created by the Common Core State Standards, there are many paths we could take. I suggest avoiding paths that cast educators as secondary decision makers or that offer quick solutions or packages. This crossroads provides an opportunity for educators to pave new paths with fresh and critical conversations about teaching and learning.

As we shape the new system and work within it, we must not lose sight of meaningful teaching and learning. There are concerns that CCSS progression might be too narrow, too prescriptive, and too detached from life in schools to allow for a positive impact. After all, meaningful teaching can only take shape in response to real children in real classrooms. So from the start we must *take hold* of these standards, *use them as a guide* rather than a formula, and *supplement* them, all in ways that have research support and that maintain students' engagement and deep learning.

Within the new system, we can still provide opportunities for students to participate in multiple forms of reading in multiple text environments. We can still offer them choice, and opportunities to experience the pleasure of reading text they see as good. We need not let standards or standardized testing take away from what we do well in classrooms or compel us to change our teaching so that students spend their school days practicing for tests, studying isolated skills, or sitting hunched over piles of work.

But as we consider the new standards, the time *is* ripe for improvement. The time *is* ripe to consider ways to shift and alter our practices, and to weed out practices that are not conducive to meaningful learning. More than ever, we must find ways to connect students with texts that they can read and that motivate them to want to read more. We must home in on carefully selected formative assessments that allow us to understand what each child needs in order to grow as a reader. We must implement instructional practices that foster deep and engaged reading. And we must take the responsibility of differentiating our instruction to ensure that each student receives well-tailored, responsive support.

Organization of the Book

The goal of *The Common Core Lesson Book* is to support K–5 teachers as they provide authentic, meaning-based, differentiated instruction related to the Common Core standards in the area of English language arts. The English Language Arts Standards are organized into six categories:

- Reading: Literature
- Reading: Informational Text
- Reading: Foundational Skills
- Writing
- Speaking and Listening
- Language

The Common Core Lesson Book offers a set of teaching strategies related to the first three categories: (1) Reading: Literature; (2) Reading: Informational Text; (3) Foundational Skills for Reading. The book is organized into three parts, one for each of these categories.

Part 1—Instructional Strategies for Reading: Literature

The Reading: Literature standards offer a focus for literature-based instruction with fiction, drama, and poetry. As shown in Table A, there are nine anchor standards for the literature category. Part 1 is organized into nine sections, one per anchor standard. Each section begins with a chart showing the specific grade-level competencies designated for the anchor at hand, followed by a comprehensive set of instructional strategies related to that standard. The strategies are organized into three categories: demonstration, collaborative engagement, and independent application.

Table A

Category	Anchor Standards for Reading: Literature K–5	Page
Key Ideas and Details	1. Read closely to determine what the text says explicitly and to make logical inferences from it; cite specific textual evidence when writing or speaking to support conclusions drawn from the text. 2. Determine central ideas or themes of a text and analyze their development; summarize the key supporting details and ideas. 3. Analyze how and why individuals, events, and ideas develop and interact over the course of a text.	**3**
Craft and Structure	4. Interpret words and phrases as they are used in a text, including determining technical, connotative, and figurative meanings, and analyze how specific word choices shape meaning or tone. 5. Analyze the structure of texts, including how specific sentences, paragraphs, and larger portions of the text (e.g., a section, chapter, scene, or stanza) relate to each other and the whole. 6. Assess how point of view or purpose shapes the content and style of a text.	**53**
Integration of Knowledge and Ideas	7. Integrate and evaluate content presented in diverse media and formats, including visually and quantitatively, as well as in words. 8. NOT APPLICABLE TO THE LITERATURE CATEGORY. 9. Analyze how two or more texts address similar themes or topics to build knowledge or to compare the approaches the authors take.	**112**
Range of Reading and Level of Text Complexity	10. Read and comprehend complex literary and informational texts independently and proficiently.	**144**

Part 2—Instructional Strategies for Reading: Informational Text

Part 2 focuses on reading informational text. The Reading: Informational Text standards offer a focus for literature-based instruction with nonfiction. As shown in Table B, there are ten anchor standards for informational text. The Informational Text standards directly match the standards for Literature, except that anchor 8 is designated as not applicable to the Literature category.

Paralleling the format of Part 1, Part 2 is organized into ten sections, one per anchor standard. As in Part 1, each section in Part 2 begins with a chart showing the specific grade-level competencies designated for the anchor standard at hand, followed by a comprehensive set of instructional strategies related to that standard. The strategies are organized into three categories: demonstration, collaborative engagement, and independent application.

Category	Anchor Standards for Reading: Informational Text K–5	Page
Key Ideas and Details	1. Read closely to determine what the text says explicitly and to make logical inferences from it; cite specific textual evidence when writing or speaking to support conclusions drawn from the text. 2. Determine central ideas or themes of a text and analyze their development; summarize the key supporting details and ideas. 3. Analyze how and why individuals, events, and ideas develop and interact over the course of a text.	**151**
Craft and Structure	4. Interpret words and phrases as they are used in a text, including determining technical, connotative, and figurative meanings, and analyze how specific word choices shape meaning or tone. 5. Analyze the structure of texts, including how specific sentences, paragraphs, and larger portions of the text (e.g., a section, chapter, scene, or stanza) relate to each other and the whole. 6. Assess how point of view or purpose shapes the content and style of a text.	**206**
Integration of Knowledge and Ideas	7. Integrate and evaluate content presented in diverse media and formats, including visually and quantitatively, as well as in words. 8. Delineate and evaluate the argument and specific claims in a text, including the validity of the reasoning as well as the relevance and sufficiency of the evidence. 9. Analyze how two or more texts address similar themes or topics to build knowledge or to compare the approaches the authors take.	**259**
Range of Reading and Level of Text Complexity	10. Read and comprehend complex literary and informational texts independently and proficiently.	**293**

Part 3—Instructional Strategies for Reading: Foundational Skills

Part 3 focuses on foundational skills for reading. The Reading: Foundational Skills category offers a focus for instruction in skills and strategies related to decoding. As shown in Table C, this category has four overarching skill areas.

Part 3 is organized into four sections, one per skill area. Each section in Part 3 begins with a chart showing the specific grade-level competencies designated for the skill area at hand, followed by a comprehensive set of instructional strategies related to that skill. The strategies are organized into three categories: demonstration, collaborative engagement, and independent application.

Table C

Category	Foundational Skills for Reading K–5	Page
Print Concepts	1. Demonstrate understanding of the organization and basic features of print.	**299**
Phonological Awareness	2. Demonstrate understanding of spoken words, syllables, and sounds (phonemes).	**320**
Phonics and Word Recognition	3. Know and apply grade-level phonics and word analysis skills in decoding words.	**340**
Fluency	4. Kindergarten: Read emergent-reader texts with purpose and understanding. Grades 1-5: Read with sufficient accuracy and fluency to support comprehension.	**356**

The Approach

The Common Core Lesson Book is designed to support differentiated instruction. Rather than presenting instructional strategies for one grade level at a time, the K–5 range is approached collectively for each standard. This allows teachers to examine a range of strategies and choose those that best match their students' needs. For example, some second-grade students may benefit from temporarily working on some Common Core competencies that are suggested for kindergarten and first-grade; or the whole class may benefit from working with these standards as a review early in the year. Others may benefit from working beyond the grade-level recommendations. The book is designed so that when planning instruction, teachers can consider the K–5 range, selecting and adapting according to their particular students' needs. Teachers working in intervention or Response to Intervention settings can select experiences that are particularly well matched with the needs of their small groups.

The Types of Instruction

Rather than providing a "curriculum" to follow, *The Common Core Lesson Book* provides a comprehensive framework of strategies for enhancing a curriculum that is already in place. For each standard/skill area, three types of experience are suggested:

- demonstration
- collaborative engagement
- independent application

This layout makes it possible to implement an approach of demonstrating various techniques for reading, exploring, and discussing text—and then encouraging a gradual takeover of responsibility by the students.

Demonstration

Teacher guidance is high during the demonstration phase, with the teacher leading the discussion and laying out explicit strategies and expectations for reading and interpreting text. Demonstration on a topic may take just one or two sessions but then be used again as students need further support.

Each demonstration section includes a general lesson that can be used with small groups or the whole class throughout the year. The lessons serve to build a common language for conversation and group activity. Along with a general lesson, most of the demonstration sections also include one or two lessons designed for intensifying the instruction. These lessons set students up to use the strategies in a guided situation with heavy teacher support. For example, Anchor 1 is focused on *close reading*. The general lesson is presented first, with the teacher demonstrating. This is followed by two lessons for intensifying the instruction. The lessons for intensifying the instruction focus on student *monitoring* and *inferring*, both of which are critical components of close reading. The students do the reading as the teacher observes and supports. All demonstration and intensifying lessons may be implemented with small groups (including intervention-based groups) or the whole class.

Collaborative Engagement

Guidance is still high in the collaborative engagement phase, but with more allowance and encouragement for students to take responsibility for their own thinking and discussion. Typically one or two days are planned for collaborative engagement, with the teacher returning to this phase as students demonstrate a need.

In the collaborative engagement sections you will find ideas for supporting group activity and conversation in relation to the concepts taught in the demonstration phase. As with the demonstration sections, the collaborative engagement sections come with starter prompts to help get conversations and activities started in meaningful directions. The prompts require that students not only talk but also use other forms of activity (viewing, drawing, labeling, mapping, reading back through the text) to complete an assignment together. At any time during this collaborative engagement phase of instruction, the teacher may come back to the demonstration phase to provide further support.

Independent Application

In the independent application phase, students work independently or with peers with much less teacher guidance, the expectation being that the strategies and concepts have been internalized. In the independent application sections, ideas are provided for supporting ongoing reading and writing experiences that will help students further explore and internalize the concepts you are teaching. It is here that students will individually or collaboratively demonstrate their knowledge in relation to the standards, and you will find numerous opportunities for assessment as well as for providing over-the-shoulder support. At any time during this independent application phase of instruction, you may come back to the demonstration phase to provide further guidance.

The Role of the Teacher

Working effectively with the standards requires the critical understanding that the teacher—not the standard or the program—is the most important variable affecting student achievement (Cunningham and Allington 2011; Wong and Wong 2010). A set of goals or materials is only as good as the instruction associated with it. The teacher makes the decisions that create the effective classroom; the teacher knows the children, their strengths, their experiences, and their needs; and the teacher can use this knowledge to create the climate, culture, and curriculum for meaningful learning.

Over the past several decades, our field has accumulated a wide body of knowledge that helps teachers and teaching teams make effective decisions, and we are just beginning to consider the implications in terms of Common Core instruction. Table D shows the characteristics of classrooms considered effective in supporting literacy (synthesized by Cunningham and Allington 2011 and Wong and Wong 2010), with implications for informing Common Core instruction. You can use the chart as a tool for evaluating areas that might warrant further development in your classroom or school.

Characteristics of Effective Classrooms	Implications for Common Core Instruction	Rating 1 = doing well 2 = almost there 3 = area to develop
Literacy instruction is balanced to include the various aspects of reading and writing (Cunningham and Allington 2011).	The Common Core standards emphasize a broad range of competencies including reading of narrative text, reading of informational text, using skills and processes for decoding, and writing in multiple genres. Plan to balance your instruction across all of these areas.	1 2 3
Children do extensive reading and writing throughout the day (Cunningham and Allington 2011).	Plan for students to spend as much time as possible during the literacy block engaged in actual reading and writing rather than in peripheral tasks that might emphasize only one standard or skill at a time. Skill practice can be helpful, but should not consume the literacy block. In addition to extensive reading and writing *during* the literacy block, also plan for reading and writing throughout the day, particularly as it supports content area learning.	1 2 3
Science and social studies maintain an important place in the school day and are integrated with reading and writing (Cunningham and Allington 2011).	Do not cut science and social studies time to lengthen the literacy block. Instead, use the Common Core literacy standards when planning content area instruction. Such integration across content areas is a way to use time efficiently, and helps ensure that careful attention is paid to children's vocabulary development, to their skill negotiating content area reading material, and to their capacity for using reading and writing as tools for learning.	1 2 3
Literacy instruction emphasizes meaningful communication and higher-level thinking skills (Cunningham and Allington 2011).	When teaching toward Common Core standards, plan for the students' activity to always be in relation to meaningful acts of reading, writing, and communicating. Rather than teaching a skill or strategy "just" so children will learn to demonstrate competency with it, teach so they can actually use the skill or strategy to support meaningful activity. Keep in mind that different children come to your classroom with different funds of knowledge. What is considered *meaningful* varies across children, classrooms, and communities.	1 2 3
Literacy skills are taught explicitly, and support is provided as children use the skills in reading and writing (Cunningham and Allington 2011).	Plan times for explicit instruction through whole-class, small-group, and one-on-one demonstration. The Common Core standards provide guidance for determining the skills to teach but the children's actual demonstrations of knowledge should inform the specifics of instruction.	1 2 3

Table D (continued)

Characteristics of Effective Classrooms	Implications for Common Core Instruction	Rating 1 = doing well 2 = almost there 3 = area to develop
Whole-class, small-group, and individual settings are used for instruction. Groups are flexible, depending on children's needs. Instruction is provided so that mastery for all students is achievable (Cunningham and Allington 2011; Wong and Wong 2010).	Determine the settings in which the different standards are most meaningfully taught and explored: whole class, small group, and individual. Use formative assessment to determine where individual students' needs lie, and group the students accordingly.	1 2 3
A wide range of materials (rather than one program or set of materials) is used to support instruction (Cunningham and Allington 2011).	Don't be afraid to make professional decisions. Standards and materials purported to help meet them are most useful when teachers understand that they have the authority to teach beyond them; to spend lots of time with some and explore others to a lesser extent; and to determine which are most appropriate for emphasis at any given time. Closely adhering to only one program or set of materials does not allow for such decision making.	1 2 3
The class is well managed so that high-quality instruction and learning can occur; students show high levels of engagement (Cunningham and Allington 2011; Wong and Wong 2010).	Implement clearly defined procedures and routines in which you guide students through a rich set of reading and writing experiences each day. Make true engagement possible by ensuring that classroom literacy experiences take into account student backgrounds and interests; allow for choice and agency; and seem meaningful and important. To hold children's attention, the texts available for reading should be accessible, with *all* of the children able to find material at their independent and instructional reading levels.	1 2 3
The teacher holds high and positive expectations for student achievement (Wong and Wong 2010).	Approach teaching as if all students "can." Differentiate instruction so that all students find classroom experiences challenging but achievable, providing extra support for those who are progressing more slowly.	1 2 3

Transforming Your Teaching

I created this book because of my desire to participate in the national conversation about teaching practices that has emerged in relation to the Common Core. I wanted to offer encouragement to stay grounded in meaningful instruction, as well as offer a set of strategies to be implemented in the interest of meaningful reading and writing.

But along the way, I really hoped for something more. I really hoped that through reading and exploring the ideas in this book, you would see with more certainty than ever that creating and adapting your *own* effective lessons and instructional designs, with standards as a guide, is within your reach. To create this book, I did little more than match strategies with standards in a way that would offer choices and possibilities for differentiation in terms of how the standards might be taught and explored. I adapted and fine-tuned in ways that I thought would honor the intent of the standards, and at the same time respect the fact that children are only five, six, seven, eight, nine, and ten years old only once in their lives. In this enchanting period they should experience deep satisfaction and pleasure in reading in the social environment of the classroom. I wanted to create opportunities that children would *want* to engage in, putting meaningful reading, writing, and inquiry at the core.

You can do the same. You can use and adjust the structure offered here to create your own lasting lessons and to continually add and adapt teaching strategies you know will have meaning to your students. To do this, you do not need to turn your attention away from your existing curriculum or from the literature you may be using—but don't be afraid to steer yourself, to step beyond scripts and programs, and to use your professional knowledge. Collaborate with your colleagues; talk about connections between your teaching and your objectives; and most important, talk about what keeps your students engaged with learning. Our task is, and always will be, to watch our students and to set the school-based learning process in motion through their interests and experiences.

PART ONE

Instructional Strategies for
Reading: Literature

The Common Core Reading: Literature standards are designed to guide instruction with fiction, drama, and poetry. The nine anchor standards (outlined in Table A) provide overarching goals for K–12 students, and the more specific sets of standards (outlined at the beginning of each section in Part 1) define the specific competencies K–5 students are expected to develop by each year's end. In general, students are expected to work with their grade-level standards, using increasingly complex text as they move through the K–5 years. This is with the understanding that some students will need extra support mastering certain competencies from earlier grades before they can demonstrate full competency with their own grade-level standards. In turn, others may be ready to move forward and explore concepts and use texts beyond the range recommended.

In Part 1 you will find nine sections, each focused on a separate literature anchor standard. Within each section, you will find a set of instructional practices involving demonstration, collaborative engagement, and independent application. These three types of experience used in sequence serve as a frame for supporting students in gradually taking control of complex thinking and activity in relation to each standard.

To support differentiation, each section begins with a decision tree to help you determine whether to pursue the lesson sequence for the anchor at hand. You may decide to use the sequence with all of your students or only a small group—or you may determine that your students are already performing well in the area and you can place your focus elsewhere. The decision tree will also help you consider whether intensified instruction may be warranted for some or all of your students in the focus area. Lessons for intensifying the instruction are provided for each standard. As you select the learning experiences, you will see that there are ideas appropriate for instruction across the K–5 range. You should pick and choose the experiences based on your students' demonstrated needs.

Category	Anchor Standards for Reading: Literature K–5	Page
Key Ideas and Details	**1.** Read closely to determine what the text says explicitly and to make logical inferences from it; cite specific textual evidence when writing or speaking to support conclusions drawn from the text. **2.** Determine central ideas or themes of a text and analyze their development; summarize the key supporting details and ideas. **3.** Analyze how and why individuals, events, and ideas develop and interact over the course of a text.	**3**
Craft and Structure	**4.** Interpret words and phrases as they are used in a text, including determining technical, connotative, and figurative meanings, and analyze how specific word choices shape meaning or tone. **5.** Analyze the structure of texts, including how specific sentences, paragraphs, and larger portions of the text (e.g., a section, chapter, scene, or stanza) relate to each other and the whole. **6.** Assess how point of view or purpose shapes the content and style of a text.	**53**
Integration of Knowledge and Ideas	**7.** Integrate and evaluate content presented in diverse media and formats, including visually and quantitatively, as well as in words. **8.** NOT APPLICABLE TO THE LITERATURE CATEGORY. **9.** Analyze how two or more texts address similar themes or topics to build knowledge or to compare the approaches the authors take.	**112**
Range of Reading and Level of Text Complexity	**10.** Read and comprehend complex literary and informational texts independently and proficiently.	**144**

KEY IDEAS AND DETAILS   ANCHOR 1

English Language Arts Standards Reading: Literature **ANCHOR 1**

Reading Anchor 1: Read closely to determine what the text says explicitly and to make logical inferences from it; cite specific textual evidence when writing or speaking to support conclusions drawn from the text.

K	First	Second	Third	Fourth	Fifth
With prompting and support, ask and answer questions about key details in a text.	Ask and answer questions about key details in a text.	Ask and answer such questions as who?, what?, where?, when?, why?, and how? to demonstrate understanding of key details in a text.	Ask and answer questions to demonstrate understanding of a text, referring explicitly to the text as the basis for the answers.	Refer to details and examples in a text when explaining what the text says explicitly and when drawing inferences from the text.	Quote accurately from a text when explaining what the text says explicitly and when drawing inferences from the text.

Decision Tree for **Reading: Literature** ANCHOR 1

Do my students need focused instruction in relation to Reading Anchor 1?

Anchor 1 requires that students *read closely, determining what the text says explicitly and making logical inferences.* (Refer to your grade-level standards for specific details.)

When some or all of your students could use support in this area, it is recommended that you start the process by implementing three types of instruction in sequence over the course of about a week:

Demonstration	**Collaborative Engagement**	**Independent Application**
Page 5	**Page 12**	**Page 14**

The initial demonstration requires just one session (to be repeated as needed), leaving one or two days for collaborative engagement and one or two days to begin the independent applications, which become ongoing as you choose. If you find during any phase of the instruction that some or all of your students could use intensified support, it is recommended that you move to the lessons for intensifying the instruction.

Do my students need intensified support with monitoring?

Monitoring is a comprehension strategy that involves keeping close track of meaning and using repair strategies when meaning gets off track. Students who need intensified support with monitoring are those who decode successfully but often come away from their independent or supported reading with an incomplete grasp of the text's key ideas and details, as demonstrated through retellings, conversation, and answering planned sets of questions. See page 10.

Do my students need intensified support with inferring?

Close reading requires not only determining what the text says explicitly, but also inferring. Inferring is a comprehension strategy that involves drawing conclusions about content and vocabulary using textual information *as well as* prior knowledge. Lessons related to inferring can be useful for all students, but particularly for those whose responses to text generally reflect lower-level thinking or little interpretation beyond what is on the page. See page 11.

Demonstration

Anchor 1 requires that students *read closely*, determining what the text says explicitly and making inferences as appropriate. Close reading involves reading for deep understanding. The goal is to enable an interpretation that includes the details as well as the bigger ideas. The present lesson is designed to help students understand what is expected in terms of close reading and to build a common language for conversation and group activity in relation to this standard. This lesson may be implemented several times, using a different text each time.

1. **Choose the text.** Choose a text for demonstration that will capture your students' interests—something that will make them *want* to read or listen closely.

2. **Introduce the text and the concept.** Let students know that you will be showing them how to engage in a process of *reading closely and responding* and that they will then be expected to do this on their own and in groups. Close reading demonstrations provide an opportunity to model and discuss key reading strategies:

   * *monitoring:* tracking comprehension and using repair strategies as needed to keep meaning on track

   * *inferring:* drawing conclusions using information from the text along with prior knowledge

   * *questioning:* asking and seeking answers to who, what, when, where, why, and how questions

   * *visualizing:* mentally representing the text events

   * *deciding what's important:* using reader purpose to determine important ideas and themes

   * *summarizing:* rethinking key ideas and details

3. **Demonstrate and discuss the concept.** Read the text aloud, pausing at points to show the students how you read closely, tracking meaning, monitoring your understandings, and thinking through any questions you may have. Let them "see" your thinking processes, and encourage them to do the same types of deep thinking as they read independently. Figure RL 1.1 offers a starter set of prompts designed to help you demonstrate and discuss the process of close reading. The prompts may be used with poetry and fiction.

READING ANCHOR 1:
Prompts to Support Teacher-Led Modeling and Discussion

Kindergarten and First Grade

- We are going to read this part closely so that we can talk through what happened. (As you read, help your students attend to detail by pausing and encouraging them to "think this through" and "picture this in your mind." Show students your thinking processes as you construct meaning.) What happened? What details did you see in your mind?

- I had a question about _____. Did you have any questions? (You may write the questions on a whiteboard to help make the process concrete.)

- After we read, I will ask you to record one important part of the story, using good detail. You may draw or write. Pay close attention because your work will be a tool for sharing your ideas with friends and talking to your family about what you have read. (Figure RL 1.2 provides a template.)

Second and Third Grades

- Let's work together to track what happens in each part and think through any questions we may have.

- We are going to work together to map out a set of who, what, where, when, why, and how questions and answers. (Figure RL 1.3 provides a template.)

Fourth and Fifth Grades

- Let's work together to track what happens in each part. Describe what happened here. Does it say that *explicitly* or are we to *infer* that? What information helps us to infer that?

- Which details and examples are we thinking about as we track meaning? What questions do we have?

- What is your opinion about this character (event)? What evidence from the text supports that? (Figure RL 1.4 provides a template for recording observations.)

I Read Closely!

Name: _____ Date: _____

Title: _____

Key Feature Map

Name: _____ Date: _____

Title: _____

Who	What

Where	When

Why	How

Evidence from the Text

Name: _____ Date: _____

Title: _____

Character or event

An opinion or observation about the character or event

Supporting evidence from the text

-
-
-
-
-

INTENSIFYING THE INSTRUCTION
Monitoring

Monitoring is a comprehension strategy that involves keeping close track of meaning and using repair strategies when meaning gets off track. To become effective at monitoring, students benefit from support that will help them *during* the act of reading (Boulware-Gooden et al. 2007; Keene and Zimmermann 2007). Ultimately, we want students to attend to meaning as they read independently and to persevere without external supports (Hiebert, Samuels, and Rasinski 2010).

1. To develop student awareness of monitoring, select a challenging text to use for demonstration and support. Choose literature that won't be just an easy read but will instead require the students to consider and reflect. Each student should have a copy of the text.

2. Let students know that they will be trying out monitoring as a comprehension strategy, and that this involves keeping close track of meaning.

3. Introduce the text. Read a portion aloud, demonstrating how you think through the key ideas and details. When a complexity or confusion arises, show ways to persevere. Strategies for persevering include *rereading, rethinking, using illustrations, using text features, thinking aloud,* and *discussing the content* when a peer or adult is available.

   Be explicit about your monitoring processes. We want students to be consciously aware of what you are doing so that they will know how to bring these strategies into their own reading.

4. After you have demonstrated with a short section of text, ask students to read segments and retell the gist on their own. If the retelling is sufficient, move on. If not, guide the students to reread and retell the key ideas and details.

   #### For English Learners

   English learners may need monitoring instruction beyond what your other students require—particularly in relation to interpreting syntax and word meanings. Such a focus is generally more meaningful after the text has been read and discussed, as students then have a general understanding of the content, and you will be more able to home in on the key aspects of the language that have presented difficulty (Gersten et al. 2007).

5. Continue instruction with students who have not yet developed effective monitoring.

Figure RL **1.6**

INTENSIFYING THE INSTRUCTION
Inferring

Inferring is a comprehension strategy that involves drawing conclusions about content using close reading of textual information as well as prior knowledge.

1. To develop student awareness of inferring, choose a text for demonstration that contains complex content or vocabulary—something just beyond what your students might be able to fully comprehend on their own. Use a sticky note to identify places that require a deep level of inferring to deeply comprehend and appreciate the piece. Each student needs a copy of the text.

2. Introduce the text and then read a segment aloud, demonstrating inferences and pointing out what you are doing. Following are some key questions to guide the process:

K–5

*   What can we infer about the character? How do we know this?
*   What can we infer about how the character is feeling? (Illustrations can be helpful.)
*   What can we infer are this character's reasons for doing this?
*   What can we infer might happen next?
*   Authors usually leave it to the reader to infer the theme or message. What can we infer about the theme?
*   What in the text supports that?

3–5

*   What does the author assume we know here?
*   What does this probably mean?
*   What evidence in the text supports that?

For English Learners

*   Write the term *infer* on the board, and help students with its meaning and pronunciation. Refer back to the written term as you use it, to help students identify it within your stream of speech. From the start, English learners should be engaged in discussions that foster comprehension of complex material and require higher-level thinking (Gersten et al. 2007), and this sometimes involves taking a little extra time to ensure they understand what they are being asked to do.
*   Allow for sharing inferences in teams of two before sharing with the whole group. You may ask students to start with a stem, "I infer . . ." or "I am inferring . . ." to support appropriate syntax, and you may ask that students paraphrase their partner's response to encourage effective listening.

3. After you have demonstrated, ask students to read to a designated stopping point and then discuss further inferences using questions of the type shown above.

4. Provide follow-up lessons for small groups as needed.

Collaborative Engagement

1. **Choose the literature and the reading context.** Select a challenging text that can be read aloud to the class and then discussed in small groups. Or provide copies of text for students to read independently. To allow for differentiation, different groups may use varying texts.

2. **Arrange for students to read or listen to the text.** Before the reading, let students know what they will be doing afterward. (See Figure RL 1.7.) This will help them focus their reading in a way that will lead to productive discussion. If you are having students read, be sure to provide support for those who may struggle with the material.

3. **Hold the meetings.** After the reading, arrange for the students to come together in groups to discuss the content. Figure RL 1.7 offers a set of starter prompts and activities.

4. **Arrange a follow-up discussion.** When all groups are working from the same text, organize for a whole-class discussion as a follow-up to the group activity.

READING ANCHOR 1:
Prompts to Support Student-Led Group Discussion

Kindergarten and First Grade

- Each student draws a picture to show one important part of the text, including as many details as possible. (Students sit together for this phase of the experience to promote dialogue.)

- Students choose one interesting event and use large chart paper to collaboratively create an illustration that shows the details. The illustration must be labeled.

Second and Third Grades

- Students use chart paper to create a group picture that shows who, what, where, when, why, and how. Different groups can be expected to create unique illustrations depending on the different directions they follow in their questions. (Figure RL 1.3 provides a template to enlarge.)

Fourth and Fifth Grades

- Students map a set of who, what, where, when, why, and how questions and answers to check their understanding. Different groups can be expected to create unique responses depending on the different directions they follow in their questions. (Figure RL 1.3 provides a template.)

- Students find quotations to represent who, what, where, when, why, and how. They record the information on a Key Feature map. (Figure RL 1.3 provides a template.)

- Students find an illustration that gives important information. Together, they write a bulleted list of important details to notice. Each detail should be important to the story.

- Students talk through the text by responding to the question "What is this about?" and then construct a twenty-word written response that includes as much key information as possible.

Independent Application

Independent Reading

Independent reading is a planned event that may be scheduled on a regular basis (three to five days per week). The goals are for students to deeply engage with text, and to read extensively.

In the interest of time, have your students organize their materials so that they always have a book ready to go. This helps prevent their spending too much time selecting a book and creates more time for actual reading. Students can choose books from the class or school library, or bring books from home. You may wish to help each student maintain a bag of books appropriate for independent reading. Large ziplock storage bags work well. Allow 15 to 30 minutes per independent reading session.

In the interest of accountability, plan for students to engage in brief forms of response during or after each session, assigning nothing that will steal too much of their reading time. Response journals, interactive journals, and key detail illustrations (see further on) can be used for this purpose.

To encourage close reading, be available to observe and confer with students, and to oversee their reading activity. A review of research shows that *close* reading does not always occur naturally when students are offered the opportunity for independent reading, but that it can be effectively cultivated when teachers do the following: provide guidance in text selection to ensure that the material students choose is interesting and appropriately challenging; keep an eye on student activity to ensure that students maintain engagement in actual sustained reading; hold students accountable to share or respond to some aspect of the reading; encourage interactions around the texts; and take the time to conference with students (Reutzel, Jones, and Newman 2010).

Response Journals

Response journals are notebooks in which students record their thoughts about a text that has been read or listened to. The journals can be used daily, or every so often, by all members of the class. An important part of the response process is having an audience with whom to share selected thoughts. This shows students that their work is valued, and that the expectation for close reading and thoughtful response is always present. To introduce response journals, provide each student with a notebook. Let students know that the journal will be a place for recording thoughts about their reading.

1. At the end of independent reading sessions, partner-reading sessions, or whole-class read-alouds, ask students to draw, write, and reflect in the response journal. Although it is generally recommended that responses be determined by the individual (Strickland 2005), be

sure to show students what is possible when you first start using the journals, or when you want them to try something new. For example, to encourage the habit of close reading, you could demonstrate and post the following:

- Draw an important character or event, using appropriate details.

- Write and answer a who, what, when, where, why, or how question of your choosing. Use details from the text to construct your response.

- Answer a who, what, when, where, why, or how question designated by the teacher, using details from the text to construct your response.

- Write a sentence to describe a part you found funny, surprising, or interesting. Write a second sentence that uses details from the text to support your opinion.

- Describe a connection you made to the book. Use details from the text and your own experience.

2. Every now and then, have students share their journals with you or with a partner. The partner need not have read the same book. You can respond by writing to the student on a sticky note placed on the appropriate page, or arrange time for partners to respond to one another in this manner.

Interactive Journals

Interactive journals are notebooks in which students participate in short written conversations about what they are reading. The journals may be used any time two or more students are reading the same text. Interactive journals encourage close reading by involving students in a cycle of reading manageable sections of text, generating questions together, and responding briefly through writing. To introduce the process, provide each student with a notebook, showing where to write or draw and where to leave room for peers to respond. Let students know that the journals will be a place for sharing ideas about their reading.

1. Instruct student teams to decide on a selected amount of text to read closely, and to then be prepared to exchange their thoughts in writing. To get the written conversations started, guide students to brainstorm some generic prompts, or offer your own. For example:

- What happened in this part?

- What was interesting or confusing?

- What do you think will happen next? Why?

- What does the illustration on page _____ tell us? How does it relate to the story?

Peers can use these generic prompts as conversation starters but may generate their own, more tailored prompts along the way.

2. At the agreed-upon stopping point, students write their responses and then trade journals to respond to the partner. They may exchange journals two to three times during a reading session, deciding on new prompts and stopping points as they go. Allow flexibility so that they may tailor their prompts to their own interests and questions in relation to the text.

Stop-and-Chats

*Stop-and-chat*s are a framework for students to read and then stop at designated points to talk about the content. Two or three students who are reading the same text can work together. Stop-and-chats encourage close reading by setting up students to read with a specific purpose in mind and fostering conversations related to that purpose. When possible, pair English learners with experienced English speakers. The students learning English will benefit from the low-risk context for using language to express ideas about manageable segments of text and the native English speakers will benefit from the need to clearly articulate their thinking.

1. Student teams place a marker at an agreed-upon stopping point. Upon reaching this point, they exchange their thoughts about what they have read so far, and then place the marker at the next agreed-upon stopping point in preparation for another chat. To get the conversations started, you and the students can brainstorm some generic prompts, or you can offer your own. For example:

- What is this about? What has happened so far?

- What kind of person is this character? What helped you conclude that?

- What do you think will happen next? Why?

2. As students gain experience with stop-and-chats, provide follow-up lessons based on observations of their performance.

Word Appreciation Readings

Word appreciation readings are sessions organized for students to revisit and closely read text with a specific aesthetic purpose in mind. Such readings are conducted after students have read or listened to a poem or story at least once. The experience involves each student in going back into the text a second time to look closely for one unique or interesting use of language.

1. Prepare students for word appreciation readings by telling them you would like them to read (or listen) closely to a familiar text to bask in the delightfulness of the author's language.

2. After the students read or listen, they note one word or phrase that stands out for them. If possible, allow students to use highlighting tape to mark their choices. Or they can write their language on a note card.

3. Students talk with a partner about the part they noted, telling why they chose it and discussing the meaning.

Key Detail Illustrations

Key detail illustrations are detailed student drawings of one key moment from a story or drama. Students may prepare such illustrations based on independent or group reading, or after listening.

Reading: Students choose one key moment from the text they are reading and create an illustration that shows the important details. They may use speech bubbles to include key quotes from the characters. Close reading is encouraged as they read and reread the key section until they are certain the illustration captures what is in the text.

Listening: Choose one key moment from a story or drama. Read the section aloud as the students listen closely for the information they will need to create an appropriately detailed illustration. You may need to reread the section several times, allowing students to add new details as they are noticed, or you can project the text so that students can reread it on their own.

Key Feature Illustrations

A *key feature illustration* is a visual representation of the who, what, where, when, why, and how of a story or poem. Such illustrations may be created as a part of students' independent reading (to encourage and support close reading) or after you have read a text aloud to the class (as a means for rethinking and discussing content). Students may use any combination of drawing, writing, and symbols to represent the key features. Figure RL 1.3 may be used as a template.

Book Advertisements

A *book advertisement* is an invitation to read a great text. Developing a book advertisement creates a meaningful context for close reading, as the process sets up students to consider and refer to key ideas and details that will convince the audience about its merit.

1. To get started, arrange for each student to choose a favorite book in preparation for developing an advertisement. Students may work collaboratively.

2. Demonstrate how to prepare a one-page advertisement featuring the title, author, and key information that will encourage others to want to read the text. Students may be required to include any combination of the following:

    *   an illustration of a key problem or goal the main character faces

    *   a description of a key problem or goal the main character faces

    *   labels, captions, or short descriptive paragraphs

    *   a description of who, what, when, where, why, and/or how

    *   quotations from the text

    *   a plot teaser that offers just the right information to entice potential readers

3. After students have created their advertisements, either post them in the room or bind them into a class book. Refer to the advertisements when helping students select literature for independent or group reading.

Book Reviews

A *book review* is an evaluative commentary focused on the merit of a single text. Writing a book review requires that students engage in close reading to present a strong stance or opinion. Students may share their reviews in small groups, or over the course of a week, with five to six students per day sharing with the class.

1. Arrange for each student to review a book. Students could choose a book they have loved, a book they have hated, or anything in between.

2. Demonstrate the process of writing a review.

- **Kindergarten.** Students illustrate and possibly write about a part of the text they liked or did not like. They must show who was in the part and what happened. They talk about their reviews as they work together in small groups, or they share the reasons behind their evaluations in a whole-class setting.

- **First grade.** Students illustrate and write about a part of the text they liked or did not like, including key details from the text. They must show who was in the part and what happened.

- **Second and third grades.** Students are instructed to either encourage or discourage others from reading the book, using details from the text to back their arguments. They may place their focus on describing the appeal (or lack thereof) of a key character or a key event.

- **Fourth and fifth grades.** Students are instructed to either encourage or discourage others from reading the book, using details and examples from the text to support their arguments.

3. The reviews may be compiled into a class book, posted on a board for viewing, or they may become part of a class literary magazine that is published more formally.

KEY IDEAS AND DETAILS

ANCHOR 2

English Language Arts Standards Reading: Literature ANCHOR 2

Reading Anchor 2: Determine central ideas or themes of a text and analyze their development; summarize the key supporting details and ideas.

K	First	Second	Third	Fourth	Fifth
With prompting and support, retell familiar stories, including key details.	Retell stories, including key details, and demonstrate understanding of their central message or lesson.	Recount stories, including fables and folktales from diverse cultures, and determine their central message, lesson, or moral.	Recount stories, including fables, folktales, and myths from diverse cultures; determine the central message, lesson, or moral and explain how it is conveyed through key details in the text.	Determine a theme of a story, drama, or poem from details in the text; summarize the text.	Determine a theme of a story, drama, or poem from details in the text, including how characters in a story or drama respond to challenges or how the speaker in a poem reflects upon a topic; summarize the text.

Decision Tree for **Reading: Literature** ANCHOR 2

Do my students need focused instruction in relation to Reading Anchor 2?

Anchor 2 requires that students *summarize the key ideas and details* in a text. (Refer to your grade-level standards for specific details.)

When some or all of your students could use support in this area, it is recommended that you start the process by implementing three types of instruction in sequence over the course of about a week:

| **Demonstration** | **Collaborative Engagement** | **Independent Application** |
| Page 22 | Page 31 | Page 32 |

The initial demonstration requires just one session (to be repeated as needed), leaving one or two days for collaborative engagement, and one or two days to begin the independent applications, which become ongoing as you choose. If you find during any phase of the instruction that some or all of your students could use intensified support, it is recommended that you move to the lessons for intensifying the instruction.

Do my students need intensified support with determining what's important?

In general, a student who is comprehending effectively can be expected to identify the key story elements. They may identify what happens at the beginning, middle, and end or the characters, setting, problem, resolution, and theme. Students who do not demonstrate such competency through retellings or conversations can benefit from intensified support with deciding what's important. See page 29.

Do my students need intensified support with summarizing?

A good summary is a concise retelling of the main points. When evaluating student summaries, we expect a logically sequenced set of ideas in which reference is made to the characters, setting, problem, key events, and resolution. Students who do not demonstrate complete retellings can generally benefit from lessons focused on summarizing. See page 30.

Demonstration

Anchor 2 requires that students *summarize key ideas and details in a text*. The goal is to determine the central message or theme and to show understanding of the path the author took to get to that point. The present lesson is designed to help build a common set of understandings and expectations related to summarization. The lesson may be utilized as many times as is helpful. You will need just one text per lesson.

1. **Choose the text.** Choose a text that your students will want to revisit and retell. When teaching summarization strategies, traditional literature provides a good start because of its tight plots and characters who are often in need of learning some type of lesson. Be sure to choose stories that have a logical sequence of events and a theme that will be appropriately challenging for the age group to identify and consider. Figure RL 2.2 provides a recommended list of texts.

2. **Introduce the text and the concept.** Let students know that they should settle in and enjoy the material as you read it aloud and that after reading, you will want to work together to *summarize* the key ideas and details. Use a graphic organizer to guide the summary and help students understand your expectations of what to include.

3. **Demonstrate and discuss the concept.** Read the text aloud, allowing time for conversation. After the reading, work with students to revisit the key ideas and details, showing them how to use an organizer to construct a retelling or summary appropriate for the grade level. Figure RL 2.1 offers a starter set of prompts to support this process.

READING ANCHOR 2:
Prompts to Support Teacher-Led Modeling and Discussion of Text

Kindergarten

Let's retell this story. What is important that happened in the beginning? Middle? End? (Figure RL 2.3 provides a template to guide student retellings.)

First and Second Grades

Many stories have a lesson or message the author wants us to think about. Instead of coming out and telling us the message, the author usually leaves it up to us to infer or figure it out ourselves. Let's retell the important parts of the story and think about what the message might be. (Figures RL 2.4 and RL 2.5 provide templates for summarizing.)

Third and Fourth Grades

Let's summarize this piece. What do we think is the central message or theme? Remember that instead of coming out and telling us the theme, the author usually leaves it up to us to infer or figure it out ourselves. Let's track how the author worked toward building a theme. (Figures RL 2.4, RL 2.5, and RL 2.6 provide templates for summarizing.)

Fifth Grade

Let's summarize this piece. What do we think is the central message or theme the author wants us to infer? Often, main characters experience challenges in relation to a theme. What are the main character's challenges in relation to this theme? How does the character respond? (Figures RL 2.5 and RL 2.6 provide templates for summarizing.)

Poetry: What is this poem about? How does this poet reflect upon the topic?

Recommended Literature for Summarizing Central Ideas and Themes

Grade	Elements	Recommended Texts
K	With prompting and support, retell familiar stories, including key details.	*The Three Billy Goats Gruff* (any version) *The Three Little Pigs* (any version) *Goldilocks and the Three Bears* (any version) *The Little Red Hen* (any version) *The Gingerbread Man* (any version) *The Napping House* (Audrey Wood)
1	Retell stories, including key details, and demonstrate understanding of their central message or lesson.	*Little Red Riding Hood* (any version) *Lon Po Po: A Red Riding Hood Story from China* (Ed Young) *The Boy Who Cried Wolf* (any version) *Betsy Who Cried Wolf* (Gail Carson Levine) *It's Mine!* (Leo Lionni) *Cuckoo: A Mexican Folktale* (Lois Ehlert)
2	Recount stories, including fables and folktales from diverse cultures, and determine their central message, lesson, or moral.	*The Empty Pot* (Demi) *The Greatest Treasure* (Demi) *The Wise Old Woman* (retold by Yoshiko Uchida) *The Green Frogs: A Korean Folktale* (retold by Yumi Iko) *The Legend of the Bluebonnet* (Tomie DePaola) *Moon Rope* (Lois Ehlert)
3	Describe characters in a story (e.g., their traits, motivations, or feelings) and explain how their actions contribute to the sequence of events.	*Mufaro's Beautiful Daughters!* (John Steptoe) *Magic Hands* (Marjorie Barker Yoshi) *Three Strong Women: A Tall Tale from Japan* (Claus Stamm) *The Secret Footprints* (Julia Alvarez) *Precious and the Boo Hag* (Patricia McKissack and Onawumi Jean Moss) *Petronella* (Jay Williams)
4	Determine a theme of a story, drama, or poem from details in the text; summarize the text.	*The Table Where Rich People Sit* (Byrd Baylor) *I'm in Charge of Celebrations* (Byrd Baylor) *The Mud Pony* (Caron Lee Cohen) *The Legend of the Indian Paintbrush* (Tomie DePaola) *The Fourth Question: A Chinese Tale* (retold by Rosalind Wang) *And Still the Turtle Watched* (Sheila MacGill-Calahan)
5	Determine a theme of a story, drama, or poem from details in the text, including how characters in a story or drama respond to challenges or how the speaker in a poem reflects upon a topic; summarize the text.	*The Bracelet* (Yoshiko Uchida) *The People Who Hugged the Trees* (adapted by Deborah Lee Rose) *Stone Soup* (Jon J. Muth) *The Tale of the Mandarin Ducks* (Katherine Paterson) *The Invisible Hunters* (Harriet Rohmer) *What You Know First* (Patricia MacLachlan)

Figure RL 2.3

I Retell Important Parts of Stories

Name: _____ Date: _____

Title: _____

Beginning →

Middle →

End →

Story Retelling Organizer

Name: _____ Date: _____

Title: _____

Message or Theme

Important events that led to the theme

Story Analysis and Summary Organizer

Name: _____ Date: _____

Title: _____

Characters	Setting

Problem or Goal	Solution or Ending

Central Message or Theme

Detailed Organizer for a Story Summary

Name: _____ Date: _____

Title: _____

Main Character

Setting

Central Message or Theme

Character Experiences Used to Convey this Theme

Figure RL 2.7

INTENSIFYING THE INSTRUCTION
Determining What's Important

Determining what's important is a comprehension strategy that is key to constructing a meaningful summary.

1. To develop student awareness of determining what's important, select a well-crafted story with a clear central message. Each student should have a copy of the text. You can use this lesson several different times with different texts.

2. Introduce the text and set a purpose for the reading. For example: *Let's settle in and enjoy this story. As we read, we'll stop to talk about the key ideas we think might be leading to a central message. Remember that instead of coming out and telling us the message* (theme), *the author usually leaves it up to us to infer it.* To help focus students' attention provide a visual, such as that featured in Figures RL 2.4, RL 2.5, or RL 2.6.

3. Ask students to read (softly or silently) to a series of designated stopping points. Or you can read aloud. Use the stopping points to discuss the author's possible progress toward building a theme. Following are some key questions to guide the process.

   - Who are the key characters?
   - Where is the story set?
   - What problem or goal or challenge does the main character face? What does the character do about that?
   - What do you think the character is going to learn from his or her experiences?
   - Do you have an idea of what the theme or central message might be? (Keep a running list of story themes and central messages visible in the classroom to help students develop a sense of what a theme is.)

4. Provide follow-up lessons for small groups as needed. Students who do not seem to get the gist of stories or have little to contribute regarding possible themes generally can benefit from intensified support in this area.

For English Learners

Teach the literacy vocabulary terms you want students to know (such as *character*, *setting*, and *theme*), and allow them to use a combination of drawing, talk, and writing to show and develop their understandings of these concepts.

INTENSIFYING THE INSTRUCTION
Summarizing

A good summary is a concise retelling of the main points. Probably the most important reason to teach summarization is that it helps students reflect on, rethink, and reconsider what they have read.

1. To develop student competency at summarizing, select a text to use for demonstration. Early on, look for stories that have a logical sequence and a clear story structure. More complex structures can be addressed after students have experience with summarizing simple structures. Each student will need a copy of the text.

2. Introduce the text. Ask students to read (softly or silently), mentally preparing to do the following upon completion:

   • Point out the author's introduction to characters.

   • Point out how the author describes the setting.

   • Point out how the author sets up the problem, goal, or challenge, point out how the characters respond, and describe how the solution is achieved.

   • Reflect on the central theme, lesson, or message.

   You may wish to create a chart or visual with these questions to be hung in the classroom to support this process. Sticky notes can be used to record key ideas and details and then be arranged to facilitate an oral summary.

For English Learners

Partnering an English learner with an experienced English speaker for structured activities such as summarizing is a promising practice (Gersten et al. 2007). Partnered students may read short passages and generate a gist statement together. If desired, they may use a retelling key (Figure RL 2.4, 2.5, or 2.6) to talk through key parts or they can turn back to the text, using the illustrations and words as a guide.

Collaborative Engagement

1. **Choose the literature and the reading context.** Gather a set of stories or poems for students to read or discuss with peers. When choosing stories, look for a clear problem-resolution sequence and a strong central message or theme. You may use a text that will be read aloud to the whole class (providing at least one copy per group), or students may be arranged in groups according to the different texts they are going to read together.

2. **Arrange for students to read or listen to the text.** Before the reading, let students know what they will be doing afterward. (See Figure RL 2.9.) If they will be inferring or discussing the theme, let them know that they should pay attention to what the key characters are learning—or should be learning—because this often provides insight into possible themes. Be sure that the texts will be accessible to all of your readers. Provide support if the texts cannot be read independently with success.

3. **Hold the meetings.** Arrange for the small groups to come together to discuss the text. Give students a guiding prompt or assignment (as in Figure RL 2.9) to help get their conversations going.

4. **Arrange a follow-up discussion.** When all groups are working on the same text, organize for a whole-class discussion as a follow-up to the group activity.

Figure RL **2.9**

READING ANCHOR 2:
Prompts to Support Student-Led Group Discussion of Text

- Students use a graphic organizer to prepare a retelling. After working as a group, they share the retelling with another group or the class. (See Figures RL 2.3, RL 2.4, RL 2.5, and RL 2.6 for possible organizers to enlarge, or students may create their own.)

- Students choose three key scenes that show how a central character's actions contribute to the overall sequence of events. They write down or draw the actions of the character at these three points in the story. Drawings may be labeled with captions or speech bubbles. Figure RL 2.3 may be enlarged and used as a template.

- Students determine what they consider to be the theme of the piece. They write down the theme and then describe the central character's experience in relation to this theme using a bulleted list to organize their description.

Independent Application

Mapping in Teams

Mapping in teams provides a forum for setting up students to summarize together. To implement, arrange for two or three students who are reading or listening to the same text to work together to reconstruct a story using an organizer. See Figures RL 2.3, RL 2.4, RL 2.5, and RL 2.6 for examples.

1. If students are doing the reading, they read silently or quietly together. Upon reaching points at which they feel they can add to the organizers, they pause and work together to fill in sections. If you are doing the reading, students work in teams to construct the map after the read-aloud.

2. As students gain experience with mapping in teams, provide follow-up lessons based on observations of their performance. For example, you might provide further support in identifying themes, guidance in pulling out the big ideas, or instruction regarding the general logistics of using mapping in teams as a tool for learning.

Choice of Media Summary

Before students read or listen to a story or drama, let them know that they will be working in groups to prepare a summary. After the text has been read, groups of students use different media available in the classroom or school to prepare the summary. Possibilities include:

- a story map that has been taught

- a bulleted list summary prepared on the computer

- a bulleted list summary written on a whiteboard

- a PowerPoint summary using one slide per key story element or event

- a set of five to eight blank sticky notes

- a web or map summary using software such as Kidspiration

- an interactive graphic organizer from ReadWriteThink:

    - Story Map: www.readwritethink.org/files/resources/interactives/storymap/

    - Doodle Splash: www.readwritethink.org/files/resources/interactives/doodle/

    - Time Line: www.readwritethink.org/files/resources/interactives/timeline/

Depending on your goals, the summaries may be used as a tool for further instruction. For example, if the whole class has read or listened to the same text, you could choose some of the strong examples and use them to discuss what should be included in a complete summary.

Theme Boards

To support your students' development of the concept of theme, you can create a *theme board*, a collection of themes that can be referred to again and again (Harvey and Goudvis 2000). Each time the class reads a book together you can consider adding a theme to the list, such as *working hard, showing respect for others, treating all groups of people fairly*, or *maintaining family traditions*. Working with such a list can help students understand what a theme is, to begin to identify themes on their own, and to compare themes across books.

What's the Theme?

After reading or listening to a story with a strong theme or central message, each student writes one sentence describing his or her conception of the theme. Then, students work in groups to compare their ideas and groups prepare a theme statement to share with the class. Often, stories contain more than one theme, and many stories have themes that can be interpreted from different angles, creating a rich opportunity for discussion.

Sketch to Stretch

After reading or listening to a story, drama, or poem, students sketch an image to represent their conception of the main idea or theme. Students then meet in small groups. Each student takes a turn to show his or her sketch to the group. The group members interpret the sketch by articulating what they think it means, and then the student who sketched the image provides his or her own interpretation (Short, Harste, and Burke 1996).

Save the Last Word for the Artist

After reading or listening to a short story, groups of students discuss what they think the story means. Each group uses a variety of art material (paper, ribbon, tape, rubber bands, yarn, paper rolls, foam pieces, stickers) to collaboratively create an image that symbolizes the meaning (or students may create their own pieces). An alternative to using the art material is to use a large piece of chart paper and pencils, allowing students to sketch. Each piece is displayed for the class while students from other groups tell what they think the group members (or individuals) were trying to convey. Finally, the creators talk about the meaning, having the last word (Short, Harste, and Burke 1996).

Retelling with Character Props

Retelling with character props allows children to draw on concrete, visual information as they structure and restructure their retellings, and such experiences increase their comprehension (Cunningham and Allington 2011). English learners especially can benefit from the opportunity to integrate oral language and concrete props with meaningful reading. To prepare for retelling with character props, students may make their own characters or you can create them ahead of time. The props can be made available during play, center, or group time. If desired, students can prepare a retelling to demonstrate for the class.

Visual Retellings

Visual retellings offer a way for children to revisit and discuss a piece of text through drawing. Students may create visuals of the following story elements, adding captions or narrative as appropriate:

- the characters
- the setting
- a key event
- the problem
- the resolution

Working in proximity with other students is probably enough to stimulate important discussion, but if you wish, you may have students formally share their visuals with a group or the class.

Dramatic Retelling

After working with the class to summarize a familiar story, provide students with simple costumes and props for dramatizing a particular scene. Focusing on one scene can be more manageable than focusing on the whole story, and retelling even a short part can be a key way for students to reflect on and demonstrate new understandings about the piece. For younger students, the costumes and props can be made available during play or center time. Older students can meet in groups to prepare a dramatic retelling that is then demonstrated for the class.

KEY IDEAS AND DETAILS

ANCHOR 3

English Language Arts Standards Reading: Literature **Anchor 3**

Reading Anchor 3: Analyze how and why individuals, events, and ideas develop and interact over the course of a text.

K	First	Second	Third	Fourth	Fifth
With prompting and support, identify characters, settings, and major events in a story.	Describe characters, settings, and major events in a story, using key details.	Describe how characters in a story respond to major events and challenges.	Describe characters in a story (e.g., their traits, motivations, or feelings) and explain how their actions contribute to the sequence of events.	Describe in depth a character, setting, or event in a story or drama, drawing on specific details in the text (e.g., a character's thoughts, words, or actions).	Compare and contrast two or more characters, settings, or events in a story or drama, drawing on specific details in the text (e.g., how characters interact).

Decision Tree for **Reading: Literature** ANCHOR 3

Do my students need focused instruction in relation to Reading Anchor 3?

Anchor 3 requires that students *describe and analyze characters and events and how they develop over the course of a text.* (Refer to your grade-level standards for specific details.)

When some or all of your students could use support in this area, it is recommended that you start the process by implementing three types of instruction in sequence over the course of about a week:

Demonstration	**Collaborative Engagement**	**Independent Application**
Page 37	Page 48	Page 49

The initial demonstration requires just one session (to be repeated as needed), leaving one or two days for collaborative engagement and one or two days to begin the independent applications, which become ongoing as you choose. If you find during any phase of the instruction that some or all of your students could use intensified support, it is recommended that you move to the lessons for intensifying the instruction.

Do my students need intensified support with predicting?

The act of predicting (using prior knowledge to think about what is coming next) can help readers stay focused on the details of events and track the ways in which characters respond to and influence these events. Students who can benefit from lessons in predicting are those who seem not to anticipate where the story is going from one moment to the next. See page 46.

Do my students need intensified support with monitoring?

Monitoring is a comprehension strategy that involves keeping close track of meaning and using repair strategies when meaning gets off track. Students who can benefit from individualized support with monitoring are often those who provide incomplete information as they attempt to describe key details and events. See page 47.

Demonstration

Anchor 3 requires that students *consider characters and events and how they interact and develop* over the course of a text. Rather than reading for facts alone, students are encouraged to analyze and describe the details that influence the major events. For example, what are this character's traits? How does this character respond to challenges? What is the character's motivation? How does he or she influence the sequence of events? Research shows that the experience of *analyzing* deepens comprehension, and students who think deeply about text find reading more rewarding and worthwhile (Applegate and Applegate 2010/2011). The present lesson may be implemented as many times as needed, using a different text each time. You will need just one text per lesson.

1. **Choose the text.** Select a piece of literature that warrants careful attention to detail. Because analysis is the goal, depth is critical. Characters need to *experience* and *feel*, acting meaningfully in relation to well-developed story events. Figure RL 3.2 features a set of recommended texts.

2. **Introduce the text and the concept.** Let students know that one way to explore a text is to consider the details of something within— usually a character or an event or the ways in which a character or situation changes over time. Choose any one of these elements to get the conversation started (your choice will depend on the text), and let students know that during and after reading you will want to discuss the details or developments.

3. **Demonstrate and discuss the concept.** Read the text aloud. During and/or after the reading, use a focused set of prompts to demonstrate and inspire thinking about key details and ideas. Figure RL 3.1 offers a starter set of prompts and organizers to use with fiction.

READING ANCHOR 3:
Prompts to Support Teacher-Led Modeling
and Discussion of Text

Kindergarten

Let's identify the characters, settings, and major events in this story. (Figure RL 3.3 provides a template to enlarge.)

First Grade

Let's describe the characters, settings, and major events. What key details of each help us understand this text? (Figure RL 3.3 provides a template to enlarge.)

Second Grade

Let's describe in detail how a character responds to the major events and challenges in the story. (Figures RL 3.4 and RL 3.5 provide templates to enlarge.)

Third Grade

Let's describe this character. What are the traits that stand out? Let's describe how this character's actions contribute to the sequence of events. What motivates these actions? (Figures RL 3.4 and 3.5 provide templates to enlarge.

Fourth Grade

Let's describe this character (or event) in depth. What are the details that matter? (Figures RL 3.5 and RL 3.6 provide templates.)

Fifth Grade

Let's compare and contrast these (characters, settings, events) in our story. (Figures RL 3.5, RL 3.6, RL 3.7, and RL 3.8 provide templates.)

Figure RL **3.2**

Recommended Literature for Analyzing Characters and Events		
Grade	**Elements**	**Recommended Texts**
K	With prompting and support, identify characters, settings, and major events in a story.	*The Stray Dog* (Marc Simont) *Widget* (Lyn Rossiter McFarland) *The Dashiki* (Gaylia Taylor) *Seven Cookies* (Lorena Iglesius Heydenburk) *Sheila Rae, The Brave* (Kevin Henkes) *Don't Need Friends* (Carolyn Crimi)
1	Describe characters, settings, and major events in a story, using key details.	*My Buddy* (Audry Osofsky) *My Rotten Redheaded Older Brother* (Patricia Polacco) *Wilfrid Gordon McDonald Partridge* (Mem Fox) *Abuela* (Arthur Dorros) *The Good Luck Cat* (Joy Harjo) *Koala Lou* (Mem Fox)
2	Describe how characters in a story respond to major events and challenges.	*Tough Boris* (Mem Fox) *The Other Side* (Jacqueline Woodson) *Tomas and the Library Lady* (Pat Mora) *Thundercake* (Patricia Polacco) *Always My Dad* (Sharon Dennis Wyeth) *Amazing Grace* (Mary Hoffman)
3	Describe characters in a story (e.g., their traits, motivations, or feelings) and explain how their actions contribute to the sequence of events.	*Heroes* (Ken Mochizuki) *The Hickory Chair* (Lisa Rowe Fraustino) *Dona Flor* (Pat Mora) *The Name Jar* (Yangsook Choi) *Sitti's Secrets* (Naomi Shihab Nye) *Miss Rumphius* (Barbara Cooney)
4	Describe in depth a character, setting, or event in a story or drama, drawing on specific details in the text (e.g., a character's thoughts, words, or actions).	*Baseball Saved Us* (Ken Mochizuki) *So Far from the Sea* (Eve Bunting) *When Lightning Comes in a Jar* (Patricia Polacco) *The Bracelet* (Yoshiko Uchida) *A Boy Called Slow* (Joseph Bruchac) *The Lotus Seed* (Sherry Garland)
5	Compare and contrast two or more characters, settings, or events in a story or drama, drawing on specific details in the text (e.g., how characters interact).	*Night Boat to Freedom* (Margot Theis Raven) *Creativity* (John Steptoe) *The Lost Lake* (Allen Say) *The Butterfly* (Patricia Polacco) *The Wall* (Eve Bunting) *Pink and Say* (Patricia Polacco)

I Can Describe Important Parts of Stories!

Name: _____ Date: _____

Title: _____

Characters   **Settings**

A Major Event

I Think About Important Events in Stories

Name: _____ Date: _____

Title: _____

Major events or challenges

How the main character responds or contributes to the events or challenges

Character Analysis Web

Name: _____ Date: _____

Title: _____

Description of Character

Major Challenge or Goal

Responses to Challenge/Goal

Character Changes over Time

Event Chart

Name: _____ Date: _____

Title: _____

Event Summary

Key Details of the Event

Compare-and-Contrast Chart

Name: _____ Date: _____

Choose two characters, events, or settings from the book you are reading. List each of your choices:

1: _____

2: _____

What are some key similarities?

What are some key differences?

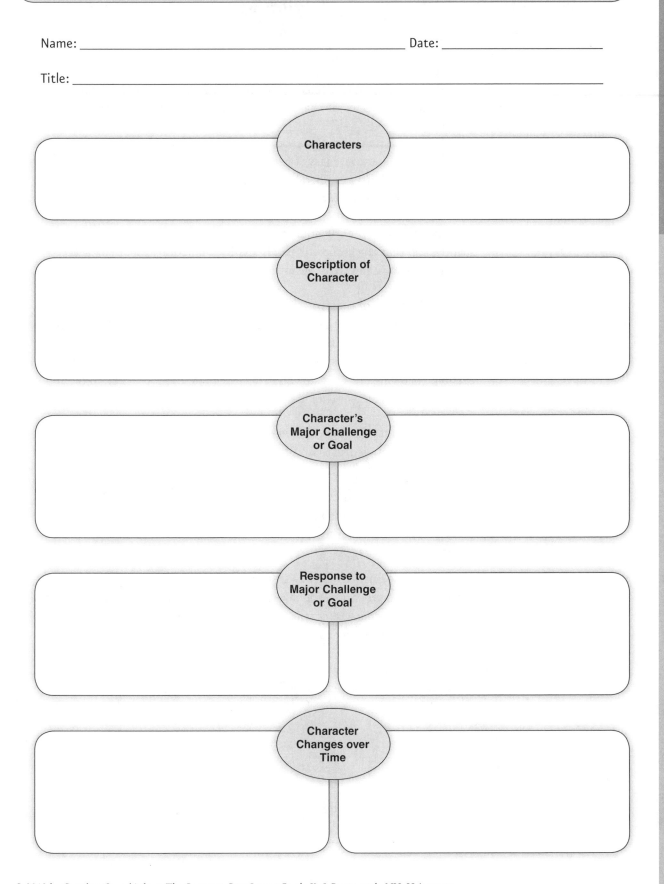

Chart for Comparing and Contrasting Characters

Name: _____ Date: _____

Title: _____

Characters

Description of Character

Character's Major Challenge or Goal

Response to Major Challenge or Goal

Character Changes over Time

INTENSIFYING THE INSTRUCTION
Predicting

Predicting is a comprehension strategy that involves using prior knowledge to consider what is coming next. Focusing on predicting can help readers stay in tune with the motivations of characters and their participation in the developing action.

1. To develop student awareness of predicting, select a text to use for demonstration. Text with a predictable sequence of events works well for this lesson. Each student will need a copy.

2. Introduce the text. Let students know that they will be reading softly or silently, and that the group will be discussing predictions about character actions based on clues that the author gives.

   Read the first part of the text aloud, stopping at a telling point to ask the students to predict how the characters might respond to the challenges the author creates for them. Then ask students to continue reading to confirm or revise their predictions. You may set two or three stopping points for discussion. Following are some key questions to guide the process of predicting in relation to Reading Anchor 3.

   • What do you predict the character will do? What is it about this character that makes you predict that?
   • How do you predict the character will respond to this problem or challenge? Has this changed over the course of the text?
   • As we read, are your predictions confirmed?

   For English Learners

   Allow English learners to work with a native English-speaking partner to talk about the predictions. You may wish to provide an explicit stem such as "I predict this character will . . . ," writing the language so students will have a visual to refer to as needed.

3. Provide follow-up lessons for small groups as needed. Students who do not make logical predictions can benefit from additional support.

Figure RL 3.10

INTENSIFYING THE INSTRUCTION:
Monitoring

Monitoring is a comprehension strategy that involves keeping close track of meaning and using repair strategies when meaning gets off track.

1. To develop student awareness of monitoring in relation to Reading Anchor 3, select a text that features interesting characters involved in interesting events. Each participating student should have access to a copy of the text.

2. Introduce the text and let the students know that they will be reading softly or silently and then discussing some key questions. Let them know the questions beforehand. For example:

   - How would you describe this character? What are this character's traits?
   - What does this character want to do, and why?
   - How does this character develop and change over time?
   - How does this character respond to challenges?
   - What details are important to include when we describe this event?

3. Read a portion of the text aloud, demonstrating how to stop at a key point to think through the question at hand. Show students how you work through complexities, rereading and thinking deeply about the content.

4. After demonstrating, team students up to discuss passages of the text together, focusing on the key questions.

For English Learners

Monitoring is one of the most important comprehension strategies for all readers. As with any reader, we want to ensure that English learners have opportunities to dig deeply into the content. When posing questions, be sure to match the student's current English language ability. For example, start with wording that allows students to point to illustrations or use one-word responses such as *yes* or *no*, gradually moving into who, what, where, when, why, and how questions. Rather than asking linguistically complex questions, break your language into meaningful parts. For example, *Who is this character? How does this character feel? How does this character feel now?*

5. Encourage independent monitoring daily, and continue instruction with students who have not yet developed effective monitoring.

Collaborative Engagement

1. **Choose the literature and the reading context.** Decide on a piece of literature that can be read aloud to all participating students and then discussed in small groups. Provide at least one copy per group. (After doing the reading with your students early on so that you can provide support with the in-depth analysis required by Anchor 3, later, when students have more experience, they may be asked to read independently.) When choosing literature to support exploration of Reading Anchor 3, look for texts that feature depth in characters or events. Figure RL 3.2 provides some recommendations.

2. **Arrange for students to read or listen to the text.** Before the reading, let students know what they will be doing afterward. (See Figure RL 1.7.)

3. **Hold the meetings.** Arrange for students to come together during or after the reading to discuss key aspects of the text. Giving students key prompts (as in Figure RL 3.11) can help them focus on the key ideas that need to be considered in preparation for their discussions.

4. **Arrange for a follow-up discussion.** When all groups are working on the same text, organize for a whole-class discussion as a follow-up to the group activity.

Figure RL **3.11**

READING ANCHOR 3:
Prompts to Support Student-Led Group Discussion of Text

Kindergarten and First Grade

Students collaboratively draw or write to describe the characters, settings, and major events. Encourage students to provide extensive detail. (Figure RL 3.3 provides a possible template to enlarge.)

Second and Third Grades

Students use the illustrations to help describe how the characters respond/contribute to the major events in the story. Students collaboratively draw or write. (Figures RL 3.4 and RL 3.5 provide possible templates.)

Fourth Grade

Students work together to describe a character (event) in depth. (Figures RL 3.5 and RL 3.6 provide possible templates.)

Fifth Grade

Students work together to compare and contrast characters, settings, or events in the story. (Figures RL 3.5, RL 3.6, RL 3.7, and RL 3.8 provide possible templates.)

Independent Application

Stop-and-Chats

*Stop-and-chat*s are student-planned opportunities to talk about text. The goal is to provide a forum for students to read with a specific purpose and to engage in conversations related to that purpose. Two or three students who are reading the same text can work together.

1. Students who are reading the same text place a marker at an agreed-upon stopping point. Upon reaching this point, they exchange their thoughts about what they have read so far and then place the marker at the next agreed-upon stopping point in preparation for another chat. To get the conversations started, you and the students can brainstorm some generic prompts to consider while reading, or you can offer your own. For example:

   * Who are the characters? Who is the main character?

   * What is the main character's problem or goal? What is the main character's role in this situation?

   * What do we know about the setting? How does the setting change over time?

   * What is a big event we should pay attention to in this section? What details are important or interesting?

2. As students gain experience with stop-and-chats, provide follow-up lessons based on observations of their performance.

Getting the Picture

Getting the picture is a way of encouraging students to enjoy the illustrations in the texts they are reading and to analyze the details in ways that will enhance their construction of meaning. The experience may occur before or after reading. For English learners, implementing the experience before reading familiarizes them with the content and vocabulary, thereby potentially making comprehension easier.

1. Guide your students to construct a generic set of questions to ask in relation to story illustrations. (Have a book available to use as an example.) Post the list somewhere in the classroom. The following questions illustrate the type that could be asked in relation to Reading Anchor 3:

   * What information does the artist give about the character(s) on this page? When we compare different parts of the text, how does the character look different?

- What information does the artist give about the setting on this page? How does the setting change across pages?

- Find an illustration that shows a character responding to a challenge.

- Compare the illustrations of two characters in the book. What are the similarities and differences? Do the characters "look" the part or does the illustrator surprise us?

- Compare the illustrations of two settings in the book. What are the similarities and differences?

- Compare the illustrations of two events in the book. What are the similarities and differences?

2. Assign students to pair up and discuss their interpretations using some or all of the questions you have constructed together.

3. Allow the students to share their observations with the class.

Story Sequence Chart

Story sequencing is a teacher-led experience that involves students in predicting the order of events in a story. The goals are to help students consider characters and how they respond to and influence the sequence of events. To prepare, write on large sticky notes six to eight events from a predictable text. Have students predict their order, placing them in a linear sequence. Read the book aloud (or students may read their own copies) and then work with the students to confirm or correct their predictions.

Story Wheel

A *story wheel* is a circular shape used to enhance comprehension of a key text by guiding a description of a character or an event and its changes over time. After students gain experience constructing story wheels with teacher guidance, they can construct them in pairs or teams.

1. Draw a large wheel-shaped figure on a whiteboard or chart paper. Leave enough room in the wheel to place sticky notes.

2. After reading a story aloud, work with students to describe a character or an event in depth. When working with characters, give students a stem such as *I feel*, *I see*, or *I am*. Have them write the sentence on a sticky note, from the perspective of the character. Then, guide students to place the sticky notes on the wheel in an order that makes sense based on the story.

3. When working with events, choose a focus character and ask students to use the character's name as the stem for describing something that happened in the story (as in *The boy left when it was dark*, or *Fergus chased the cat*). Then, guide students to place the sticky note on the wheel in the order in which the events occurred.

Feelings Map

One of the most rewarding parts of reading a story is connecting with the feelings that a character undergoes over time. A *feelings map* is a visual depiction of a character's feelings and how the feelings change over time. To implement, each student draws three to five faces of a character to indicate the changes in feelings the character undergoes over the course of the story. Students may either orally describe their images to a partner or write captions describing the images.

Written Character Sketch

Characters in literature can be memorable for many reasons. They may be silly, wise, stubborn, generous, brave, greedy, or cowardly or any combination of these. Writing a sketch that describes a memorable character can deepen comprehension by helping students tune into the intricacies of the personality and the character's unique ways of approaching situations.

1. Choose a text to use for modeling—one you have already read aloud in part or whole. The text should feature characters with interesting depth.

2. Let students know that you will be using the text to show how to prepare a character sketch and to give them a chance to try their own. As your students observe, make a chart with three headings to show that a good sketch (1) provides **background information;**

(2) creates strong mental **images**; (3) identifies notable **traits** (ways the character talks, approaches situations, views the world), providing supporting details and examples for each identified trait.

3. Have the students help you jot information under each header:

   - **Background Information**. Name the character and list key introductory information (age, sex, role in family, role in story). If you are working with younger students, you may wish to draw the character and use labels for any key information that should be shared.

   - **Images.** Tell how the character looks, sounds, smells, and/or feels to touch. Students can use sentences, phrases, labels, or one-word descriptors.

   - **Traits.** List personality characteristics, interests, and ways of interacting with others. Older students can use sentences or phrases; younger students can use labels or one-word descriptors.

4. Have students work in teams using the three-header framework to provide a sketch of a *different* character in the text you are using, or assign students to write their own sketches from the books they are reading.

Projects

Each member of the class chooses a character or an event to analyze from a story/drama the class has read/observed together. Students create multimedia studies of their chosen entity, using multiple lenses of consideration.

For example, a *character study* might include any of the following: a written sketch (see above), a detailed drawing of the character at a key point in time (or three points in time), a list of items that were important to the character, a set of quotations showing the nature of the character, a comparison to another character, a narrative written from the character's perspective describing a small but important moment in the story.

An *event study* might include a detailed drawing of a critical moment, a sketch with captions, a written description from the perspectives of two different characters, or a written description surrounded by the faces of different characters to show their feelings about the event. The ultimate goal of character and event projects is to help students consider the material in depth and develop new insights.

CRAFT AND STRUCTURE

ANCHOR 4

English Language Arts Standards Reading: Literature **ANCHOR 4**

Reading Anchor 4: Interpret words and phrases as they are used in a text, including determining technical, connotative, and figurative meanings, and analyze how specific word choices shape meaning or tone.

K	First	Second	Third	Fourth	Fifth
Ask and answer questions about unknown words in a text.	Identify words and phrases in stories or poems that suggest feelings or appeal to the senses.	Describe how words and phrases (e.g., regular beats, alliteration, rhymes, repeated lines) supply rhythm and meaning in a story, poem, or song.	Determine the meaning of words and phrases as they are used in a text, distinguishing literal from nonliteral language.	Determine the meaning of words and phrases as they are used in a text, including those that allude to significant characters found in mythology (e.g., Herculean).	Determine the meaning of words and phrases as they are used in a text, including figurative language such as metaphors and similes.

Decision Tree for **Reading: Literature** ANCHOR 4

Do my students need focused instruction in relation to Reading Anchor 4?

Anchor 4 requires that students *determine and interpret the meanings of key words and phrases* in text. (Refer to your grade-level standards for specific details.)

When some or all of your students could use support in this area, it is recommended that you start the process by implementing three types of instruction in sequence over the course of about a week:

Demonstration
Page 55

Collaborative Engagement
Page 66

Independent Application
Page 68

The initial demonstration requires just one session (to be repeated as needed), leaving one or two days for collaborative engagement and one or two days to begin the independent applications, which become ongoing as you choose. If you find during any phase of the instruction that some or all of your students could use intensified support, it is recommended that you move to the lessons for intensifying the instruction.

Do my students need intensified support with vocabulary-learning strategies?

When students do not have a strong repertoire of strategies for dealing with unfamiliar words, they can benefit from the vocabulary-learning strategy lessons. We often see this need in students who do not pause at critical words or take action even though they clearly do not know their meaning. See page 59.

Do my students need intensified support to develop vocabulary?

Vocabulary studies are used to help develop students' comprehension and content knowledge in relation to the texts they are reading. English learners especially can benefit from this extra boost in vocabulary instruction. See page 60.

Demonstration

Anchor 4 requires that students *determine and interpret the meanings of key words and phrases* in text. It is widely recommended that instruction related to word meanings be steeped in an effort to develop a *word consciousness*—an awareness of and an interest in learning and using new words. Word consciousness is not only critical for vocabulary growth, it also extends reading comprehension (Graves and Watts-Taffe 2008; Scott and Nagy 2004; Tompkins 2011).

The present lesson is designed to help you support your students in developing their word consciousness and building their vocabularies. It may be implemented several times over the course of the year, using different texts that are read aloud.

The lesson requires planning ahead in two areas. First, have your specific focus for vocabulary instruction in mind beforehand. Check your grade level standards for guidance. For example, is it time to address the importance of asking questions about unknown words? Do your students need help distinguishing literal from nonliteral language? Would they benefit from support considering the phenomenon of metaphors and similes? Your chosen focus will shape the lesson. Second, determine whether to use the lesson as the frame for creating or adding to a word wall or chart. Through this lesson, you may create a variety of word wall *types* (see Sidebar).

> **WORD WALL TYPES**
>
> Synonyms
>
> Homonyms
>
> Onomatopoeic words
>
> Words with multiple meanings
>
> Feeling words
>
> Five-sense words
>
> Contractions
>
> Tricky words
>
> Interesting verbs
>
> Interesting adjectives
>
> Science words
>
> Math words
>
> Social studies words
>
> Words that sound good
>
> Words related to the books the class reads together

1. **Choose the text.** Choose a text that could be used to achieve your lesson goals.

2. **Introduce the text and the concept.** Let students know that you will be showing them some words you found to be interesting, confusing, or particularly important—and that you will want them to help you interpret their meanings. Because rich vocabulary instruction takes time, short word lists for any one lesson are recommended (Gersten et al. 2007).

3. **Demonstrate and discuss the concept.** Read the whole text through once before backing up to discuss the words and phrases of interest. On a first read, students generally benefit from focusing on making meaning from the whole. On a second read, they are generally more ready to attend to word-level specifics.

   When reading through the text the second time, pause to discuss and show how you think about the key words and phrases you (and the students) have noted. If you are working with a word wall or chart, be prepared to write the key words on note cards and place them on the wall. Figure RL 4.1 offers a starter set of prompts designed to guide your discussion.

READING ANCHOR 4:
Prompts to Support Teacher-Led Modeling and Discussion

Kindergarten and First Grade

We are going to look back through the text to talk about some of the interesting words. (We will be putting some of these words on our word wall.)

I noticed _____. What do you think it means? I think it means _____ because _____.

Did you have any questions about words? Let's listen again . . .

Let's listen for words that tell us about feelings.

Let's listen for words that make us use our senses.

What do you feel when I read this word/these words? What do you see in your mind?

Figure RL 4.2 offers a template for students to record words.

Second Through Fifth Grades

We are going to think together about how this author uses words in special ways. I've chosen a text with interesting (rhymes, alliteration, imagery, repetition, beats, onomatopoeia, metaphors, similes, nonliteral language, word meanings). I want to point out some of this language and discuss what it means. I also want *you* to draw our attention to any interesting words you notice. (We will be putting some of the language on our word wall.)

I noticed _____. What do you think it means? I think it means _____ because _____.

What questions do you have about the words in this text? What are some ways we could answer these questions? (Use the surrounding context; break the words into meaningful parts; use a dictionary; discuss with others.)

Figure RL 4.3 offers a template for students to record words and meanings, as well as noting any specific characteristics such as similes, metaphors, or alliteration.

I Notice Interesting Words When I Read!

Name: _____ Date: _____

Title: _____

Words Worth Noticing

Name: _____ Date: _____

Title: _____

Word or Phrase	**Meaning**	**Special Characteristic**

Figure RL 4.4

INTENSIFYING THE INSTRUCTION
Vocabulary-Learning Strategies

The vocabulary-learning strategy lessons are designed to help students understand what to do with potentially important unfamiliar words.

1. Select a text that contains vocabulary you know will challenge the participating students. This could be a text you are reading with the whole class. Each student should have access to a copy.

2. Read a portion of the text, demonstrating your thinking processes for dealing with vocabulary:

   - Is this a word I should try to understand or is it not important here?
   - Can I use my own logic to figure out what it means?
   - Do the surrounding sentences provide any clues to the meaning?
   - Do I recognize any of the word parts?
   - Does the author provide information anywhere else?
   - Is there someone I could ask?
   - Should I check the dictionary?

   Be explicit about your processes. We want students to be consciously aware of what you are doing so that they will know how to bring these strategies into their own reading.

3. After demonstrating, ask students to read and discuss a passage of the text together, identifying unfamiliar words and discussing the best strategies for determining their meanings. Students can use highlighting tape or document words on sticky notes or note cards.

4. Continue instruction with students who do not demonstrate understanding of effective strategies for learning about new words.

INTENSIFYING THE INSTRUCTION
Vocabulary Studies

A new word is best learned as a concept, rather than through a process of isolated word study. The vocabulary-learning strategy lessons are designed as frameworks for students to study words in the wider context in which they appear.

To implement vocabulary studies, select words that are critical to understanding the key concepts in a text and use the graphic organizers featured in figures RL 4.6 to RL 4.10 to guide students to explore them from a variety of angles. Or students may select their own words for vocabulary study. The organizers are examples of materials you may use. Ideally, you will create your own to suit your particular needs.

As you develop your instruction and create your materials, take into consideration the following effective strategies for facilitating vocabulary learning (synthesized from research by Jitendra et al., 2004).

1. Ensure that students read often.

2. Provide instruction related to words students will need to deeply comprehend the material they are reading.

3. Focus not on a casually chosen *set* of words, but on a key word with multiple connections to other words.

For English Learners

Intervention research suggests that "English Learners will benefit most from rich, intensive vocabulary instruction that emphasizes 'student-friendly' definitions, that engages students in the meaningful use of word meanings in reading, writing, speaking, and listening, and that provides regular review" (Gersten et al. 2007).

Semantic Web

Name: _____ Date: _____

Title: _____

Write the key word in the middle and write words and phrases to describe it in the circles.

Semantic Web with Questions

Name: _____ Date: _____

Title: _____

Write the key word in the middle.

What does it mean?

What is it like?

What are some examples?

Vocabulary Star

Name: _____ Date: _____

Title: _____

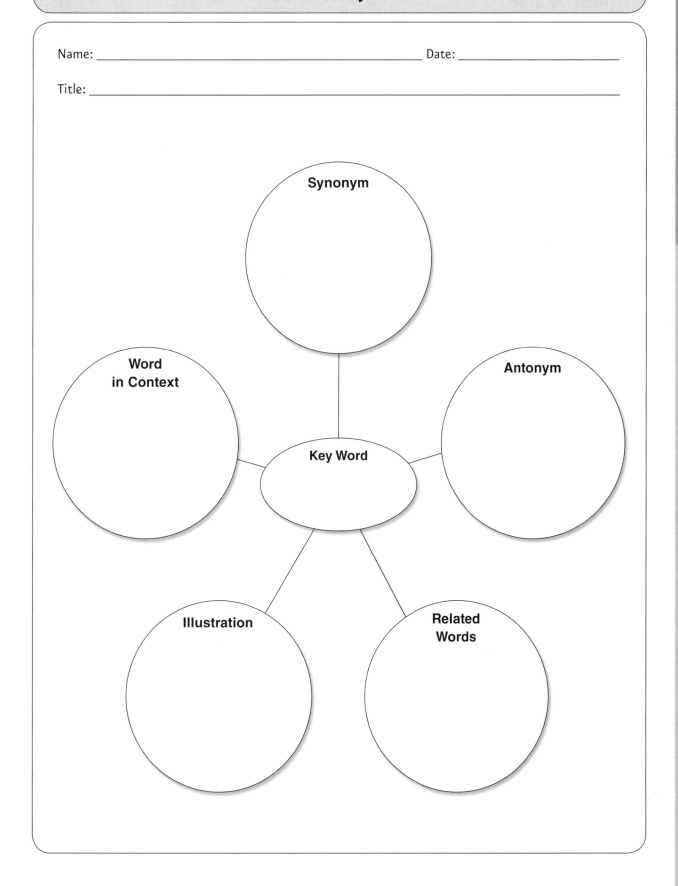

Figure RL **4.9**

Considering Word Meaning

Name: _____ Date: _____

Title: _____

> **Word**

Word in Context

Definition in My Own Words

An Example That Helps Create a Picture in My Mind

Activating Prior Knowledge for Vocabulary

Name: _____ Date: _____

Title: _____

Focus Word:

**What I
Knew Before
the Study**

**What I Have
Learned**

Collaborative Engagement

1. **Choose the literature and the reading context.** Select a book or a poem to read aloud to the whole class. Or plan for students to read together in their groups. If students are to do the reading, the text need not be the same across groups. You can differentiate across groups by choosing the literature based on student interest or on text difficulty.

2. **Arrange for students to read or listen to the text.** Before the reading, let students know what they will be doing afterward. (See Figure RL 4.11.) Note: With some of the collaborative engagements, students complete the reading after the group initially meets.

3. **Hold the meetings.** Arrange for students to come together to discuss key words and phrases from the text. Figure RL 4.11 offers a set of starter prompts.

4. **Arrange a follow-up discussion.** When all groups are working on the same text, or the same concept, organize for a whole-class discussion as a follow-up to the small-group activity.

READING ANCHOR 4:
Prompts to Support Student-Led Group Discussion of Text

Word Illustrations (Grades K–5)

Groups choose three key words or phrases from the text and work as a team to create a visual representation of each. (Or the teacher can choose the words/phrases and post them for the class.)

Graphic Organizers (Grades K–5)

Students are given a vocabulary-related graphic organizer to enlarge and complete as a team. Use organizers you have modeled with the whole class, as in Figures RL 4.2, 4.3, and RL 4.6 to RL 4.10. After they gain experience with organizers, allow students to create their own.

Vocabulary Sorts (Grades K–5)

Students are given a set of pictures, words, or phrases (prewritten on note cards) to sort. The cards should be created to represent important concepts in the story. Depending on your goals, the cards may be sorted in a number of ways. Students may:

- Place the cards in categories in any way that makes sense. Develop a title for each category.
- Place the cards in categories representing the character they best match.
- Place the cards in categories based on the sense the author is appealing to (taste, touch, smell, hearing, sight).
- Place the cards in four categories representing characters, setting, problem, and solution.
- Place the cards in categories representing literal versus figurative language.

Knowledge Rating Charts (Grades 2–5)

Before reading or listening, students individually rate their knowledge in relation to a teacher-chosen set of words. (See chart below for an example). They discuss their ratings with peers and share understandings related to words they know well.

While reading, they seek new meanings by using background knowledge, context clues, more information from peers, and the dictionary.

After reading, the words are discussed again and rated again on the chart, using a different color of pen.

Word	Know it Well	Have Heard It	Don't Know It
hospitable			
greedy			
desire			
uneasily			
dread			
foolish			
forgive			

Words from *The Golden Touch: The Story of Bacchus and King Midas* (Osborne)

Independent Application

Independent Reading

Students who read independently for at least 10 minutes per day show higher rates of vocabulary growth than students who do little independent reading (Jitendra et al. 2004). To implement *independent reading*, have your students organize their materials so that they always have a book ready to read. They may choose books from the class library or bring books from home. Or if you have a specific topic or concept in mind, provide a bin from which students may choose. Allow 10 to 30 minutes for quiet reading.

To support word consciousness, for each independent reading session, you can ask students to choose one key word or phrase that was important to the text. They record the word/phrase on a hole-punched note card and record the book title on the back. The cards are kept on a key ring for future reference.

Interactive Journals

Interactive journals are notebooks in which students record interesting ideas from their reading and explore them with a partner. The journals may be used any time two or more students are reading the same text. In support of Reading Anchor 4, interactive journals can be used as a tool for recording words and phrases that have special sounds or meanings. You can ask students to reserve a section of the journal for this purpose.

1. Instruct students to decide on a selected amount of text to read. As they read, they are to choose one or two key words or phrases to record. Depending on your curricular goals, you may wish to ask the students to look for *particular* types of words or phrases. For example:

   Kindergarten: Words you have seen before.

   Grade 1: Words or phrases that appeal to the senses or suggest feelings.

   Grade 2: Phrases that have a great sound or beat or are fun to read. The phrases may be characterized by regular beats, alliteration, rhymes, or repeated lines.

   Grades 3–5: Phrases that reflect nonliteral uses of language.

2. Peers record their words or phrases and then exchange journals. Kindergarten students then read the words together and show where they are located in the book. Students in grades 1–5 can use a plus (+) or minus (–) to indicate whether they agree or disagree that the recorded words/phrases fit the assigned criteria. They then discuss any differing points of view or understandings.

Winning Words Box

Encourage students to talk about words and their special sounds and meanings by having available a special bin with books containing "winning words." The books may be used for independent or partner reading. Start with a small collection of your favorites. Figure RL 4.12 offers some suggestions to get you started. Encourage students to add a book to the bin when they come across one they feel lives up to the "winning" criterion. As you read these books with your students, stop and discuss why certain words and phrases appeal.

Stop-and-Chats

Stop-and-chats provide a useful forum for setting up students to read with a specific purpose in mind and fostering conversations related to that purpose. They can be tailored to support students' exploration of words.

1. Two or three students who are reading the same text place a marker at an agreed-upon stopping point. As they read, they use a sticky note to write down unfamiliar words or phrases. Generally, just one or two key choices will provide enough substance to sustain a rich conversation.

2. Upon reaching the stopping point, students discuss possible meanings of their documented words and then place the marker at the next agreed-upon stopping point in preparation for another chat.

3. As a possible follow-up, the words may be revisited through whole-class or small-group discussion with the teacher.

Recommended Books and Poems for the Winning Words Box

Books for Kindergarten and First and Second Grades

Catalina Magdalena by Tedd Arnold

Chrysanthemum by Kevin Henkes

Lilly's Purple Plastic Purse by Kevin Henkes

Fancy Nancy by Jane O'Connor

Cassie's Word Quilt by Faith Ringgfold

Dr. Seuss' ABC Book by Dr. Seuss

Rain Talk by Mary Serfozo

Quick as a Cricket by Audrey Wood

The Way I Feel by Janan Cain

When Sophie Gets Angry—Really, Really Angry . . . by Molly Bang

Jamberry by Bruce Degen

My Many Colored Days by Dr. Seuss

Books for Third, Fourth, and Fifth Grades

Word Wizard by Cathryn Falwell

Miss Alaineaus: A Vocabulary Disaster by Debra Fraser

A Chocolate Moose for Dinner by Fred Gwynne

Many Luscious Lollipops by Ruth Heller

Scranimals by Jack Prelutsky

Martin's Big Words by Doreen Rappaport

The Great Fuzz Frenzy by Janet Stevens

Max's Words by Kate Banks

Quick as a Cricket by Audrey Wood

Doodle Dandies by J. Patrick Lewis

I Am America by Charles Smith

When Winter Comes by Robert Maass

Poems

Covers by Nikki Giovanni

Prickled Pickles Don't Smile by Nikki Giovanni

Horned Lizard by Pat Mora

Who Has Seen the Wind by Christina Rosetti

The World's Fastest Bicycle by Ken Nesbitt

My Gerbil Seemed Bedraggled by Jack Prelutsky

Fog by Carl Sandberg

Little Red Riding Hood and the Wolf by Roald Dahl

Word Appreciation Readings

Word appreciation readings are sessions organized for students to revisit text with a specific aesthetic purpose in mind. After students have read or listened to a poem or story at least once, they go back into the text a second time to look closely for particularly rich or interesting uses of language.

1. Prepare students for word appreciation readings by telling them you would like them to read (or listen) closely to bask in the delightfulness of an author's language. In relation to Reading Anchor 4, you might ask that they read/listen for particular literary techniques such as the following:

    K–2

    - rhyme
    - alliteration
    - special beats
    - imagery
    - appeals to the senses or feelings

    3–5

    - alliteration
    - assonance
    - rhythm
    - onomatopoeia
    - repetition
    - figurative uses of language
    - metaphors
    - similes

2. After the students read or listen, they use highlighting tape to mark one to three words or phrases that stand out for them.

3. Students talk with a partner about the part they marked, telling why they think that part adds value to the piece.

Wow Word Wall

Wow word walls are collections of words that are studied based on student interest. Regardless of the other word walls being developed in your classroom at any given time, you may want to keep the wow word wall throughout the year as a way to increase student awareness and interest in authors' word choices. Word consciousness will grow through this experience.

1. Select a piece of literature with interesting words and phrases. Read a section of the text, asking students to give you a "thumbs-up" when they hear an interesting word or phrase. Be sure to choose a section with lots of scintillating words.

   - Discuss as a class why students connect to their chosen words.

   - Write one of the words on an index card with a scented marker in large print. (You can reserve these markers for wow words only.)

   - Write a student definition of the word under the word in smaller print.

   - On the back side of the card, write the dictionary definition of the word.

2. Place the card in a library pocket on the wow word wall bulletin board.

3. To continue building the wall, students in grades K–1 can continue as a class or in guided reading groups. Have one card per guided reading group or story. Students in grades 2–5 can each have a wow library card pocket. Multiple cards can be placed in each pocket and pulled out every so often to share with a partner or group.

Dictionary Entries

We know that the direct teaching or copying of definitions is not a useful strategy for developing word knowledge or comprehension. Still, dictionaries do serve important functions, and students need to learn to use them. Maintaining a collection of dictionary-entry words that have been studied in their appropriate contexts can be enriching and empowering.

1. Teach your students to read and write dictionary entries by preselecting a set of words from a children's dictionary and then showing them the professionally constructed definitions, the illustrative sentences, and any lists of related words that are included.

2. Arrange for students to build their own dictionaries over the course of the school year. Provide each child with a key ring and a large

stack of note cards with a hole punched in one corner. This allows students to add words in alphabetic order at any time. Keeping the entries meaningful and limited to just a few key words per week will sustain engagement over the course of the year.

Illustrated Definitions

Each student chooses a key word or phrase from a text the class is reading together, writes it in large print on a piece of paper, and creates an illustration to help show the meaning. Students may write the word in a sentence or write a definition using their own wording. To help students choose appropriate words from a read-aloud, you can list several possibilities, having the students choose just one. Or you can require that they choose a particular type of word or phrase (such as feeling words or figurative language). Student creations can be shared in small groups or stapled together to form a class book.

Focused Word Studies

Kindergarten: Students choose three words from the word wall and draw a picture that helps show what each word means. (*Note:* The word wall should be of the type that focuses on vocabulary and meanings rather than the type that is focused on teaching students to read and write commonly used words.)

Grade 1: Students choose a poem from a set selected by the teacher. They read the poem many times to notice the images and feelings the author creates. They record three words or phrases that suggest feelings or appeal to the senses and create an illustration for each.

Grade 2: Students choose a poem from a set selected by the teacher. They read the poem many times to notice the interesting ways the author uses language. They record two words or phrases that have "punch," create an illustration for each, and write down why they like them. As students consider devices such as sound, beat, alliteration, rhyme, or repeated lines, you can help them use the appropriate vocabulary to describe these devices.

Grade 3: Students choose a poem from a set selected by the teacher. They read the poem many times to notice the interesting ways the author uses language. Specifically, they are to look for nonliteral uses of language. They record two or three phrases that show a rich use of nonliteral language and write down what they think the phrases mean.

Grade 4: Place each student with a partner. Invite each partner-team to choose a character found in mythology and to search online and in books and dictionaries to find words related to the name of the character. Each team organizes its findings onto one page. The pages are compiled to form a class book. Using the following list of characters yields some interesting results:

Achilles	Hygeia	Odysseus
Alcyone	Iris	Pan
Arachne	Janus	Pandora
Ceres	Maia	Phobos
Echo	Midas	Somnos
Helios	Morpheus	Typhon
Heracles	Narcissus	

Figure RL **4.13**

Recommended Books for Teaching About Greek Myths

Favorite Greek Myths (Mary Pope Osborne)

Classic Myths to Read Aloud (William F. Russell)

The Greek Gods (Bernard Evslin, Dorothy Evslin, and Ned Hoopes)

Greek Myths and Legends (Cheryl Evans and Anne Millard)

Greek Myths (Ingri d'Aulaire and Edgar Parin d'Aulaire)

Percy Jackson and the Olympians (Rick Riordan)

Grade 5: Students choose a poem from a set selected by the teacher. They read the poem many times to notice the interesting ways the author uses language. Specifically, they are to look for nonliteral uses of language. They highlight two or three phrases that show a rich use of nonliteral language and write down what they think the phrases mean.

CRAFT AND STRUCTURE

ANCHOR 5

English Language Arts Standards Reading: Literature ANCHOR 5

Reading Anchor 5: Analyze the structure of texts, including how specific sentences, paragraphs, and larger portions of the text (e.g., a section, chapter, scene, or stanza) relate to each other and the whole.

K	First	Second	Third	Fourth	Fifth
Recognize common types of texts (e.g., storybooks, poems).	Explain major differences between books that tell stories and books that give information, drawing on wide reading of a range of text types.	Describe the overall structure of a story, including describing how the beginning introduces the story and the ending concludes the action.	Refer to parts of stories, dramas, and poems when writing or speaking about a text, using terms such as *chapter*, *scene*, and *stanza*; describe how each successive part builds on earlier sections.	Explain major differences between poems, drama, and prose and refer to the structural elements of poems (e.g., verse, rhythm, meter) and drama (e.g., casts of characters, settings, descriptions, dialogue, stage directions) when writing or speaking about a text.	Explain how a series of chapters, scenes, or stanzas fits together to provide the overall structure of a particular story, drama, or poem.

Decision Tree for **Reading: Literature** ANCHOR 5

**Do my students need focused instruction
in relation to Reading Anchor 5?**

Anchor 5 is aimed at helping students learn to *use text structure to support meaning making*. (Refer to your grade-level standards for specific details.)

When some or all of your students could use support in this area, it is recommended that you start the process by implementing three types of instruction in sequence over the course of about a week:

| **Demonstration**
Page 77 | **Collaborative Engagement**
Page 81 | **Independent Application**
Page 85 |

The initial demonstration requires just one session (to be repeated as needed), leaving one or two days for collaborative engagement, and one or two days to begin the independent applications, which become ongoing as you choose. If you find during any phase of the instruction that some or all of your students could use intensified support, it is recommended that you move to the lessons for intensifying the instruction.

Do my students need intensified support with considering structure?

Considering structure is a comprehension strategy that supports students in connecting the different parts of a text into a meaningful whole. Students who seem to have difficulty holding meaning across the pages of a text can benefit from support with considering structure. See page 80.

Demonstration

Anchor 5 is aimed at helping students learn to *use text structure to support meaning making*. Having a sense of a structure—an idea about how texts are organized—can do two important things: It can support students in holding meaning across the pages of a text, and it can support them in pulling together all of the critical pieces of information. For example, when reading stories or dramas, students learn to expect a plot. Knowledge of plot structures provides a mental frame for organizing the material and pulling together the parts of the story. With poetry, the same holds true. Understanding the purpose of structural elements such as verses, stanzas, and line breaks can help students pull together ideas and consider how they are related.

When teaching students about text structure, we don't want to send the message that readers should consider the parts of a text simply to demonstrate their knowledge of such. Instead, we allow students to read for meaning and, when they are intrigued, to discuss the particular devices that author has used to create the dramatically or aesthetically pleasing effects. The present lesson builds a common language for discussing and analyzing text structure in ways that contribute to aesthetic appreciation and meaning making.

1. **Choose the text.** Any text can be used to teach about structure, but the key over time is variety in terms of the elements that are represented. Gather a set of texts that represent the structural elements you are to teach at your grade level. Figure RL 5.2 features an example set of elements. You will need just one text per lesson.

2. **Introduce the text and the concept.** Show students how you do a quick preview that highlights the overarching structure. You may wish to read the whole text (or a meaningful segment) aloud before discussing its structure in depth. This allows for a full focus on enjoyment and meaning. Either before or after reading the text or segment, on chart paper, write the structural features you want to highlight.

3. **Demonstrate and discuss the concept.** Use the text to show students how you make use of the key structural features you are highlighting for the lesson. Figure RL 5.1 offers a starter set of prompts.

READING ANCHOR 5:
Prompts to Support Teacher-Led Modeling and Discussion of Text

Kindergarten and First Grade

Stories, Poetry, and Informational Books

Why do you think the author wrote this?

Look at where the author put the writing (refer to structural elements such as titles, stanzas, captions, and so on). Why did the author do this? What looks like writing you have seen before? Which parts are different?

What stands out about the format? What are the words or phrases or sentences like?

What are the illustrations for?

Just for Poetry

How are line breaks used? Let's listen to what the poem sounds like without the line breaks.

Why do you think the poet chose this format?

What makes this poem fun to say? Why does it make us want to move?

Second Grade

Stories

Let's examine how the story was introduced. How did we meet the characters? How/when was the problem set up? How/when was it solved? (Figures RL 2.3 and RL 2.5 provide templates for summarizing.)

Third, Fourth, and Fifth Grades

Stories, Dramas, and Poetry

Look at the way the author organized this (refer to structural elements such as stanzas and line breaks in poetry, scenes in dramas, and chapters in stories). Why do you think the author organized the ideas this way?

Let's jot down the big idea from each section. This will help us think about how the author organized this whole piece.

Some Important Elements of Structure

Elements to Teach and Discuss in Relation to Stories

- **Title**. A heading that gives insight into the content of the story

- **Plot**. The series of events: a beginning that draws in the reader and provides information about the characters and setting; a middle that develops a conflict; a high point in action when the conflict is about to be solved; and an ending or resolution

- **Theme**. The often unstated idea, meaning, or message that ties together the characters, setting, and plot. Stories often have more than one theme

- **Caption**. A description of what is happening in an illustration

- **Speech or thought bubbles**. Graphic features showing the speech or thought of a given character

- **Chapter**. Sections of text grouping the ideas into logical parts

Elements to Teach and Discuss in Relation to Poetry

- **Title**: A heading that gives insight into the content of the poem

- **Rhyme**: Words that sound alike, often linking one concept to another

- **Rhythm**: The beat that results from the stress pattern of syllables

- **Meter**: The rhythm in a line of poetry

- **Line breaks**: Where lines of poetry end; a way to create and enhance meaning

- **Stanza**: A grouping of lines in poetry

- **Verse**: A line or division/grouping of lines in a poem

Elements to Teach and Discuss in Relation to Drama

- **Title**: A heading that gives insight into the content of the drama

- **List of characters**: A listing of information about the characters

- **Scene**: A description of the setting

- **Stage directions**: Directions throughout a script that offer information about the characters' actions

- **List of props:** A listing of items the characters use on stage

- **Dialogue**: What the characters say

- **Plot**: The series of events: a beginning that draws in the audience and provides information about the characters and setting; a middle that develops a conflict; a high point in action when the conflict is about to be solved; and an ending or resolution

INTENSIFYING THE INSTRUCTION
Consideration of Structure

Considering structure is a comprehension strategy that involves attending to the structure of text and the ways in which its parts are related.

1. Choose a book or poem for demonstration and have available a bin of books/poems for partners to use. You may wish to have all students use *either* fiction, poetry, or nonfiction the first few times you teach the structure lesson. You can differentiate by having books representing a range of difficulty.

2. Show students the surface structure of the book/poem you are using for demonstration, and tell them everything you notice (title, author, chapter headers, speech bubbles, captions, stanzas, verses). (See Figure RL 5.2.)

3. Ask the students to turn through their books and note any special features. Students may work with a partner for this step of the lesson.

4. Have students report their observations back to the whole group and remind them that previewing before reading can help them begin to build understanding.

5. Read the demonstration text and discuss the deeper structural elements such as plot or meter. (See Figure RL 5.2.) Help students understand that authors use particular structures to help organize their writing and create aesthetically or dramatically pleasing effects.

For English Learners

- Before reading, use conversations about structure as a frame for discussing content or vocabulary that may be unfamiliar.
- For step 3 of this lesson, place English learners with experienced English speakers.

Collaborative Engagement

The prompts in Figure RL 5.4 are designed to help students explore structure together. Students should work in small groups.

Figure RL 5.4

READING ANCHOR 5:
Prompts to Support Student-Led Group Discussion of Text

Kindergarten and First Grade

- Gather a bin of books for each group. Each bin should contain ten to twelve books. Students sort the books into three piles: stories, poetry, and books that give information. They may read from any pile.

- Create enough storyboards for each group. A storyboard is made up of cut-apart pages of a picture book. You may use fiction or informational text. Be sure the sequence is predictable (as with a life cycle or plant growth). Students place the storyboard pictures in order. You can select key pages for the group to work with. You may wish to laminate the pages on colored construction paper, placing pictures from the beginning on green, middle on yellow, and end on red (Tompkins 2001).

First Grade

- Gather a bin of books for each group. Each bin should contain five to seven books. Students sort the books into two piles: stories and informational books. They go through the two piles and make a chart to show what is the same and different in the two types of books. (Figure RL 5.5 provides a template.)

- Students take turns reading aloud from the pages of a story or an informational text. Choose texts that students can easily read with success.

- Students read a professionally published reader's theatre script.

Second Grade

- Prepare a set of cards with some typed-out beginnings and endings from stories. (Type them out rather than photocopying the pages.) Students read the parts and match the beginnings with the endings. (This may occur before or after the stories have been read in full.)

(continues)

Second Grade (continued)

- Students collaborate to draw a picture of the beginning and the ending of a familiar story on large chart paper. They write one sentence to describe each.

- Create enough storyboards for each group. A storyboard is made up of cut-apart pages of a picture book. Students place the storyboard pictures in order. You can select key pages for the group to work with. You may wish to laminate the pages on colored construction paper, placing pictures from the beginning on green, middle on yellow, and end on red (Tompkins 2001).

- Students take turns reading aloud from the pages of a story or an informational text. Choose texts that students can easily read with success.

- Students read a professionally published reader's theatre script.

Third, Fourth, and Fifth Grades

- Each group member draws a picture from one part of the text and writes one detail-rich sentence to describe it. Students work with their group to place their pictures in order. When the groups are finished, the whole class works through the same process, placing the pictures in order. The piece is then bound into a class book.

- Give each group a set of lines or passages from a text that has been cut into several parts. Students read the parts and place them in logical order. (This may occur before or after the piece has been read. The whole text need not be used.)

- Students work together to fill in a semantic feature analysis chart that contains key text elements from different genres. (Figure RL 5.6 provides an example.) Students place checks in the appropriate boxes. After they have placed the checks, they add five terms of their own, and place checks in the appropriate boxes.

- Students take turns reading aloud from the pages of a story or an informational text. Choose texts that students can easily read with success.

- Students read a professionally published reader's theatre script.

Comparing Stories and Informational Text

Name: _____ Date: _____

Stories

Informational Text

Semantic Feature Analysis of Three Genres

Name: _____ Date: _____

1. Place a check in the appropriate boxes.

2. Add five of your own elements and place a check in the remaining boxes.

Elements	Poetry	Drama	Prose/Stories
Chapters			
Dialogue			
Line breaks			
Meter			
Plot			
Rhythm			
Scenes			
Stage directions			
Stanzas			
Theme			

Independent Application

Browsing Bins

Provide your students with the resources necessary to develop familiarity with different types of texts by organizing bins of books by genre. Offer browsing time to the whole class, and discuss with students which bins they favor and why.

To encourage expanding tastes and preferences, take a little class time to allow students to make recommendations from the bins. This can be as simple as having every child show a book and tell what they liked about it. For upper elementary grades, you might set up a time for students to use the books to create bulleted lists of three things each that they like about reading fiction, nonfiction, and poetry.

Plot Charts

A *plot chart* is a visual depiction of the rising and falling action of a story or drama. Plot charts can be created based on picture books, chapter books, scripts, or movies, as a way of helping students see the overall structure. To get started, choose a story with a well developed plot. Figure RL 5.7 provides a recommended starter list. Read the entire story aloud, and then work with your students to fill out the plot chart that best works for your grade level. See Figures RL 5.8 and RL 5.9 or use interactive materials from ReadWriteThink such as a plot diagram (www.readwritethink.org/classroom-resources/student-interactives/plot-diagram-30040.html) or a graphic map (www.readwritethink.org/classroom-resources/student-interactives/graphic-30039.html). If you are using a chapter book, work with your students to fill in the chart one chapter at a time. Help students understand that it will take careful thinking to choose just the key elements to describe. After filling out one or more plot charts with the whole class, your students can begin to work through plot charts on their own.

Figure RL 5.7

Recommended Literature for Plot Charts	
K–2	**3–5**
The Three Snow Bears by Jan Brett	*Henry and the Buccaneer Bunnies* by Carolyn Crimi
Strega Nona by Tomie DePaola	*The Hickory Chair* by Lisa Rowe Fraustino
Mole's Hill by Lois Ehlert	*Martin's Big Words* by Doreen Rappaport
Millions of Cats by Wanda Gag	*The Great Fuzz Frenzy* by Janet Stevens
The Snowy Day by Ezra Jack Keats	*The Other Side* by Jacqueline Woodson
Shortcut by Donald Crews	*Precious and the Boo Hag* by Patricia McKissack

Plot Chart for Story Highs and Lows (K–2)

Name: _____ Date: _____

Title: _____

	Event	Event	Event	Event
+++				
++				
+				
0				
–				
– –				
– – –				

Draw or write about four important events. Color the plot chart to show highs and lows.

Plot Chart for Story Highs and Lows (3–5)

Name: _____ Date: _____

Title: _____

+++							
++							
+							
0							
–							
– –							
– – –							
Describe five to seven important events and rate each as a story high or low on the plot.	Event	Event	Event	Event	Event	Event	Event

Charting with Props

Charting with props involves students using character props or puppets to retell a story. To prepare the props, scour author websites for characters to print (see suggested sites below or photocopy and laminate cardstock characters from your students' favorite books). Before asking students to use the props, work with them to create a wall-size plot chart with sketches to cue them into key parts of the story. For example, with *The Three Little Pigs*, you might create four sketches: the exterior of the straw house, the exterior of the stick house, the exterior of the brick house, and the interior of the brick house. The high point of the story occurs in view of the brick house exterior, so this could be placed a bit higher than the other sketches.

Recommended Websites for Props
www.janbrett.com/
www.kevinhenkes.com/default.asp
www.patriciapolacco.com/
www.janetstevens.com/flash/images/Coloring_Pages.pdf

Important Parts

Important parts is a useful strategy for helping students build meaning across the pages of a chapter book. After reading a key chapter—or each chapter—students pause to consider the event that stands out the most for them. Choosing key events across chapters helps students think about how the parts fit together. Figure RL 5.10 provides a frame for analysis of four chapters.

Story Structure in Chapter Books

Name: _____ Date: _____

Title: _____

Chapter
_____

Name a key event.

Describe it in one to two sentences.

Chapter
_____

Name a key event.

Describe it in one to two sentences.

Chapter
_____

Name a key event.

Describe it in one to two sentences.

Chapter
_____

Name a key event.

Describe it in one to two sentences.

Scripting a Story for Reader's Theatre

Scripting a story for reader's theatre leads children to a deep examination of the internal structure and format of a script.

1. Select a piece of literature for the class to use to learn to prepare a script. When working with reader's theatre, choose stories with tight plots, clear endings, interesting characters, and lots of dialogue. Figure RL 5.11 provides a list of recommendations. Decide whether to focus on the whole text or a particularly memorable scene or sequence of events.

2. Spend time reading and discussing the text, as a good understanding of the story will facilitate the scripting process. Engage with the students in a discussion of characterization, setting, and plot, helping them see why all are necessary to a meaningful presentation. Using a story map or graphic organizer can help to pull out key information and ideas.

3. Using chart paper, invite the students to help you list the cast of characters and to determine whether a narrator is needed.

4. Work with the students to tell the story using dialogue. Write speaker names in the margin, and discuss whether it would make sense to copy the dialogue directly or change it into your own words. Show students how dialogue is written (without "he said" and "she said"). Original book ideas can be revised as long as you maintain the basic theme, character descriptions, and sequence of events. Encourage continued evaluation of whether the audience will understand what is happening.

5. You may wish to construct scripts with the whole class and then divide students into groups to rehearse and perform the same piece. Or after they gain experience, student groups (upper elementary) can prepare their own scripts to perform

Collaborative Sequencing

Collaborative sequencing is a whole-class effort involving putting together the pieces of a story or drama to replicate the original structure. After viewing a dramatic presentation or listening to a story read aloud, each student draws one part of the story, writes one rich and detailed sentence about that part, and determines where the event falls best: the beginning, middle, or end.

Recommended Books for Crafting Reader's Theatre Scripts

First and Second Grades

"Fire! Fire!" Said Mrs. McGuire (Bill Martin Jr.)

Duck Soup (Jackie Urbanovic)

Mouse Was Mad (Linda Urban)

It's Mine! (Leo Lionni)

The Flying Dragon Room (Audrey Wood)

Geraldine's Big Snow (Holly Keller)

Click, Clack, Moo: Cows That Type (Doreen Cronin)

The Three Billy Goats Gruff (any version)

The Three Little Pigs (any version)

Goldilocks (any version)

Third, Fourth, and Fifth Grades

The Day the Earth Was Silent (Michael McGuffee)

The Great Kapok Tree (Lynne Cherry)

Fleas (Jeanne Steig)

The True Story of the 3 Little Pigs! (Jon Scieszka)

The Seven Chinese Brothers (Margaret Mahy)

I Wish I Were a Butterfly (James Howe)

The class then meets in three groups (whose membership is based on who has depicted parts from the beginning, middle, and end) to determine an order for each piece within that group. The class then stands in a circle around the room and reads the combined pieces in sequence. Adjustments in sequence may be made before reading the piece again, and students may add helpful terms such as *first* and *next* to help clarify the order of events. Lead the class to discuss whether the plot has been captured. The pieces are bound together into a class book and kept in the classroom library.

Poetry Appreciation Readings

Poetry in the classroom should be an experience that involves reading for the joy of reading and writing for the joy of writing. When the time is right—when children have an interest in the sounds, meanings, and formats—then more formal instruction on style reasonably can begin.

1. Prepare students for poetry appreciation by telling them you would like them to revisit an already-read text to bask in the delightfulness of the poet's craft. In relation to Reading Anchor 5, you might ask that they consider questions related to the connections between format and meaning (See Figure RL 5.12.)

2. As students revisit the text, they use a sticky note to mark one part that stands out for them in relation to the questions. They may use the sticky note to record their reasons for selecting the part.

3. Students talk with a partner about the part they marked, telling why they think that part adds value to the piece.

Questions for Considering Poetry

Poetry is a unique genre in that its visual layout contributes to its meanings and sounds. Poets use spaces and line breaks to speed us up, slow us down, change our intonation, create a rhythm, keep us on a thought, or shift our focus (Kohl 1999). As you discuss poetry formats with students, show them how you read through the selection once or twice to get an overall picture of what it looks like and how it is organized. An initial examination helps readers get their bearings within the poem and become familiar with its language and structure (Kohl 1999). On a second or third reading, students can explore the following:

- What looks like writing you have seen before? What breaks this pattern?
- Why do you think the poet chose this format?
- How are spaces and line breaks used?
- Read the poem without line breaks. How is it different?
- How are verses or stanzas used?

Poetry Center

To encourage wide reading, establish a *poetry center* that includes children's poetry anthologies, photocopied poems, child-written poems, paper, pencils, and materials for illustrating. Also make available a selection of very short poems for children who wish to experiment with performing. Arrange for students to keep a special notebook for copies of their favorite poems. They can print poems from the Web and tape them into their notebooks and/or copy their own. Personal poetry anthologies make excellent individualized reading, and kids tend to return to them again and again.

Storyboard Center

Create a center for students to sequence familiar text using storyboards. A *storyboard* is made up of cut-apart pages of a picture book. Students place the storyboard pictures in order. You can select key pages rather than placing all pieces at the center. You may wish to laminate the pieces on colored construction paper and to place pictures from the beginning on green, middle on yellow, and end on red (Tompkins 2001). Before placing the materials in the center, model the process with a small group.

Comparative Reviews

To prepare a *comparative review*, students review a text by comparing it with a second piece. If you teach in the early grades, all students may review the same two texts that you have read aloud, or students may choose two to review from a small set of familiar texts that you display. If you teach older students, students may read and review their own texts.

Not only can students review two pieces of text written within the same genre, they can also review across genres. When asking students to review across genres, you may wish to keep the topics similar, to help emphasize that different genres suit different purposes. Figure RL 5.13 provides a suggested set of literature for review across genres.

Kindergarten: Let students know that they will be considering two texts that you have read aloud to them and choosing one favorite. (Choose two different genres.) Write the genre and title of each choice on a piece of chart paper and display the texts underneath. Ask students to choose one favorite, write the title and genre at the top of the page, and then draw something they liked about the favorite piece. After the students have completed their reviews, hold a whole-class session, using a graph to determine which text was the overall favorite.

First Grade: Let students know that they will be considering two texts that are written in different genres but about similar topics (choose literature, informational text, or poetry). Write the genre and title of each choice on chart paper and display the texts underneath. Students choose the text they like the best and write the title and then indicate one thing they like about the piece through drawing and writing a sentence. After the students have completed their reviews, hold a whole-class session to graph the two choices and determine which text was the overall favorite.

Figure RL **5.13**

Comparing Fiction, Nonfiction, and Poetry		
Fiction	**Nonfiction**	**Poetry (Available Online)**
The Sun Is My Favorite Star (Frank Asch)	*The Sun* (Melvin and Gilda Berger	"A Pizza the Size of the Sun" (Jack Prelutsky)
The Butterfly (Anna Milbourne)	*Monarch Butterfly* (Gail Gibbons)	"Fake Tattoo" (Nikki Grimes)
The Apple Pie Tree (Zoe Hall)	*Apples* (Gail Gibbons)	"The Cow in Apple Time" (Robert Frost)
It's Pumpkin Time! (Zoe Hall)	*The Pumpkin Book* (Gail Gibbons)	"Spaghetti Seeds" (Jack Prelutsky)
The Snowy Day (Ezra Jack Keats)	*When Winter Comes* (Robert Maass)	"Snow Day!" (Kenn Nesbitt)
A Color of His Own (Leo Lionni)	*Chameleon, Chameleon* (Joy Cowley)	"I Have a Pet Chameleon" (Kenn Nesbitt)
Diary of a Worm (Doreen Cronin)	*Wiggling Worms at Work* (Wendy Pfeffer)	"The Worm" (Ralph Bergengren)
Dolphin's First Day (Kathleen Zoehfeld)	*Dolphins* (Sylvia James)	"Sea Creatures" (Meish Goldish)
Cats, Cats, Cats (Leslea Newman)	*Cats* (Anna Milbourne)	"I've Got a Three-Thousand-Pound Cat" (Jack Prelutsky)
The Great Kapok Tree (Lynne Cherry)	*Rain Forest Babies* (Kathy Darling)	"If You Catch a Firefly" (Lilian Moore)

Second Grade: Let students know that they will be considering two stories and deciding which ending they like the best. Display both texts. Students choose one favorite and prepare an evaluation by drawing the ending, describing what makes it good, and explaining why they prefer it over the other ending. After the students have completed their reviews, hold a whole-class session to graph the two choices and determine which ending was the overall favorite.

Third Grade: Let students know that they will be comparing two texts written in the same genre. Write the genre and title of each on chart paper, and display the texts underneath. Ask students to choose a favorite and to prepare a written rationale by referring to each text as they comment on an assigned set of elements. For example:

- Which opening pages/line did you prefer? Why?

- Which ending did you prefer? Why?

- Which language was more aesthetically pleasing to you when read aloud? Why?

- Which would you want to read again? Why?

Fourth Grade: Let students know that they will be considering three texts: one story, one informational text, and one poem. Write the genre and title of each choice on chart paper and display the texts underneath. Students choose their favorite and prepare a rationale for their choice by commenting on an assigned set of elements. For example:

- Which format do you generally prefer? Why? Use examples from the three texts to explain your preference.

- Which content do you generally prefer? Why? Use examples from the three texts to explain your preference.

Fifth Grade: Let students know that they will be comparing two texts written in the same genre. Students choose a favorite and prepare a written rationale by commenting on an assigned set of elements. For example:

- Which opening did you prefer? Use examples from the texts to show why.

- Which ending did you prefer? Use examples from the texts to show why.

- Which sounds more pleasing to you when read aloud? Use examples from the texts to show why.

- Which would you want to read again? Use examples from the texts to show why.

CRAFT AND STRUCTURE

ANCHOR 6

English Language Arts Standards Reading: Literature ANCHOR 6

Reading Anchor 6: Assess how point of view or purpose shapes the content and style of a text.

K	First	Second	Third	Fourth	Fifth
With prompting and support, name the author and illustrator of a story and define the role of each in telling the story.	Identify who is telling the story at various points in the text.	Acknowledge differences in points of view of characters, including by speaking in a different voice for each character when reading dialogue aloud.	Distinguish their own point of view from that of the narrator or those of the characters.	Compare and contrast the point of view from which different stories are narrated, including the difference between first- and third-person narrations.	Describe how a narrator's or speaker's point of view influences how events are described.

Decision Tree for **Reading: Literature** ANCHOR 6

**Do my students need focused instruction
in relation to Reading Anchor 6?**

Anchor 6 requires that students *consider the ways in which point of view affects content and style.* (Refer to your grade-level standards for specific details.)

When some or all of your students could use support in this area, it is recommended that you start the process by implementing three types of instruction in sequence over the course of about a week:

Demonstration
Page 97

Collaborative Engagement
Page 101

Independent Application
Page 108

The initial demonstration requires just one session (to be repeated as needed), leaving one or two days for collaborative engagement and one or two days to begin the independent applications, which become ongoing as you choose. If you find during any phase of the instruction that some or all of your students could use intensified support, it is recommended that you move to the lessons for intensifying the instruction.

Do my students need intensified support with evaluating?

Evaluating is a comprehension strategy that involves establishing opinions, considering author intents and viewpoints, and preparing to smartly discuss and apply new information gained from reading. Students who rarely show critical thinking, seem hesitant to identify authors' viewpoints, or hesitate to express agreement/disagreement can benefit from support with evaluating. See page 100.

Demonstration

Stories and poems are written from particular points of view. Whether the author chooses to narrate in third person, or chooses a character to narrate in first person, we "see" the story depending on who is telling it. Approaching text with an eye on "whose perspective" leads to enhanced enjoyment and deepens critical thinking.

Anchor 6 requires that students *consider the ways in which point of view affects content and style*. For elementary grade students, this means considering who is telling the story and how this might affect the way events are described. The present lesson is designed to help K–5 students consider point of view and to build a common language for conversation and group activity in relation to this standard. This lesson may be implemented several times, using a different text each time.

1. **Choose the text.** Choose a text for modeling that will lead to interesting discussions about point of view. Text with easy-to-see points of view, and familiar tales told from varied perspectives, work well for this lesson. Figure RL 6.2 features a recommended starter list.

2. **Introduce the text and the concept.** Let students know that you would like to discuss the point of view from which the story is told and that they will later be expected to follow up with a related activity in a small group.

3. **Demonstrate and discuss the concept.** Work with students to consider and assess various aspects of point of view. Figure RL 6.1 offers a starter set of prompts designed to support this process.

READING ANCHOR 6:
Prompts to Support Teacher-Led Modeling and Discussion

Kindergarten and First Grade

Who is the author of this book/poem? Who is the illustrator? What did the author and illustrator do to create this book/poem?

First person: After reading this first part, we can see that one of the characters is telling the story. Who is telling the story? How do you know? What do we know about this character? How do we know?

Third person: After reading this first part, we can see that the *author* is narrating the story. When authors narrate stories, they let us know how certain characters feel and see things. Which characters do we know about? How are they feeling? How do we know?

First and Third Person: Illustrators help us know how characters feel and see things, too. Looking back through the illustrations, how has the illustrator helped us understand what characters are thinking and feeling?

Second Grade

First person: After reading this first part, we can see that one of the characters is telling the story. Who is telling the story? How is the character feeling right now? How would this character sound? What would the character's actions probably be like?

Third person: After reading this first part, we can see that the *author* is narrating the story. When authors narrate stories, they let us know how certain characters feel and see things. Which characters do we know about? What are their views? How are they feeling? How would these different characters sound? What would their actions probably be like?

Third Grade

Who is telling this story? Is it written in first person or third person?

What is the problem or goal? What led to it? Whose perspective are we seeing? What are other points of view someone might have about the problem or goal?

How does the character feel about what is happening? How do we know? How would you feel?

Fourth and Fifth Grades

Who is telling this story? Is it written in first person or third person?

First person: This story is written in first person. Who is telling the story? How does the teller's point of view influence the ways in which events are described? What does the narrator *not* tell us?

Third person: This story is written in third person. What different points of view do the characters have regarding the issue at hand? Does the author help us understand one point of view more than the others?

Figure RL **6.2**

Recommended Literature for Teaching Point of View	
Elements	**Recommended Texts**
Stories with easy-to-see points of view	*From Here to There* (Margery Cuyler) *Dragon Scales and Willow Leaves* (Terryl Givens) *George Shrinks* (William Joyce) *Diary of a Wombat* (Jackie French) *Diary of a Worm* (Doreen Cronin) *Diary of a Spider* (Doreen Cronin) *The Little Red Hen* (Jerry Pinkney) *Two Bad Ants* (Chris Raschka) *Dear Mrs. LaRue: Letters from Obedience School* (Mark Teague) *Help Me, Mr. Mutt!* (Janet Stevens and Susan Stevens Crummel) *The Frog Princess* (Rosalind Allchin) *Princess Smartypants* (Babette Cole) *The Other Side* (Jacqueline Woodson) *One Green Apple* (Eve Bunting) *Encounter* (Jane Yolen)
Poems with easy-to-see points of view	*I'm Not Afraid of the Dark* (Ken Nesbitt) *Don't Bring Camels in the Classroom* (Ken Nesbitt) *Bed in Summer* (Robert Louis Stevenson) *The Sloth* (Theodore Roethke) *Looking Forward* (Robert Louis Stevenson) *Granny Is* (Valerie Bloom) *I, Too* (Langston Hughes) *Little Red Riding Hood and the Wolf* (Roald Dahl) *A Noiseless Patient Spider* (Walt Whitman)
Stories to read after students have heard the original versions: a different point of view	*The Eensy Weensy Spider Freaks Out! (Big-Time!)* (Troy Cummings) *The True Story of the Three Little Pigs* (Jon Scieszka) *The Wolf's Story: What Really Happened to Little Red Riding Hood* (Toby Forward) *The Truth About Hansel and Gretel* (Karina Law) *A Very Smart Pea and the Princess-to-Be* (Mini Grey) *Cinderella's Rat* (Susan Meddaugh)

INTENSIFYING THE INSTRUCTION
Evaluating

Evaluating is a comprehension strategy that involves establishing opinions, considering author intents and viewpoints, and preparing to smartly discuss and apply new information gained from reading.

1. Choose a text for discussion. (This may be a text you have already read with the class, or one you choose to read solely for the purposes of this lesson.) Let students know that you want to talk with them about the author's *purpose* or *point of view*.

2. During or after reading, use questions such as the following to support students in evaluating the text and thinking critically about the impact that point of view has on content and style.

   - What topic did the author write about?

   - Who does the author have telling the story? Why do you think the author chose this narrator?

   - How do you think the narrator feels about the topic? How can you tell?

   - Do you agree with this narrator's views?

   - How might another character describe this part differently?

   - What does this narrator *not* tell us?

   - Do you think that people or issues are fairly portrayed in this book? Why?

   - Are people from parallel cultures (boys and girls, men and women, people of color) presented realistically or in stereotypical roles?

   - How does this compare with other accounts you have read?

   - How can you use the information in this book?

   - How can you effectively critique it? What language could you use to encourage others to consider your ideas?

Collaborative Engagement

1. **Choose the literature and the reading context.** You may use a text that has been read aloud to the whole class (providing at least one copy per group) or students may be arranged in groups to read different texts. When choosing literature to support exploration of Reading Anchor 6, look for texts with interesting perspectives and points of view. Starting out with obvious perspectives and points of view will help build a foundation for considering more complex concepts. Figure RL 6.2 features a recommended list for getting started.

2. **Arrange for students to read or listen to the text.** Before the reading, let students know what they will be doing afterward. (See Figure RL 6.4.) Be sure that the texts are accessible to all of your readers. Provide support for students who cannot read the material independently with success.

3. **Hold the meetings.** Arrange for students to come together after the reading to discuss issues related to point of view. Giving students key prompts (as in Figure RL 6.4) can help them engage in focused discussions.

4. **Arrange for a follow-up discussion.** When all groups are working on the same text, organize for a whole-class discussion as a follow-up to the group activity.

READING ANCHOR 6:
Prompts to Support Student-Led Group Discussion of Text

Kindergarten

- Each group member draws the storyteller. Students compare their illustrations. As an option, students may be encouraged to use a speech bubble to write something the storyteller would say.

First Grade

- **Preparation:** Gather a bin of four or five familiar books for each group. Some of the books should be narrated by the author and some by a character.

  Students sort through the books in their bin to make two piles: stories narrated by the author and stories narrated by a character. Then, they read through the books and write down one sentence from each that helps show who is telling the story. Instruct the students to include terms such as "he said," "she said," and "I," and to use the punctuation marks appropriately. As an option, make time at the end of your small-group session for students to read their work aloud so classmates can guess the narrators. Figure RL 6.5 provides a template.

Second Grade

- **Preparation:** Gather a bin of four or five familiar books for each group. Some of the books should be narrated by the author and some by a character.

  Students sort through the books to make two piles: stories narrated by the author and stories narrated by a character. Then, they read through the books and write down one sentence from each that helps show the point of view of the narrator. Students practice reading the sentences aloud in the voices of the characters. Figure RL 6.5 provides a template.

Third Grade

- Students work with their group to record a response to the following questions: What is one major problem or goal the main character faced? What did the character do about the problem or goal? What would you have done? Instruct students to come to a consensus on these three issues and record their findings and decisions. Figure RL 6.6 provides a template. As an option, they can share their findings with the class.

- Students read through a book that is familiar to the whole class, writing down one or more quotations from each important character. After recording the quotations, they practice reading their quotations aloud in the voices of the characters, preparing to read the lines aloud for the class. The class guesses which characters said those lines.

Third Grade (continued)

- Students work with their group to record a response to the following: Who narrates the story? Describe the point of view. How would things be different if the story were told from a different character's perspective or from your own perspective? Figure RL 6.7 provides a template. Some excellent stories for considering point of view include:

  - *The Eensy Weensy Spider Freaks Out! (Big-Time!)* (Troy Cummings)
  - *The Little Red Hen* (Jerry Pinkney)
  - *Diary of a Wombat* (Jackie French)
  - *Diary of a Worm* (Doreen Cronin)
  - *Diary of a Spider* (Doreen Cronin)
  - *Two Bad Ants* (Chris Raschka)
  - *Dear Mrs. LaRue: Letters from Obedience School* (Mark Teague)
  - *Help Me, Mr. Mutt!* (Janet Stevens and Susan Stevens Crummel)
  - *Encounter* (Jane Yolen)
  - *The Pain and the Great One* (Judy Blume)
  - *The Whipping Boy* (Sid Fleischman)

Fourth and Fifth Grades

- Students work with their group to compare and contrast the different points of view presented in a conventional fairy tale and its related counterpart. Figure RL 6.8 provides a template. Some excellent fractured tales to compare with their more conventional counterparts include:

  - *The True Story of the Three Little Pigs* (Jon Scieszka)
  - *The Wolf's Story: What Really Happened to Little Red Riding Hood* (Toby Forward)
  - *A Very Smart Pea and the Princess-to-Be* (Mini Grey)
  - *Cinder Edna* (Ellen Jackson)
  - *The Three Horrid Little Pigs* (Liz Pichon)

- Groups use an interactive program from ReadWriteThink to compose a fractured fairy tale: http://www.readwritethink.org/classroom-resources/student-interactives/fractured-fairy-tales-30062.html

Identifying Point of View

Name: _____ Date: _____

Title: _____

Book Title

Who tells the story? Record one sentence from the narrator.

Considering Our Own Points of View

Name: _____ Date: _____

Title: _____

One Major Problem Experienced by the Main Character

What the Character Did About This Problem/Goal

What I Would Have Done

Considering Different Points of View

Name: _____ Date: _____

Title: _____

Who narrates the story?	

Record the page number of one illustration or section to show the narrator's point of view regarding an important event. Describe the point of view. **Page:** _____	

How would things be different if the story were told from a different character's perspective or from your own perspective? **Choose one:** ___ **Different character** ___ **You or your group**	

Point-of-View Comparison Chart

Name: _____ Date: _____

Title: _____

Two Stories

Title 1   Title 2

Characters

Narrator

Troublemaker(s)

How the Trouble Starts

Describe how the narrator's point of view influences how the events are described.

Independent Application

Point-of-View Character Illustrations

Point-of-view character illustrations are student-created pictures of characters drawn from a variety of perspectives. The purpose is to support consideration of the ways in which point of view can be communicated through illustration.

> **Kindergarten:** Students draw a picture of a character at a particular point in time, using details from the author to guide the illustration. As students are drawing, you can read aloud the author's description several times, asking them to "show what the character is thinking."

> **First Grade:** Students draw a picture of a character at a particular point in time, using details from the author to guide the illustration. As students are drawing, you can read aloud the author's description several times. After drawing, students use thought bubbles to write what the character is thinking.

> **Second, Third, Fourth, and Fifth Grades:** Students draw pictures of characters from the probable perspectives of other characters. For example, although the "three little pigs" are usually depicted as cute, the wolf might depict them as menacing, as in Jon Scieszka's *The True Story of the Three Little Pigs*. Or although some artists might depict Cinderella's prince as charming, others might portray him as vain and rather silly, as in Ellen Jackson's *Cinder Edna*. Both of these books can be used as models for considering the ways in which illustrations take shape depending on the point of view of the author or narrator.

Character Evaluations

Character evaluations are written reflections designed to encourage students to consider a character from multiple perspectives. Students choose a character from a text you are reading aloud to the whole class or from a text they are reading independently. They write the character's name at the top, and then either draw or write in response to three questions:

- What do you think about this character?

- What does another character think about this character?

- What does the author think about this character?

Character Interviews

In *character interviews*, students take on the persona of a character and write responses to a set of interview questions. You may create the set of questions or brainstorm a list with your students and allow them to choose three to six to answer. Allow time for performance, as the responses to questions inspire reflection on characters and their points of view and often generate lots of laughter.

Letters from Characters

In *letters from characters*, students consider the point of view of one character in relation to a particular issue and write a letter to another character from that persona. For example, in Leo Lionni's *Frederick*, all the field mice except for Frederick gather goods for winter. With this text, students either write a letter from Frederick to the field mice or from the field mice to Frederick, using the point of view and the "voice" of the character(s). Letters from characters support students in distinguishing among different points of view in a story.

Letters from Authors

Letters from authors are written after students read or listen to a story, drama, or poem. Students consider the point of view of the author and compose a letter "from" the author, telling the class the reason for writing the piece. Students discuss their rationales in small groups or with the whole class.

News Articles

To create a *news article*, students write about a story event from the perspective of an outside reporter. Articles should consist of a clever title and a description of the event. Students can be encouraged to use a who, what, when, where, why, how format.

Diary Entries

Diary entries provide a frame for students to deeply consider the point of view of a key character.

1. Show students what a diary entry typically sounds like. You may use professionally published literature to suit this purpose. For example, with grades K–2, you could use *Diary of a Wombat* (French) or *Diary of a Worm* (Cronin), discussing how to record the date and write about one moment of the day. With grades 2–5, you could use *Dork Diaries* (Russell) or *Diary of a Wimpy Kid* (Kinney), showing how to use the diary for more extended reflection.

2. Choose a favorite story and demonstrate how to write a main character diary entry of the type you wish for your students to create. (Let them know that later they will be creating their own entries for a character in the book they are currently reading.)

3. Have students record an entry for the same character you used, at a different time in the story. The entry should focus on one particular event. For example, they might record an entry from the Wolf just before he pursues the three little pigs, or from Red Riding Hood telling why she opted to disobey her mother.

4. Arrange time for students to record entries on their own. Allow time for sharing and use this as an opportunity to discuss the idea that different points of view influence the ways in which events are described.

Narrated Illustrations

Narrated illustrations are first-person accounts of one illustration from the perspective of a character. Students choose an illustration and write a first-person description of what is happening. To compare two different characters' perspectives, students can narrate the illustration from the two perspectives. Engaging in narrated illustrations provides a structured medium for considering different points of view.

Perspective Writing

Perspective writing provides a medium for students to identify and consider different points of view in relation to the texts they are reading.

1. After reading or listening to a story, students identify who is telling the story.

2. Students choose a paragraph or page and rewrite it to show a *different* point of view. For example, *The Cats in Krasinski Square* (Hesse) is a first-person narrative of a young Jewish girl's experience in Warsaw during World War II. The girl has burned her Jewish armband in an attempt to become invisible in the city. The page reads:

   I wear my Polish look,
   I walk my Polish walk.
   Polish words float from my lips and I am almost safe,
   almost invisible,
   moving through Krasinski Square
   past the dizzy girls riding the merry-go-round.

   In perspective writing, students rewrite the scene from the perspective of any character in the text. For example, they could write from the point of view of a member of the Gestapo who might be suspicious about all who pass through the square, or from the perspective of a passerby or a girl on the merry-go-round, who might be equally as fearful as she.

3. Allow students to share their pieces with the whole class, a small group, or a partner. Use this opportunity to emphasize the concept that the point of view that is presented is influenced by who is telling the story.

INTEGRATION OF KNOWLEDGE AND IDEAS

ANCHOR 7

English Language Arts Standards Reading: Literature ANCHOR 7

Reading Anchor 7: Integrate and evaluate content presented in diverse media and formats, including visually and quantitatively, as well as in words.

K	First	Second	Third	Fourth	Fifth
With prompting and support, describe the relationship between illustrations and the story in which they appear (e.g., what moment in a story an illustration depicts).	Use illustrations and details in a story to describe its characters, setting, or events.	Use information gained from the illustrations and words in a print or digital text to demonstrate understanding of its characters, setting, or plot.	Explain how specific aspects of a text's illustrations contribute to what is conveyed by the words in a story (e.g., create mood, emphasize aspects of a character or setting).	Make connections between the text of a story or drama and a visual or oral presentation of the text, identifying where each version reflects specific descriptions and directions in the text.	Analyze how visual and multimedia elements contribute to the meaning, tone, or beauty of a text (e.g., graphic novel, multimedia presentation of fiction, folktale, myth, poem).

Decision Tree for **Reading: Literature** ANCHOR 7

Do my students need focused instruction in relation to Reading Anchor 7?

Anchor 7 requires that students *integrate and evaluate the different media featured in text*, considering all the parts that give it meaning. (Refer to your grade-level standards for specific details.)

When some or all of your students could use support in this area, it is recommended that you start the process by implementing three types of instruction in sequence over the course of about a week:

Demonstration	**Collaborative Engagement**	**Independent Application**
Page 114	**Page 118**	**Page 121**

The initial demonstration requires just one session (to be repeated as needed), leaving one or two days for collaborative engagement and one or two days to begin the independent applications, which become ongoing as you choose. If you find during any phase of the instruction that some or all of your students could use intensified support, it is recommended that you move to the lessons for intensifying the instruction.

Do my students need intensified support with interpreting the different media featured in texts?

Media previews are a way to encourage use of the full display of information to make meaning. They can be especially beneficial for English learners, for students who need a boost in vocabulary in relation to the topic being read, and for students who tend to rush rather than allowing themselves quality time with a text. See page 117.

Demonstration

Anchor 7 requires that students *integrate and evaluate the different media featured in text*. This means that they must consider all of the parts that give a text meaning, including words, illustrations, and other media such as sound or video, and use those parts to construct an integrated understanding. The present lesson may be implemented toward this goal as many times as would be beneficial, using one or more different texts each time.

1. **Choose the text.** Select a print or digital text with illustrations (and possibly other media) that students are likely to be interested in discussing. An excellent introductory text for this lesson is *No Mirrors in My Nana's House*, by Ysaye Barnwell (http://storylineonline.net/).

2. **Introduce the text and the concept.** Briefly show all of the relevant media in the text, and let students know that to really dig into and fully live through a piece of literature, we must closely consider all of its parts.

3. **Demonstrate and discuss the concept.** As you work through the text, show students how you attend to and consider the illustrations/contributions of other media, and how they connect with the author's words. Figure RL 7.1 offers a starter set of prompts.

READING ANCHOR 7:
Prompts to Support Teacher-Led Modeling and Discussion of Text

Kindergarten

Let's discuss what we notice in this illustration. What part of the story does this illustration help us understand?

First and Second Grades

Let's discuss what this illustration tells us about the characters/the setting?

Let's discuss what this illustration tells us about this event.

Let's discuss what this illustration tells us about the problem/the solution?

Third and Fourth Grades

Let's discuss how the illustrations help create the mood.

Let's discuss how the illustrations contribute to what the author tells us about the characters/setting.

Let's discuss how the oral (or dramatic/video/sound) version reflects or differs from the text version.

Let's discuss the artist's techniques. What shapes does the artist use? Where are the different parts of the illustration placed on the page? How does the artist use colors and shading? How does the artist use size? What else does the artist do? (See information for analyzing illustrations in Figure RL 7.2.)

Fifth Grade

Let's discuss how the different media contribute to the meaning of the piece/to the tone of the piece/to the beauty of the piece.

Let's discuss the artist's techniques. What shapes does the artist use? Where are the different parts of the illustration placed on the page? How does the artist use colors and shading? How does the artist use size? What else does the artist do? (See information for analyzing illustrations in Figure RL 7.2.)

Analyzing Illustrations

Teach your students to analyze details in illustrations by inviting them to consider how the artist uses shape, space, color, and size. Bang (2000) offers some guidance for analyzing the art in children's literature.

Prompts for Teaching	Technique	Effect
What shapes does the artist use?	Smooth, flat, horizontal shapes	Creates a sense of stability and calm
	Vertical shapes	Creates a sense of excitement and activity
	Diagonal shapes	Creates a sense of motion or tension
	Pointed shapes	Creates a sense of feeling scared
	Rounded shapes or curves	Creates a sense of security and comfort
Where are the different parts of the illustration placed on the page?	Objects at center of page	Draws attention
	Objects at edges and corners	Creates tension
	Top half of picture	Conveys freedom, happiness, triumph
	Bottom half of picture	Conveys a sense of threat, heaviness, sadness, constraint
	Object placed higher on page	Conveys importance
How does the artist use colors and shading?	White or light backgrounds	Creates a sense of safety
	Dark backgrounds	Creates a sense of danger
	Different objects on page with same color	Creates a sense of connection
	Contrasts	Draws attention
How does the artist use size?	Larger objects	Conveys strength

Figure RL 7.3

INTENSIFYING THE INSTRUCTION
Media Previews

Media previews are a way to encourage students to use the entire display of information presented in a text.

1. Choose a text for modeling that contains illustrations or other visual features that greatly enhance the meaning.

2. Before reading, walk through the pages of the section to be read, discussing with students the details in the display and pointing out the importance what you are doing together:

K–2

- Discuss what you see in the illustrations.
- Discuss the characters you notice.
- Discuss the setting.
- Discuss whether you can anticipate the problems the characters are going to face.

3–5

- Discuss what stands out for you in the illustrations (or other media).
- Discuss what you think the artist is trying to show about the setting.
- Discuss what you think the artist wants the audience to notice about the characters.
- Discuss the mood or tone the artist is probably trying to convey.

For English Learners

- Use the illustrations to discuss specific vocabulary relevant to the text.
- Use small (half-inch-by-two-inch) sticky notes to label key parts of the illustrations that will appear in the written text. For example, before reading *Stellaluna* (Cannon), you might work with students to label key illustrations such as *fruit bat, clutched, limp and useless, upside down, right side up, branches, twig, limb,* and *nest*.
- Use transparency tape to highlight a few key words or phrases and discuss their meanings before reading. Show the connections between the words/phrases and the illustrations.
- Before reading, place English learners with experienced English speakers to discuss the illustrations in the story and make predictions about the content.

3. Regularly remind students that media previews are an important part of reading. Provide follow-up lessons for small groups as needed.

Collaborative Engagement

1. **Choose the literature and the reading context.** Gather a set of texts to read aloud and/or for students to read with peers. When choosing literature to support students in integrating text with visual media, look for material with visual or multimedia elements that are likely to capture students' interest and lead to discussion. We want the illustrations and the graphics to inspire the talk.

2. **Arrange for students to read or listen to the text.** Before the reading, let students know what they will be doing afterward. (See Figure RL 7.4.) Provide support for students who may struggle with reading the material independently.

3. **Hold the meetings.** Arrange for students to come together after the reading to discuss key aspects of the illustrations in relation to the written text. Give students key starter prompts (as in Figure RL 7.4) to help them focus on the ideas that are critical to integrating and evaluating information from the visual display.

4. **Arrange for a follow-up discussion.** When all groups are working on the same text, organize for a whole-class discussion as a follow-up to the group activity.

READING ANCHOR 7:
Prompts to Support Student-Led Group Discussion of Text

Preparation

- Secure an extra paperback copy of five to seven key picture books you can use to teach in relation to Reading Anchor 7. Cut apart and laminate the pages so that students can manipulate them and use them to analyze and discuss key connections between the print and the visual display. You may wish to laminate on colored construction paper, placing pages from the beginning on green, the middle on yellow, and the end on red (Tompkins 2001).

- For some of the experiences described below, you will want to mix together illustrations from several different books. Coding the pages, such as by placing a colored dot or a number in the corner of each, will help you stay organized.

Kindergarten

- Students put four to eight key pages in order and use them to retell the story. Students need not use all of the pages from the entire text.

- Students review all of the illustrations from the story, each choosing and describing one that represents a part of the story they enjoyed. Each student describes the moment the illustration depicts.

First and Second Grades

- Students review all of the illustrations provided, choosing and describing three that provide helpful or telling images of the characters.

- Students review all of the illustrations provided, choosing and describing three that provide good images of the setting.

- Students review all of the illustrations provided, choosing and describing three that show important events.

- Students review all of the illustrations provided, choosing and describing three that help show the problem and resolution.

- Students write a retelling of one page of the text, using the illustration as a guide.

Third Grade

- Students review all of the illustrations provided, choosing and describing three that show how the artist works in collaboration with the illustrator to create the mood.

- Students review all of the illustrations provided, choosing and describing three that help explain how the artist emphasizes what the character is like.

- Students review all of the illustrations provided, choosing and describing three that show how the artist emphasizes what the setting is like.

(continues)

Third Grade (continued)

- Using illustrations from one or more books, students sort the illustrations into categories based on color. They reflect on the following: Are the colors cool, warm, dark, bright, natural, artificial, gentle, vibrant? What does this do for the meaning? If the colors change across the pages of the same book, why do you think the artist made this choice?

Fourth Grade

- Students review all of the illustrations provided, choosing and marking three that show how the artist helps create the mood. They use highlighting tape to show key language that might have informed the illustrations.
- Students review all of the illustrations provided, choosing and marking three that show how the artist emphasizes character traits. They use highlighting tape to show key language that might have informed the illustrations.
- Students review all of the illustrations provided, choosing and marking three that show how the artist emphasizes what the setting is like. They use highlighting tape to show key language that might have informed the illustrations.
- Students write a description of the techniques the illustrator uses, considering the following: Are the colors cool, warm, dark, bright, natural, artificial, gentle, vibrant? Why do you think the illustrator chose these colors? What textures are used? Why do you think so? Do they appear soft, rough, smooth, harsh, fragile? How does the illustrator's choice of color and texture connect with the written text?
- Students write or perform a retelling of one page of the text, using the illustration as a guide. They may be asked to create a two-column chart of what is included in the performance/retelling and what is not.

Fifth Grade

- Students choose one illustration that shows the artist's contribution to meaning. They use highlighting tape to show the specific part of the text that is enhanced by the artist's work on this page.
- Students choose one illustration that shows the artist's contribution to the beauty of the piece. They use highlighting tape to show the language that best connects with the illustration.
- Tone is generally thought of as the narrative voice in which the story is told. It creates the mood for the piece. Students highlight one part of the narrative that is a good example of the overall tone. They write a statement that describes the tone of the piece.
- Students write a description of the techniques the illustrator uses, reflecting on the following: Are the colors cool, warm, dark, bright, natural, artificial, gentle, vibrant? Why do you think the illustrator chose these colors? What textures are used? Why do you think so? Do they appear soft, rough, smooth, harsh, fragile? How does the illustrator's choice of color and texture shape the meaning, tone, and beauty of the text?

Independent Application

Stop-and-Chats

Stop-and-chats provide a useful forum for setting up students to read with a specific purpose in mind and fostering conversations related to that purpose. To use stop-and-chats to support students in integrating ideas from the written text with the visual display, two or three students who are reading the same text should work together.

1. Before they read, students turn through the illustrations and place a marker at an agreed-upon stopping point for discussion. Upon reaching this point, they exchange their thoughts about the ways in which the text connects with the illustrations or graphics and then place the marker at the next agreed-upon stopping point in preparation for another chat. Students generally need little prompting to talk about interesting illustrations, but to get the conversations started, you and the students can brainstorm some generic prompts, or you can offer your own. For example:

Kindergarten and First and Second Grades

- What does this illustration tell us about the characters?
- What does this illustration tell us about the setting?
- What does this illustration tell us about the important events?
- Let's use the illustration to retell what has happened.

Third and Fourth Grades

- How does this illustration help create the mood?
- How does this illustration relate to what the author tells us about the setting?
- How does this illustration relate to what the author tells us about the characters?

Fifth Grade

- How does this visual display contribute to the meaning of the piece?
- How does this visual display contribute to the tone of the piece?
- How does this visual display contribute to the beauty of the piece?

2. As students gain experience with stop-and-chats, provide follow-up lessons based on observations of their performance.

Cover Studies

Cover studies are conversations between two students designed to help facilitate meaningful entry into a text.

1. Work with your students to create a list of questions to consider as they study a book cover with a partner. Keep the list short and manageable for the age group. For example, if you teach third grade, you might post the following:

    *   Based on the cover illustration, what expectations do you have for this book?

    *   Does the illustration give any information about the characters?

    *   What information does it give about the setting?

    *   What colors stand out? What might these colors mean?

    *   What mood does the artist set for the book?

2. Before starting a new book, students find a partner with whom to engage in a cover study. The partnered students need not be reading the same books. Or this activity can be done before you do a read-aloud.

Create a Cover

Arrange time for your students to create a cover for a piece of their own writing. Instruct students to include the name of the author and title and to use artistic techniques you have been studying through whole-class instruction and small-group discussions (such as creating certain moods with carefully chosen colors and shading or emphasizing what to pay attention to when considering placement on the page). Figure RL 7.2 provides some guidelines.

Art Appreciation Readings

Art appreciation readings are conducted after students have read or listened to a story at least once. The focus is on having students go back into the text a second time, with the intent of finding particularly appealing or telling illustrations. The chosen illustrations are discussed, leading to new appreciation and understanding of the literature.

1. Prepare students for art appreciation by telling them you would like them to revisit an already-read text to bask in the delightfulness of the artist's work. Turn through the pages while the group observes. In relation to Reading Anchor 7, ask that they consider questions such as the following:

- What medium does the artist use?

- What colors does the artist use?

- What shapes does the artist use?

- What textures does the artist create?

- What moods does the artist create? How?

- How does the work of the artist relate to the work of the author?

2. Students turn through the pages of their own text and use a bookmark or sticky note to mark one page that stands out for them in relation to the focus question(s). They may use the sticky note to record their reasons for selecting the page.

3. Students talk with a partner about the part they marked, telling how they think that part relates to or enhances the written text.

4. As an optional follow-up, each student may show the chosen example to the class. Allow time for class discussion.

Graphing Favorites

Choose two or three texts your students have recently read or listened to. Display the texts and ask students to choose a favorite based on visual elements such as aesthetic appeal, mood, beauty, or humor. Graph the favorites, and discuss student rationales for the choices they made.

Outstanding Illustrator Projects

Outstanding illustrator projects help students develop their tastes and preferences for art, as well as help them integrate the different information presented by authors and illustrators.

1. Allow your students time to identify an outstanding picture-book illustrator. Give them the choice of bringing in a book from home (send a note to facilitate this process) or choosing one from the classroom collection. The books will need to remain on display in the classroom for one to two weeks.

2. When the books have been chosen, allow students time to work on the projects. Some possibilities follow:

Kindergarten

- Create a bookmark with your name on it. Use it to mark an important part. Tell why it is important.

First and Second Grades

- Choose an illustration. Using a half-piece of paper, write three sentences that tell why the illustrator did a good job of portraying a character on this page. Use your writing to mark your chosen page in the book.

- Choose an illustration. Using a half-piece of paper, write three sentences that tell why the illustrator did a good job of portraying the setting on this page. Use your writing to mark your chosen page in the book.

- Choose an illustration. Using a half-piece of paper, write three sentences to tell why the illustrator did a good job of portraying the story problem or solution attempt on this page. Use your writing to mark your chosen page in the book.

Third, Fourth, and Fifth Grades

- Work with the class to create a list of questions to evaluate illustrations. Remind students of the types of questions you have encouraged them to consider in your whole-class instruction and in their small-group discussions. (See Figures RL 7.1, RL 7.2, and RL 7.4.) Students choose three to five questions. Using a half-piece of paper, they write their evaluations in bulleted-list format, using their writing to mark the chosen pages.

3. Display the books and evaluations for viewing and arrange time for all students to visit the display.

Illustrator Awards

Students work in teams of two to create an *illustrator award* for a book in the classroom library. To get started, work with students to brainstorm a list of possible awards, such as the following:

- best overall
- best detail
- best match to the story the author tells
- best parallel storytelling
- best creation of mood
- best depiction of a character
- best depiction of a setting

Awards may be created in the form of certificates, ribbons, or medals and displayed with the books. Hold an awards ceremony to share the awards.

Book Quilts

Select a piece of literature for a class read-aloud. After listening to and discussing the text, each student creates a picture representing a part of the content and just a few words to describe it. Give students white paper and crayons to create their designs. Before sending them off to work, discuss the general mood of the text, and ask them to re-create it with their color choices. Put the pieces together to create a class quilt, and discuss the meaning of the illustrations.

Comic Strip Retellings

Comic strip retellings are a combination of visuals and words used to retell key parts of a story. Students can be encouraged to retell in three or six frames, dividing their pages as follows:

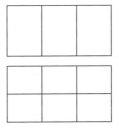

As students create their comic strip retellings, encourage them to honor the tone and mood of the original piece.

Illustration Center

Use an *illustration center* to allow your students to informally explore the illustrator's craft. To prepare, work with students to create a set of challenges. For example:

- Create a sense of motion.
- Create a sensation of heat or cold.
- Create a sense of calm.
- Create a sense of excitement and activity.
- Create an illustration that draws attention to one character.
- Convey a sense of threat or danger.
- Use the materials to show a mood of your choice. For example, you may choose happy, silly, dark, informative, serious, fun, reflective, or uncertain.

Post the possibilities on the wall near the center, make several supplies available, and allow all students the opportunity to explore the materials and activities.

INTEGRATION OF KNOWLEDGE AND IDEAS

ANCHOR 8

English Language Arts Standards Reading: Literature ANCHOR 8

Reading Anchor 8*: Delineate and evaluate the argument and specific claims in a text, including the validity of the reasoning as well as the relevance and sufficiency of the evidence.

*Anchor 8 is not applicable to the Reading: Literature category. See Reading: Informational Text for information related to teaching toward this anchor.

INTEGRATION OF KNOWLEDGE AND IDEAS

ANCHOR 9

English Language Arts Standards Reading: Literature ANCHOR 9

Reading Anchor 9: Analyze how two or more texts address similar themes or topics to build knowledge or to compare the approaches the authors take.

K	First	Second	Third	Fourth	Fifth
With prompting and support, compare and contrast the adventures and experiences of characters in familiar stories.	Compare and contrast the adventures and experiences of characters in stories.	Compare and contrast two or more versions of the same story (e.g., Cinderella stories) by different authors or from different cultures.	Compare and contrast the themes, settings, and plots of stories written by the same author about the same or similar characters (e.g., in books from a series).	Compare and contrast the treatment of similar themes and topics (e.g., opposition of good and evil) and patterns of events (e.g., the quest) in stories, myths, and traditional literature from different cultures.	Compare and contrast stories in the same genre (e.g., mysteries, and adventure stories) on their approaches to similar themes and topics.

Decision Tree for **Reading: Literature** ANCHOR 9

Do my students need focused instruction in relation to Reading Anchor 9?

Anchor 9 requires that students *compare, contrast, and integrate information from different texts.* (Refer to your grade-level standards for specific details.)

When some or all of your students could use support in this area, it is recommended that you start the process by implementing three types of instruction in sequence over the course of about a week:

Demonstration	**Collaborative Engagement**	**Independent Application**
Page 129	**Page 138**	**Page 140**

The initial demonstration requires just one session (to be repeated as needed), leaving one or two days for collaborative engagement and one or two days to begin the independent applications, which become ongoing as you choose. If you find during any phase of the instruction that some or all of your students could use intensified support, it is recommended that you move to the lessons for intensifying the instruction.

Do my students need intensified support with making connections between texts?

Because making connections between texts is so important to children's development of all kinds of knowledge, just about any student can benefit from intensified instruction in this area. English learners especially can benefit, as working with two texts that have related content provides an opportunity for repeated use of vocabulary that is focused on a particular topic. See page 137.

Demonstration

Anchor 9 requires that students *compare, contrast, and integrate information from different texts*. When working with literature (fiction), this generally involves comparing and contrasting settings, characters, events, plots, and themes. The present lesson is designed to help K–5 students meet this goal through meaningful reading. This lesson may be implemented several times, using a different text set each time.

1. **Choose the text set.** A text set is a grouping of two or more texts that are related in some way, such as by topic, theme, or genre. For this lesson, choose two texts that will allow students to explore the key narrative elements recommended for your grade level. Figure RL 9.2 features a recommended list matched with the common core grade-level elements. Allow at least two days for the lesson.

2. **Introduce the texts and the concept.** Show students the texts, indicating that you will be reading them over the course of two days and comparing them on some key elements. Let them know the elements you will be focusing on (as listed in Figure RL 9.2).

3. **Demonstrate and discuss the concept.** On day one, read the first book and place an emphasis on discussing your focus element. For example, if you teach kindergarten or first grade, emphasize attention to the characters' adventures. If you teach fourth or fifth grade, emphasize attention to the topic or theme. On day two, introduce the second book, reminding students that you will be comparing it with the first on the focus element. Read the text, focusing your discussion on comparing and contrasting the elements across books. Figure RL 9.1 offers a starter set of prompts.

Figure RL **9.1**

READING ANCHOR 9:
Prompts to Support Teacher-Led Modeling and Discussion

Kindergarten and First Grade

Let's compare the adventures/experiences of the two main characters in our two books. (Figure RL 9.3 provides a template for drawing and writing.)

- Overall, what is similar about the two stories. Let's state that in one sentence starting with "Both stories. . . ."
- Who are the main characters we are comparing?
- What kinds of adventures/experiences do both characters have? How are the experiences similar/different?

(continues)

Second Grade

- Let's compare and contrast the two stories. (Figure RL 9.3 and 9.4 provide templates.)

- Overall, what is similar about the two stories? Let's state that in one sentence starting with "Both stories are about. . . ."

- What is similar/different about the settings?

- What major problem or goal do the two main characters face? How are these similar/different? How are their responses to the problem/goal similar or different?

- How do other characters respond to these characters? Do you notice similarities in the way the two characters are treated?

- How are the endings similar or different?

Third Grade

- Let's compare and contrast the (plot, setting, themes) of the two stories. (Figures RL 9.4 and 9.5 provide templates.)

- Overall, what is similar about the two stories? Let's state that in one sentence starting with "Both stories. . . ."

- What is similar/different about the themes?

- What is similar/different about the settings?

- What major problem or goal do the two main characters face? How are these similar/different? How are their responses to the problem/goal similar or different?

- How do other characters respond to these characters? Do you notice similarities in the way the two characters are treated?

- How are the endings similar or different?

Fourth and Fifth Grades

- Let's compare and contrast the ways the two authors portray the (themes, topics) of the two stories. (Figures RL 9.4 and RL 9.5 provide templates.)

- What do we think is the central theme or message (or topic) in each story? How are the messages/themes/content similar/different?

- How does each author convey the theme/address the topic?

Grade	Elements	Recommended Text Sets
Recommended Literature for Comparing and Contrasting		
K	Compare and contrast the adventures and experiences of characters in familiar stories.	**Spunky Kids** *It Takes a Village* (Jane Cowen-Fletcher) *Oh, No, Toto!* (Katrin Hyman Tchana and Louise Tchana Pami) *No, David!* (David Shannon) **Spunky Pets** *Mittens* (Lola Schaefer) *Cookie's Week* (Cindy Ward) **Cumulative Tales—Animals Sharing Space** *Move Over, Rover!* (Karen Beaumont) *The Mitten* (Jan Brett) **Cumulative Tales—Voracious Cats** *Gobble, Gobble, Slip, Slop: A Tale of a Very Greedy Cat* (Meilo So) *Fat Cat: A Danish Folk Tale* (Margaret Read MacDonald) **Friendships Across Borders** *Yo! Yes?* (Chris Raschka) *The Knight and the Dragon* (Tomie DePaola) **Mother Separated from Young** *Stellaluna* (Janell Canon) *Owl Babies* (Martin Waddell)
1	Compare and contrast the adventures and experiences of characters in stories.	**Spunky Kids** *Lilly's Purple Plastic Purse* (Kevin Henkes) *Too Many Tamales* (Gary Soto) *Shortcut* (Donald Crews) **Spunky Pets** *Good Boy, Fergus!* (David Shannon) *Muldoon* (Pamela Duncan Edwards) *Catch That Goat!* (Polly Alakija) **Stray Animals** *The Stray Dog* (Marc Simont) *McDuff Moves In* (Rosemary Wells) **Sharing Food** *Mama Panya's Pancakes: A Village Tale from Kenya* (Mary Chamberlain) *Stone Soup* (John Muth) **Friendships Across Cultures** *The Other Side* (Jacqueline Woodson) *Henry and the Kite Dragon* (Bruce Edward Hall)

(continues)

KNOWLEDGE AND IDEAS : ANCHOR 9

1	Compare and contrast the adventures and experiences of characters in stories.	**Fantasy Flights** *Chavela and the Magic Bubble* (Monica Brown) *Abuela* (Arthur Dorros) *Tar Beach* (Faith Ringgold) **Finding Beauty in the Home Environment** *Something Beautiful* (Sharon Dennis Wyeth) *All the Places to Love* (Patricia Maclachlan)
2	Compare and contrast two or more versions of the same story by different authors or from different cultures.	**Cinderella Text Set for Second Grade** *Cinderella* (James Marshall) *Mufaro's Beautiful Daughters: An African Tale* (Jon Steptoe) *Yeh-Shen: A Cinderella Story from China* (Ai-Ling Louie) *The Rough-Face Girl* (Rafe Martin) *The Golden Sandal: A Middle Eastern Cinderella Story* (Rebecca Hickox) **Little Red Riding Hood Text Set for Second Grade** *Little Red Riding Hood* (Jerry Pinkney) *Lon Po Po: A Red Riding Hood Story from China* (Ed Young) *Pretty Salma: A Little Red Riding Hood Story from Africa* (Niki Daly) *Little Red Riding Hood* (Trina Schart Hyman) *Little Red Riding Hood: A New Fangled Prairie Tale* (Lisa Campbell Ernst) **The Three Little Pigs Text Set for Second Grade** *The Three Little Hawaiian Pigs and the Magic Shark* (Donivee Martin Laird) *The Three Little Pigs* (James Marshall) *The True Story of the Three Little Pigs* (Jon Scieszka) *The Three Little Wolves and the Big Bad Pig* (Eugene Trivizas) *The Three Little Javelinas* (Susan Lowell)
3	Compare and contrast the themes, settings, and plots of stories written by the same author about the same or similar characters.	**Author Sets** *A Chair for My Mother* (Vera B. Williams) *Something Special for Me* (Vera B. Williams) *Junkyard Wonders* (Patricia Polacco) *Thank You, Mr. Falker* (Patricia Polacco) *Rotten Richie and the Ultimate Dare* (Patricia Polacco) *My Rotten, Redheaded Older Brother* (Patricia Polacco) *Dear Mrs. LaRue* (Mark Teague) *LaRue for Mayor* (Mark Teague) *The Table Where Rich People Sit* (Byrd Baylor) *The Desert Is Theirs* (Byrd Baylor) *Mercy Watson Goes for a Ride* (Kate DiCamillo) *Mercy Watson to the Rescue* (Kate DiCamillo) *Flossie and the Fox* (Patricia McKissack) *Precious and the Boo Hag* (Patricia McKissack)

Figure RL 9.2 (continued)

4	Compare and contrast the treatment of similar themes and topics in stories, myths, and traditional literature from different cultures.	**Related Stories Collections** *When Birds Could Talk and Bats Could Sing* (told by Virginia Hamilton). A collection of traditional folktales from the southern United States, all centered around birds. *The People Could Fly: American Black Folktales* (Virginia Hamilton). A collection divided into four topic areas: animal tales, fanciful tales, supernatural tales, and slave tales. *Favorite Greek Myths* (retold by Mary Pope Osborne). A collection of Greek myths featuring many of the best-known characters. *Keepers of the Animals* (Michael Caduto and Joseph Bruchac). A collection of traditional Native American stories emphasizing the interdependence of living things.
5	Compare and contrast stories in the same genre on their approaches to similar themes and topics.	**Biographical Information on Martin Luther King** *Martin's Big Words* (Doreen Rappaport) *My Brother Martin* (Christine King Farris) **Issues of Slavery and Freedom** *January's Sparrow* (Patricia Polacco) *Pink and Say* (Patricia Polacco) **Escape from Slavery** *Henry's Freedom Box* (Ellen Levine) *Ain't Nobody a Stranger to Me* (Ann Grifalconi) *Night Boat to Freedom* (Margot Theis Raven) **Children Learning About Civil Rights** *Grandmama's Pride* (Becky Birtha) *A Sweet Smell of Roses* (Angela Johnson) **Gender Issues** *She's Wearing a Dead Bird on Her Head* (Kathryn Lasky) *Roses Sing on New Snow* (Paul Yee) **Issues of Poverty** *Fly Away Home* (Eve Bunting) *An Angel for Solomon Singer* (Cynthia Rylant) **Conservation** *The Great Kapok Tree* (Lynne Cherry) *The People Who Hugged the Trees* (adapted by Deborah Lee Rose) **The Meaning of "Rich"** *The Gold Coin* (Alma Flor Ada) *The Table Where Rich People Sit* (Byrd Baylor) *The Greatest Treasure* (Demi)

READING: LITERATURE

I Can Compare Characters!

Name: _____ Date: _____

Title: _____

Character

Character

Comparison of Two Texts

Name: _____ Date: _____

Title 1: _____

Title 2: _____

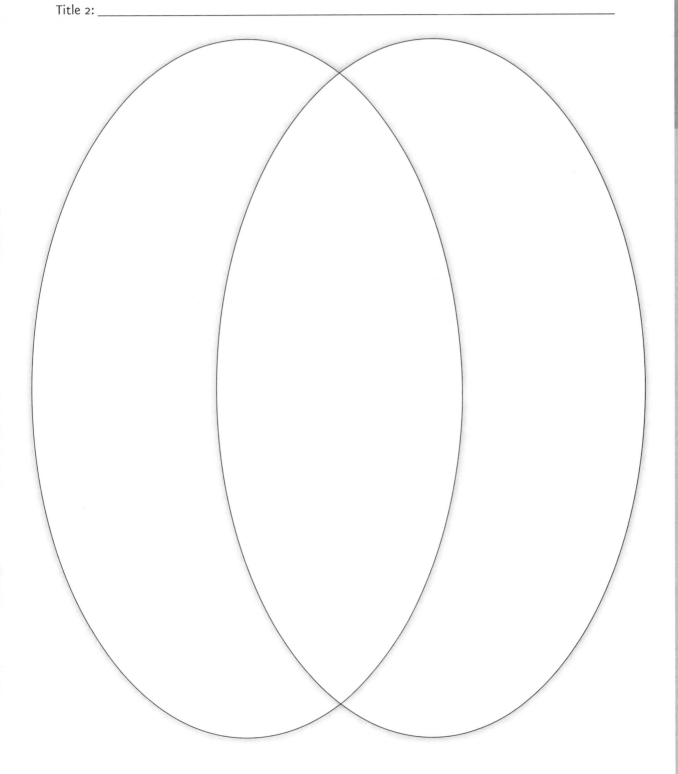

READING: LITERATURE

Alike and Different

Name: _____ Date: _____

Book 1: _____

Book 2: _____

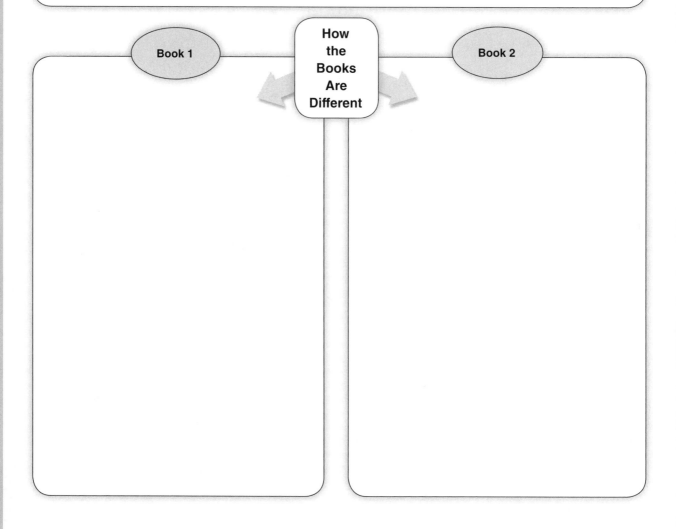

How the Books Are Alike

Book 1   How the Books Are Different   Book 2

INTENSIFYING THE INSTRUCTION
Connections Between Texts

Making Connections Between Texts is a comprehension strategy that is ideal for supporting student development in relation to Reading Anchor 9. Connections may be made between characters, settings, themes, topics, genres, or two books by the same author. Allow two days for this lesson.

1. Select two familiar texts that are related in some way. See Figure RL 9.2 for a starter set of ideas. You may read the texts aloud or students may read them silently or with a partner.

2. If you are working with a small group, give the students a large piece of chart paper; if working with the whole class, arrange students in groups, each with a large piece of chart paper in the middle.

3. Give students a set of two or three guiding questions and ask them to use a bulleted list to jot down their ideas about ways in which the texts connect. Following are some key questions to guide the process.

   - What is similar about the topics?
   - What is similar about the characters?
   - What is similar about the settings?
   - What is similar about the themes?
   - What is similar about the problem-resolution sequences?
   - What similarities do you notice in the way the books are organized?
   - These texts are written by the same author. What similarities do you notice?

   For English Learners

   If possible, place English learners with native English speakers for this activity.

4. Ask groups or partners to work together to make a statement about what they have learned by comparing and contrasting two texts.

Collaborative Engagement

1. **Choose the literature and the reading context.** Gather a set of texts that you want your students to compare. Look for texts that will lead to interesting comparisons of characters, events, topics, or themes. See the list of recommended books in Figure RL 9.2.

2. **Arrange for students to read or listen to the text.** You may use texts that have been read aloud to the whole class (ideally providing at least one copy of each per group) or students may be arranged in groups to read different texts. Because of the complexity of comparing two books, it is recommended that you read the books aloud to K–2 students and talk them through the comparison before setting them off on their own. For older students, be sure that the texts are accessible to all, providing support for those who cannot read the material independently with success.

3. **Hold the meetings.** Arrange for students to come together after the reading to compare the two texts in ways you have modeled. Giving students key prompts before reading (as in Figure RL 9.7) can help them focus on key ideas to consider in preparation for their discussions.

4. **Arrange a follow-up discussion.** When all groups are working on the same text, organize for a whole-class discussion as a follow-up to the group activity.

READING ANCHOR 9:
Prompts to Support Student-Led Group Discussion of Text

Kindergarten

- Set up a center containing puppets or props from two stories (such as *Goldilocks* and *Little Red Riding Hood*). Allow students to merge the materials and dramatize as they wish.

- After students listen to two or three stories (or more), guide each student to choose a character from one book and draw that character engaged in an experience/adventure from the book. Students should write the character's name at the top of the page. As students work, encourage talk that compares and contrasts the character's experiences and adventures. Staple all the adventures together to create a class book.

First Grade

- Students work together to record one key experience that was similar for the two main characters in two different books. You may ask that they use drawing and/or writing. Figure RL 9.3 provides a template that may be reproduced on large chart paper or given to each student for documentation.

Second Grade

- Students work together to compare and contrast two versions of the same story on one key element (topic, characters, setting, problem/goal). Students should write enough detail to show both similarities and differences. Figures RL 9.3 and RL 9.4 provide templates that may be reproduced on large chart paper or given to each student for documentation.

Third Grade

- Students work with their group to compare and contrast the settings, themes, or plots of two stories written by the same author. Figures RL 9.4 and RL 9.5 provide templates that may be reproduced on large chart paper or given to each student for documentation.

Fourth and Fifth Grades

- Students work with their group to compare and contrast the ways in which two authors portray similar themes or topics in two different stories. Figures RL 9.4 and RL 9.5 provide templates that may be reproduced on large chart paper or given to each student for documentation.

Independent Application

Browsing Bins

Create *browsing bins* featuring sets of texts you want your students to compare and contrast. Label each bin according to the topic or theme of books it contains (such as Goldilocks stories, books about pets, books about funny characters). Allow students to use the bins during independent or paired reading times, pointing out the topics on the bins and taking time to ask about the observations they are making across books. To ensure accountability and reflection, you may wish to ask that they record their observations using a compare-and-contrast organizer, as featured in Figures RL 9.3 to RL 9.5. Or each student could be required to record one or two text-to-text connections.

Graphing Favorites

Display two to four stories your students have read or listened to, and ask them to choose a favorite. Work with students to graph their favorites, encouraging them to use comparisons among the texts to provide rationales for their choices. Have students then write a comparative statement indicating why they chose one text over the other(s).

Graffiti Boards

Graffiti boards (Short, Harste, and Burke 1996) serve the important function of helping students identify and organize connections between texts.

1. Arrange for students to sit in small groups with a large piece of paper in the middle. Each group should have a text set (a collection of different texts that are related in some way, such as by topic or setting).

2. As students read, they work alone, recording words and phrases and sketching ideas and images that come to mind. To differentiate, include texts representing varying levels of difficulty and allow English learners to read in the first language if possible.

3. After the reading session, students discuss their graffiti with the group as a way to build knowledge on the topic.

Text Link Talks

Text link talks provide a structured opportunity for students to think together about different authors' approaches to similar themes and topics. For this lesson you will need five or six copies each of two books that are related by theme. Each student will also need a piece of paper that's been folded in half.

1. Read aloud and discuss the two related texts over the course of two days. After each day, guide students to use one half of the page to write down what they see as a key message or lesson from the book. They may be asked to illustrate as well. Do not work as a class to convene on a key theme/message; allow students to do this on their own and use the opportunity to assess their understandings. Students will bring their individual work to a small-group meeting on day 3.

2. On the third day, place students in groups and give each group a copy of each book and a piece of paper for recording their ideas. Present the students with the following prompts:

    *   What does your group see as the central message or theme of each book? Write down your response.

    *   How do the themes connect? Write down your response.

3. Bring the class together to compare their findings. Follow up with a discussion regarding the groups' different interpretations, showing that texts often can be interpreted in more than one way.

What's the Connection?

After the class reads or listens to two stories that connect in some way, each student writes or draws on a sticky note one or two observations about the ways in which the two texts connect. Then, students work in small groups to create a group web featuring their sticky-note observations. The notes are placed on a large piece of paper to form the web. If two students have observed the same connection, the notes are stacked. After each group creates a web, the same process is followed with the whole class, leading to a classwide web featuring all the connections students have made between the books.

Comparative Reviews

In preparing *comparative reviews*, students analyze and compare various elements of two or more texts through drawing or writing. It is recommended that these reviews be discussed with the class and then compiled as part of a class literary magazine that is published and kept on the classroom shelf. Publishing the reviews shows students that their own work is valued and allows them to gain new insights by reviewing the work of peers.

Kindergarten and First Grade: Let students know that they will be drawing two characters from two different texts that you have read aloud to them. Help them choose characters that are similar in some way. Students are to divide their paper in half and write the titles of the two books at the top. Then, they draw each character in an important part of the story. You may ask that they write words that describe each character. Encourage talk and collaboration as students work.

Second Grade: Let students know that they will be comparing two versions of the same story. Ask students to draw the main character of one of the stories—at one point in time—using as much detail as possible. They then draw the same main character from the other version—at the most similar point in time—again using as much detail as possible. Students then describe in writing what is happening in each of their illustrations, showing the similarities and differences.

Third Grade: Let students know that they will be comparing two texts written by the same author, about the same or similar characters. To format the comparison, they should create a two-column page, with one column for each book. It is suggested that students use the following prompts.

- Describe the setting for each book.

- Describe the problem/goal faced by each main character.

- Describe how each problem/goal was addressed.

- Describe the theme or lesson of each book.

Fourth Grade: Let students know that they will be comparing two stories/myths/pieces of traditional literature written on a similar topic. To format, students use two columns to the following questions (suggested by Norton 2011, 71) for each text:

- Is this a good story?

- Did the main character overcome the problem, but not too easily?

- Did I understand the characters' personalities and the reasons for their actions?

- Did the characters in the story grow?

- Did I feel that I was really in that time or place?

- Was the theme worthwhile?

To conclude:

- Which seems to be the stronger text?

Fifth Grade: Let students know that they will be comparing two stories written in the same genre and on a similar topic. Historical and contemporary realistic fiction work well, but other genres may be used as well. Students prepare a written evaluation of each text by writing a narrative describing each author's approach to the topic and answering the following questions (suggested by Norton 2011, 71) for each text:

- Is this a good story?

- Is the plot believable?

- Did the main character overcome the problem, but not too easily?

- Did the characters seem real?

- Did the characters grow?

- Did I feel I was really in that time or place?

- Was the theme worthwhile?

To conclude:

- Which seems to be the stronger text?

RANGE OF READING AND LEVEL OF TEXT COMPLEXITY

ANCHOR 10

English Language Arts Standards Reading: Literature ANCHOR 10

Reading Anchor 10: Read and comprehend complex literary and informational texts independently and proficiently.

K	First	Second	Third	Fourth	Fifth
Actively engage in group reading activities with purpose and understanding.	With prompting and support, read prose and poetry of appropriate complexity for grade 1.	By the end of the year, read and comprehend literature, including stories and poetry, in the grades 2–3 text complexity band proficiently, with scaffolding as needed at the high end of the range.	By the end of the year, read and comprehend literature, including stories, dramas, and poetry, in the grades 2–3 text complexity band independently and proficiently.	By the end of the year, read and comprehend literature, including stories and poetry, in the grades 4–5 text complexity band proficiently, with scaffolding as needed at the high end of the range.	By the end of the year, read and comprehend literature, including stories, dramas, and poetry, in the grades 4–5 text complexity band independently and proficiently.

Recommendations for Instruction 145

Recommendations for Working Toward Reading Anchor 10

The goal for Anchor 10 is that students will *read and comprehend literature considered to be within an appropriate range of complexity for their grade level*. Although all of the teaching strategies in this book are aimed at supporting this goal, their strongest impact will be felt if implemented within a wider context that makes use of what is known about reading development. With this in mind, the following research-informed recommendations are provided to aid you in implementing the strategies effectively.

- Ensure that each student finds material of interest in the classroom library.

- Arrange the classroom day so that students read extensively.

- Ensure that each student has regular access to text that can be read with success.

- Know your students' particular instructional needs.

- Ensure that your students have opportunities to talk and collaborate to enrich their reading experiences.

Ensure that each student finds material of interest in the classroom library. Research in the field of reading shows a strong connection between engagement and achievement (Braunger and Lewis 2006; Guthrie and Wigfield 2000). When students are interested in what they are reading, they process the text more deeply and show deeper levels of learning (Taboada, Tonks, Wigfield, and Guthrie 2009). They are also likely to read more (Allington 2012).

To capture and maintain interest, multiple text types are recommended: picture books, chapter books, reference books, textbooks, magazines, comic books, electronic texts, and text related to television, film, visual art, and performance art. The ultimate goal is to use text that has meaning in children's lives and at the same time to expand their access to new varieties (Wade and Moje 2001).

Arrange the classroom day so that students read extensively. When more-effective elementary classrooms are compared with less-effective classrooms, a key distinguishing feature is that students in high-achievement classrooms read more (Allington 2012). Yet, research over the past thirty years has shown that students spend disturbingly little time reading at school; only about 10 to 20 minutes per day (Allington 2012; Hiebert, Samuels, and Rasinski 2010). One recent study showed students spending on average 18 minutes reading per day, which constituted only 20 percent of a daily 90-minute reading block. About half of this time was spent reading orally and half silently, with a number of different books/topics being read during this time. Such routines leave little time for development of new strategies or for in-depth engagement with the content (Hiebert, Samuels, and Rasinski 2010).

We know that more effective teachers schedule more time for reading. Although literacy-related activities such as word study and literature response can serve important functions, they should consume considerably less time during the reading block than actual reading. Virtually any effort at scheduling that increases the amount of time students spend reading is likely to lead to gains in achievement (Allington 2012).

Ensure that each student has regular access to text that can be read with success. Reading develops most readily when the text used for instruction is neither too hard nor too easy; when it is challenging but achievable. Text that is *accessible* supports comprehension, fluency development, and consolidation of developing skills and strategies (Allington 2009; Clay 1991; Fountas and Pinnell 2006; Mesmer and Cuming 2009). Unfortunately, in many classrooms, *only* grade-level material is used for both instruction and independent reading—making the text regularly inaccessible for some students (Allington 2009). When students find themselves in a position in which most of the material they attempt to read cannot be successfully decoded and/or comprehended, they soon lose interest and often become frustrated.

At the other end of the spectrum, although there is nothing wrong with a student reading a great deal of material that feels easy in terms of decoding and comprehending, if the student has no opportunity to read material that offers challenging new vocabulary and concepts, growth cannot progress as it should.

Effective teachers use decoding and comprehension assessments to identify the types and levels of text with which students can work successfully. They move students along a gradient as they continue to expand their competencies. This is with the understanding that the difficulty of the material may be adjusted up or down depending on the situation. For example, when students are learning or solidifying new skills and strategies, easier text may be warranted. A variety of factors can make a text easy or difficult: genre, text structure, content, vocabulary, themes and ideas, literary features, book and print features, sentence complexity, words, illustrations, student motivation, and the context for reading (Fountas and Pinnell 2006; Glasswell and Ford 2011). The effective teacher understands that no gradient is perfect for any child. Professional judgment carries more weight than leveling formulas when it comes to making effective decisions about text appropriateness.

Know your students' instructional needs. Working to connect students with an abundance of literature that is *personally interesting* and *appropriately challenging* are two important parts of the instructional puzzle. Working to connect students with *just-right instruction* is yet another. "Instructional levels are not the same as instructional needs, and they are not magic bullets that ensure quality teaching around the small-group reading table" (Glasswell and Ford 2011, 211). Along with identifying a generally appropriate range of text difficulty for each student, teachers must engage in formative assessment of students' strengths and needs to effectively plan, differentiate, and revise instruction.

Formative assessment involves the collection of a broad range of information within the areas of decoding, comprehending, and personal factors affecting reading (such as interests, attitudes, approaches to learning, and outside-of-school language and literacy practices). In effective classrooms, this assessment leads to differentiation that involves not only varying the text difficulty and the topic, but also the types of instructional support provided.

Valencia and Buly (2005) identified six different profiles of readers who struggle:

- *Automatic word callers* can decode quickly and with accuracy, but do not read for meaning.
- *Struggling word callers* have difficulty with both word identification and meaning.
- *Slow word callers* decode well, but slowly, and do not read for meaning.
- *Word stumblers* have trouble with word identification but are strong comprehenders.
- *Slow comprehenders* decode accurately and comprehend well, but process text slowly.
- *Disabled readers* experience difficulty with word identification, comprehension, and fluency.

Children's needs as readers differ vastly—far beyond the "level" of text at which they are reading. Thus, not only the text and the topic but also nature of the support they are receiving should differ accordingly.

Ensure that your students have opportunities to talk and collaborate to enhance their reading experiences. Talk is a critical part of learning. It is the primary medium through which children extend their thinking beyond themselves and construct knowledge about the world (Vygotsky 1978). Research in elementary classrooms shows that exemplary teachers encourage lots of talk. High-quality talk is purposeful and connected to curricular topics, but it is conversational rather than being characterized by teachers doing all the asking and evaluating and children doing all the responding (Allington 2002; Braunger and Lewis 2006). Textual agency—the freedom to control literary discussions by initiating topics and changing topics at will—has shown to be important to children's literacy development and critical to students' viewing reading comprehension as an ongoing, fluid, social, cognitive, and linguistic process rather than a discrete set of skills and strategies (Santori 2011). Students benefit from opportunities to talk about literature on their own terms, shaping their discussions from what has moved them, intrigued them, provoked them, and raised questions in their developing minds.

Instructional Strategies for Reading: Informational Text

The Common Core Reading: Informational Text standards are designed to guide instruction with nonfiction text. The ten anchor standards (outlined in Table B) provide overarching goals for K–12 students and the more specific sets of standards (outlined at the beginning of each section in Part 2) define the specific competencies K–5 students are expected to develop by each year's end. In general, students are expected to work with their grade-level standards, using increasingly complex text as they move through the K–5 years. This is with the understanding that some students will need extra support mastering certain competencies from earlier grades before they can demonstrate full competency with their own grade-level standards. In turn, others may be ready to move forward and explore concepts and texts beyond the range recommended.

In Part 2, you will find ten sections, each focused on a separate Informational Text anchor standard. Within each section, you will find a set of instructional practices involving demonstration, collaborative engagement, and independent application. These three types of experience used in sequence serve as a frame for supporting students in gradually taking control of complex thinking and activity in relation to each standard.

To support differentiation, each section begins with a decision tree to help you determine whether to pursue the lesson sequence for the anchor at hand. You may decide to use the sequence with all of your students or only a small group—or you may determine that your students are already performing well in the area and you can place your focus elsewhere. The decision tree will also help you to consider whether intensified instruction may be warranted for some or all of your students in the focus area. Lessons for intensifying the instruction are provided for each standard. As you select the learning experiences, you will see that there are ideas appropriate for instruction across the K–5 range. You should pick and choose the experiences based on your students' demonstrated needs.

A key point to keep in mind is that because the lessons in Part 2 focus on strategies for reading informational text, they serve a dual purpose: They help students develop both content knowledge and literacy knowledge. Therefore, make a point to use literature related to your content curriculum as you teach the lessons in the informational text category. The lessons are designed to support your science, social studies, and math curriculum.

Category	Anchor Standards for Reading: Informational Text K–5	Page
Key Ideas and Details	**1.** Read closely to determine what the text says explicitly and to make logical inferences from it; cite specific textual evidence when writing or speaking to support conclusions drawn from the text. **2.** Determine central ideas or themes of a text and analyze their development; summarize the key supporting details and ideas. **3.** Analyze how and why individuals, events, and ideas develop and interact over the course of a text.	**151**
Craft and Structure	**4.** Interpret words and phrases as they are used in a text, including determining technical, connotative, and figurative meanings, and analyze how specific word choices shape meaning or tone. **5.** Analyze the structure of texts, including how specific sentences, paragraphs, and larger portions of the text (e.g., a section, chapter, scene, or stanza) relate to each other and the whole. **6.** Assess how point of view or purpose shapes the content and style of a text.	**206**
Integration of Knowledge and Ideas	**7.** Integrate and evaluate content presented in diverse media and formats, including visually and quantitatively, as well as in words. **8.** Delineate and evaluate the argument and specific claims in a text, including the validity of the reasoning as well as the relevance and sufficiency of the evidence. **9.** Analyze how two or more texts address similar themes or topics to build knowledge or to compare the approaches the authors take.	**259**
Range of Reading and Level of Text Complexity	**10.** Read and comprehend complex literary and informational texts independently and proficiently.	**293**

English Language Arts Standards　Reading: Informational Text　ANCHOR 1

Reading Anchor 1: Read closely to determine what the text says explicitly and to make logical inferences from it; cite specific textual evidence when writing or speaking to support conclusions drawn from the text.

K	First	Second	Third	Fourth	Fifth
With prompting and support, ask and answer questions about key details in a text.	Ask and answer questions about key details in a text.	Ask and answer such questions as who, what, where, when, why, and how to demonstrate understanding of key details in a text.	Ask and answer questions to demonstrate understanding of a text, referring explicitly to the text as the basis for the answers.	Refer to details and examples in a text when explaining what the text says explicitly and when drawing inferences from the text.	Quote accurately from a text when explaining what the text says explicitly and when drawing inferences from the text.

Decision Tree for
Reading: Informational Text ANCHOR 1

Do my students need focused instruction in relation to Reading Anchor 1?

Anchor 1 requires that students *read closely, determining what the text says explicitly and making logical inferences.* (Refer to your grade-level standards for specific details.)

When some or all of your students could use support in this area, it is recommended that you start the process by implementing three types of instruction in sequence over the course of about a week:

Demonstration
Page 153

Collaborative Engagement
Page 163

Independent Application
Page 165

The initial demonstration requires just one session (to be repeated as needed), leaving one or two days for collaborative engagement and one or two days to begin the independent applications, which become ongoing as you choose. If you find during any phase of the instruction that some or all of your students could use intensified support, it is recommended that you move to the lessons for intensifying the instruction.

Do my students need intensified support with monitoring?

Monitoring is a comprehension strategy that involves considering the purpose of the reading event and then keeping close track of meaning to ensure that the purpose is being met. Students who need intensified support with monitoring are those who often come away from their reading not having fully met a purpose or showing partial understanding as demonstrated through retellings, conversation, and answering planned sets of questions. See page 161.

Do my students need intensified support with inferring?

Close reading requires not only determining what the text says explicitly, but also inferring. *Inferring* is a comprehension strategy that involves drawing conclusions about content using textual information as well as prior knowledge. Lessons related to inferring can be useful for all students, but particularly for those whose responses to text often reflect lower-level thinking or little interpretation beyond what is on the page. See page 162.

Demonstration

Anchor 1 requires that students *read closely*, determining what the text says explicitly and making logical inferences. Close reading involves reading for deep understanding. The goal is to enable an interpretation or explanation that includes the details as well as the bigger ideas.

When working with close reading of informational text, we must keep in mind that our *purpose* has a strong influence on *what* and *how* we read. Sometimes we need to pay close attention to detail, as when looking for a critical piece of information or seeking to answer a specific question; but sometimes we are looking for general information or ideas, and we find that skimming is sufficient; and other times we need not read the actual text at all to meet our goals for the event: just the pictures suffice. How we read—or how we *should* read—depends on the purpose we set. Considering *purpose* is an important part of close reading.

The present lesson is designed to help you demonstrate what close reading of informational text looks like and to build a common language to support group activity in relation to this standard. The lesson may be implemented several times, using a different text each time.

1. **Choose the text.** Use material that relates to your content-area curriculum or text that reflects a topic in which your students have expressed interest. If you use a textbook, be sure to supplement your instruction in the area of close reading with a variety of engaging informational books, articles, and Web-based information. This will help your students see the many different contexts in which close reading is warranted.

2. **Introduce the text and the concept.** Let students know that you will be showing them ways of engaging in a process of *reading closely to meet your purpose* and that they will then be expected to do this on their own and in groups. Clearly articulate the purpose of the reading event. Is the purpose to gain broad knowledge on a topic? Is it to answer a specific question? Is it to learn how to do something? Is it to learn about a story from the past? In light of your established purpose, show how you preview the text features such as tables of contents, illustrations, subheads, and the index to locate the parts you want to read. For example:

    *   "This website has all kinds of information about dinosaurs, but our focus is on learning about the fossil record. So I'm going to use *fossil record* as a search term and then read that part closely."

- "There is a lot of information about moths in this article, but we are focused on learning how physical characteristics help an organism survive. We'll use the subheads to find that section and discuss/take notes about that part."

- "We have been learning about stories from the past. This is a biography. We want to learn all we can about this story so it makes sense to closely read the whole text, knowing that some parts will be more important than others."

3. **Demonstrate and discuss the concept.** Read the text aloud, showing students how you stay focused on your purpose. Demonstrate how you track meaning, monitor your understandings, and think through any questions you may have, all in light of your purpose. Let them "see" your thinking processes, and encourage them to do the same types of deep thinking as they read independently. Figure RIT 1.1 offers some prompts to support the process.

READING ANCHOR 1:
Prompts to Support Teacher-Led Demonstration and Discussion

Kindergarten and First Grade

Our goal is to learn about _____. We are going to read this part closely so that we can talk through what the author is teaching about that. (As you read, you may help your students attend to detail by pausing and encouraging them to "think this through" and "picture this in your mind.")

I had a **question** about _____. Did you have any questions? (You may write the questions to help make the process concrete, and then show how you read with the purpose of answering them. You may document questions and answers using Figure RIT 1.2.)

We are reading to learn about _____. After we read, I will ask you to record one important thing the author taught about that. You may draw or write. Pay close attention because your work will be a tool for sharing what you are learning with other people. (Figure RIT 1.3 provides a template.)

Second and Third Grades

What is our purpose for reading this? What questions do we have?

Let's work together to track what the author taught in this part. How does that relate to our purpose? (Figures RIT 1.2 and 1.3 provide templates for documentation.)

We are going to read closely to map out a set of who, what, where, when, why, how questions and answers. This is a way to help you focus on key issues during your reading and to think back through the key information. (Figure RIT 1.4 provides a template for documentation.)

Fourth and Fifth Grades

What is our purpose for reading this? Let's work together to track the important ideas in relation to our purpose. What evidence or examples does the author use to support these ideas? Are there any specific words we might *quote* to help us explain? (Figures RIT 1.5 and RIT 1.6 provide templates for recording observations and sharing information with others.)

Question and Answer Chart

Name: _____ Date: _____

Title: _____

What I Wonder

What I Have Learned

What I Wonder

What I Have Learned

What I Wonder

What I Have Learned

I Read Closely!

Name: _____ Date: _____

Title: _____

Here is something important the author taught.

Key Feature Map

Name: _____ Date: _____

Title: _____

Who	**What**
Where	**When**
Why	**How**

I Explain

Name: _____ Date: _____

Title: _____

Tell about an interesting piece of information you found in this text.

Share three details or examples the author uses in relation to the information.

-

-

-

Share a quotation from the text that relates to the information.

Evidence from Informational Text

Name: _____ Date: _____

Title: _____

In one sentence, summarize a key argument, opinion, or piece of information presented by the author.

What specific information/details/examples does the author present in relation to this argument, opinion, or piece of information?

-

-

-

-

-

INTENSIFYING THE INSTRUCTION
Monitoring with Informational Text

Monitoring is a comprehension strategy that involves considering the purpose of the reading and then keeping close track of meaning to ensure that the purpose is being met.

1. To develop student awareness of monitoring, select challenging material related to a content-area topic you are exploring. Choose literature that won't be just an easy read but will require that students consider and reflect, getting a conscious feel for what close reading entails. Each student needs a copy of the text.

2. Work with the students to set a purpose for the reading. For example, if you want them to answer a set of questions, review it first. If you are reading for general information or to understand a whole text (such as a biography), make that clear. If you are reading to inform work on a project, discuss the information that needs to be obtained.

   Let students know that they will be trying out monitoring as a reading strategy and that when we monitor with informational text, we do so with a specific purpose in mind.

3. Introduce the text. Read a portion aloud, demonstrating how you think through the key ideas and details in light of your purpose. Rather than recounting every detail, show how you think through the *gist*. If you are pursuing answers to specific questions, show how answers are found:

   - by looking at one place in the text
   - by piecing together different parts
   - by using some information from the text and some from our own knowledge base

   When complexities or confusions arise, show ways to persevere. Strategies for persevering include rereading, rethinking, questioning, using illustrations, using text features, thinking aloud, and discussing the content when a peer or adult is available.

4. After you have demonstrated, turn the responsibility over to the students. Help them consider their purpose, and then read short segments and retell the gist in relation to that purpose. If the retelling is sufficient, move on. If not, guide the students to reread.

   For English Learners

   When monitoring with informational text, English learners often need support with word meanings and syntax. Allow time for rereading portions of text and retelling the gist with support. Use gesture, movement, illustrations, and conversation to help clarify meaning. If it is helpful, students can write meanings in their first language (sticky notes work well) as a scaffold for pulling and holding the ideas together.

5. Continue instruction with students who have not yet developed effective monitoring.

INTENSIFYING THE INSTRUCTION
Inferring

Inferring is a comprehension strategy that involves drawing conclusions about content using close reading of textual information as well as prior knowledge.

1. To develop student awareness of inferring, choose a text for demonstration that requires some "reading between the lines" or interpretation beyond what the author states directly in order to fully appreciate the content.

2. Introduce the text and read a portion aloud, pointing out and discussing the process of inferring. Following are some key questions to guide the process:

   • What do we think might happen next? What evidence leads us to think so?

   • What can we infer about this individual? How do we know this?

   • What can we infer are this person's reasons for making this decision?

   • What would happen if . . . ?

   • What does this probably mean? What evidence in the text supports that?

   • Why do you think the author (illustrator) included this?

   For English Learners

   Provide support enabling English learners to engage in higher-order discussion. When working with inferring, write the term on the board, and help students with its pronunciation. Show its meaning with simple examples such as "Infer how this person feels" or "Infer what would happen if. . . ." Refer back to the written term as you use it, to help students identify it within your stream of speech. English learners need not master conventional English before exploring high-level concepts written in English. From the start, they should be engaged in discussions that foster comprehension of complex material and require higher-level thinking (Gersten et al. 2007).

3. Provide follow-up lessons for small groups as needed.

Collaborative Engagement

1. **Choose the literature and the reading context.** Choose a piece of informational text, or a text set, that is relevant to a current content-area study in your classroom. Determine whether to read aloud or provide copies for students to read independently. Different discussion groups may use different texts as long as the class is focused on the same general content (such as *water*, *endangered species*, *females in history*, *celebrations*).

2. **Arrange for students to read or listen to the text.** Before reading, help students articulate the purpose. Are they seeking to collect information on a specific topic; answer a set of questions; learn how to do something; enjoy a good historical account of an event? They should focus their attention accordingly and prepare to come to the group with ideas for discussion. Figure RIT 1.9 provides a suggested set of starter prompts and activities to facilitate close reading. If you are having students do the reading, be sure to provide support for those who may struggle with the material.

3. **Hold the meetings.** Arrange for the students to come together in groups to discuss the content as assigned.

4. **Arrange a follow-up discussion.** When all groups are working from the same text, or focusing on similar content, organize for a whole-class discussion as a follow-up to the group activity.

Figure RIT **1.9**

READING ANCHOR 1:
Prompts to Support Student-Led Group Discussion

Kindergarten and First Grade

- Sitting together in a group, each student draws a picture to show something important the author taught in relation to the established purpose for reading. Students include as many details as possible. (Students sit together to promote informal dialogue about the text.) Each student then describes his or her work to the other members of the group. Discussion is encouraged.

- Students turn through the pages of the text and talk through the concepts the author taught, discussing any questions they have. Together, they choose one interesting concept and using large chart paper they create an illustration that shows the details. The illustration must be labeled.

(continues)

- Students turn through the pages of a text set looking for answers to one or two questions the class has discussed with teacher guidance. For example, "What do birds eat?" "What is their habitat?" "What are the types of homes people live in?" They draw or write to record a response. Figure RIT 1.3 may be used.

Second and Third Grades

- Students work together on large chart paper to create a picture showing each of the following: who, what, where, when, why, and how. (Figure RIT 1.4 provides a template that may be enlarged.)

- Students turn through the pages of a text set looking for answers to one or two questions the class has discussed with teacher guidance. For example, "What natural resources are found in our state?" "How do people help improve the environment?" They use sticky notes to web a group response, placing the question in the middle and parts of the answer in the spokes.

Fourth and Fifth Grades

- Students map a set of who, what, where, when, why, and how questions and answers to check and build their understanding. (Figure RIT 1.4 provides a template.)

- Students find quotations to represent who, what, where, when, why, and how. They record the information on a key feature map. (Figure RIT 1.4 provides a template.)

- Students find an illustration that gives important information in relation to the purpose that has been set for the reading. Together, they write a bulleted list of important details to notice, based on information the illustrator has provided.

- Students talk through a text (or section) by responding to the question "What is this about?" The group creates a twenty-word response that includes as much information as possible.

- Students respond to a set of questions posed by the teacher.

- Students turn through the pages of a text set looking for answers to one or two questions the class has discussed with teacher guidance. For example, "What role does mimicry play in animal survival?" "How is mimicry different from and similar to camouflage?" Students use sticky notes to map a response. For a descriptive structure, a web with spokes works well. For compare and contrast, two columns work well. For a sequence of events, the pieces may be placed in a linear array.

- Groups prepare to share with the class the most pertinent information from a portion of the text. They mark details and examples with sticky notes, writing down points that will help explain the key information. They also mark specific quotations (no more than a sentence or two) to help explain the information.

Independent Application

Independent Reading

Research evidence is clear: the more time students spend reading, the higher their reading achievement (Anderson, Fielding, and Wilson 1988). *Independent reading* is a planned event that is scheduled on a regular basis (three to five days per week). The goals are for students to deeply engage with content and to read extensively.

Students benefit most when independent reading time is carefully planned and monitored. Reutzel, Jones, and Newman (2010) offer some recommendations. First, have an appropriate set of materials always ready for use. This prevents students from spending too much of their time selecting material. You can have bins of content-area books from which children may choose (it's okay to mix social studies, science, and math), or students may read from a particular collection focused on a particular topic.

Second, make your expectations clear. Close reading can be encouraged by familiarizing students with the general procedures you expect and then monitoring their activity to be sure they are following through. To get started, work with your students to create a chart that shows the key processes you want them to follow. For example:

> • Set a purpose.
> • Preview.
> • Read.
> • Review your purpose.

Demonstrate the process, and provide opportunities for follow-up discussion regarding student use of the strategy.

Third, plan for students to engage in brief forms of response during or after each session. Having students write or orally share their thinking has been found to help keep them on task. Along these same lines, it can also be helpful to conference with students (Reutzel, Jones, and Newman 2010). This can be accomplished through brief over-the-shoulder conversations asking students to read a short section or tell you about what they are reading.

Response Journals

Response journals are notebooks in which students record their thoughts about a text that has been read or listened to. The journals can be used daily, or every so often, by all members of the class. They may be used to support independent reading or other reading experiences.

To get started, provide each student with a notebook. Let students know that the journal will be a place for recording key information and thoughts about their reading. At the end of independent reading sessions, partner-reading sessions, or whole-class read-alouds, allow students time to draw, write, and reflect in the response journal. Demonstrate the process first, as students might not have a good idea of what to write until they see the possibilities. It can be tempting to ask that they jot down the *main ideas* from a text, and you may sometimes want to do that to be sure they are getting the gist, but there are many other useful forms of response to nonfiction that will also provide indicators of comprehension:

- Write one word that was important to your reading today.

- Write one sentence that shows what was important in your reading today.

- Write a fact or piece of information about one part that would be interesting to discuss with a partner or group.

- Sketch one part you found to be interesting. Use captions or labels to show what is happening.

- Write your opinion about this book or section. Use ideas from the text to support your thinking.

- Write down what you think are the main ideas.

- Write about a connection you made to the book.

- Write about a connection between this book and another book.

Provide opportunities for students to share their journals with you or with a partner. You can respond by writing to the student on a sticky note placed on the appropriate page or arrange time for partners to respond to one another in this manner. Providing regular opportunities for sharing shows students that their work is valued and that the expectation for close reading is always present. It also provides an opportunity for students to build knowledge together.

Interactive Journals

Interactive journals are notebooks in which students participate in short written conversations about what they are reading. The journals may be used any time two or more students (or even all students in the class) are reading the same text. Interactive journals encourage close reading by involving students in a cycle of reading manageable sections of text, generating questions together, and responding briefly through writing. To introduce the process, provide each student with a notebook, showing where to write or draw, and where to leave room for a peer to respond. Let students know that the journals will be a place for sharing ideas about their reading.

1. Instruct student-teams to decide on a selected amount of text to read closely and to then be prepared to exchange their thoughts in writing. To get the written conversations started, the students can brainstorm some generic prompts or you can offer your own. For example:

   - Choose one word that represents an important concept.

   - Choose one sentence that represents what you think is the most important concept in this section.

   - Given our purpose, what have we learned so far?

   - What did the author teach in this section?

   - What do you think will happen next?

   - What do the visuals on page _____ tell us?

   Peers can use these generic prompts as conversation starters but may generate their own more tailored prompts along the way. Allow flexibility so that they may tailor their prompts to their own interests and questions in relation to the text.

2. At the agreed-upon stopping point, students write their responses and then trade journals to respond to the partner. They may exchange journals two or three times during a reading session, deciding on new prompts and stopping points as they go.

Stop-and-Chats

*Stop-and-chat*s are a framework for students to read and then stop at a designated point to discuss the content with a partner. They may be used any time two or more (even thirty) students are reading the same text. The process encourages close reading by setting up students to read with a specific purpose in mind and fostering conversations related to that purpose. When possible, pair English learners with experienced English speakers. The English learners will benefit from the low-risk context for using language to express ideas about manageable segments of text.

1. Student teams place a marker at an agreed-upon stopping point. Upon reaching this point, they exchange their thoughts about what they have read so far and then place the marker at the next agreed-upon stopping point in preparation for another chat. To get the

conversations started, you and the students can brainstorm some generic prompts, or you can offer your own. For example:

- Given our purpose, what have we learned so far?

- What is this part about?

- What did the author teach in this section?

- What do you think will happen next?

- Is there a word that is either important or confusing?

2. As students gain experience with stop-and-chats, follow up with lessons based on observations of their performance.

Information Gathering

Information gathering involves inviting students to closely read a text or its illustrations to meet a specific whole-class purpose.

1. Collect a text set on a topic you are exploring through your social studies or science curriculum. Use one of the texts to show students how you read for specific information the class needs. For example, the class may be working to collect information on the ways individuals can conserve resources or on an important person in history. Show how you read the text and/or view the illustrations with this goal in mind.

2. Provide each student with a form for documenting information in relation to the question at hand. Figure RIT 1.10 provides an example. Allow students to work in teams to search for answers to the question.

3. As a follow-up, bring the class back together to use the information that has been collected. For example, the class might web the information, forming categories along the way. Or individual students/ teams might use the information to write a particular page for what will be eventually compiled into a class book.

Information Gathering

Name: _____ Date: _____

Title: _____

Topic or Question

Information from the Text

Key Feature Illustrations

A *key feature illustration* is a visual representation of the who, what, where, when, why, and how of an informational text. Such illustrations may be created as a part of students' independent reading (to encourage and support close reading) or after you have read a text aloud to/with the class (as a means for rethinking and discussing the content). Students may use any combination of drawing, writing, colors, and symbols to represent the key features. Figure RIT 1.3 may be used as a template.

Number One Sentence!

Encourage close reading by giving students a sentence challenge. Students use highlighting tape or an erasable highlighter to mark what they think is the most important sentence in a designated section of text or in the whole text. You can teach students to choose a sentence that signifies an important concept worth considering or one that best signifies the main idea. After students have individually highlighted key sentences (or done so in teams) allow discussion time with a small group or the whole class.

Number One Word!

Encourage close reading by giving students a word challenge. Students use highlighting tape or an erasable highlighter to mark what they think is the most important word in a designated section of text or the whole text. After students have individually highlighted key words (or done so in teams), allow discussion time with a small group or the whole class.

Notes to the Author

In *notes to the author*, students use sticky notes to comment to the author on what they are thinking as they read. For example, they may comment on feelings: "This part is so sad!" They might comment on the content: "So, whales migrate to warm water to have their babies? That makes sense." They may even have a little advice for the author: "You could have written more about that. It would have been interesting." "I wish you would have defined *echidna*." Close reading is encouraged as students have an "audience" (albeit imagined) with whom to share their thinking. Of course, it's always fun for students to share their notes with one another, and this can encourage creativity and a desire to keep writing.

English Language Arts Standards Reading: Informational Text ANCHOR 2

Reading Anchor 2: Determine central ideas or themes of a text and analyze their development; summarize the key supporting details and ideas.

K	First	Second	Third	Fourth	Fifth
With prompting and support, identify the main topic and retell key details of a text.	Identify the main topic and retell key details of a text.	Identify the main topic of a multiparagraph text as well as the focus of specific paragraphs within the text.	Determine the main idea of a text; recount the key details and explain how they support the main idea.	Determine the main idea of a text and explain how it is supported by key details; summarize the text.	Determine two or more main ideas of a text and explain how they are supported by key details; summarize the text.

Decision Tree for
Reading: Informational Text ANCHOR 2

Do my students need focused instruction in relation to Reading Anchor 2?

Anchor 2 requires that students *identify and summarize the main topics or ideas* in a text. (Refer to your grade-level standards for specific details.)

When some or all of your students could use support in this area, it is recommended that you start the process by implementing three types of instruction in sequence over the course of about a week:

Demonstration	Collaborative Engagement	Independent Application
Page 173	**Page 181**	**Page 183**

The initial demonstration requires just one session (to be repeated as needed), leaving one or two days for collaborative engagement and one or two days to begin the independent applications, which become ongoing as you choose. If you find during any phase of the instruction that some or all of your students could use intensified support, it is recommended that you move to the lessons for intensifying the instruction.

Do my students need intensified support with determining what's important?

In general, a student who is comprehending effectively can be expected to identify the general topic as well as most of the key ideas. Students who generally do not demonstrate such competency can benefit from support with deciding what's important. See page 179.

Do my students need intensified support with summarizing?

A good summary is a concise retelling of the main points and reflects the structure the author used (such as description or cause-effect). Students who do not demonstrate complete or coherent retellings can benefit from lessons focused on summarizing. See page 180.

Demonstration

Anchor 2 requires that students *summarize the main topics or ideas in a text*. The goal is to consider the big picture in each key section of a text and to talk or write about it in knowledgeable ways. The present lesson is designed to help you demonstrate ways of summarizing and to help students build a common set of strategies to draw from as they develop their own summaries. The lesson may be utilized as many times as is helpful. You will need just one text per lesson.

1. **Choose the text.** Because summarizing requires an intense process of thinking and rethinking, choose material that you want students to understand and consider in depth. Working closely with material to summarize its content builds deep understanding. The lesson will work with a textbook, but other literature (including online material) should be used as well, to show students the range of reasons we might summarize a text.

2. **Introduce the text and the concept.** Before reading, discuss your purpose. Let students know that this is an important piece you want them to explore in depth, and one good way to do that is to rethink it by creating a summary. Your purpose is to read for understanding and rethink the important content.

3. **Demonstrate and discuss the concept.** Work with students to identify the key ideas and details. Jot down key information, along the way crossing off any information you discover is not critical. When you decide on the key ideas, use your notes to concisely retell the information. If necessary, number the ideas so they can be presented in a logical order. Figure RIT 2.1 offers a starter set of prompts and graphic organizers to support students as they learn to summarize nonfiction text.

READING ANCHOR 2:
Prompts to Support Teacher-Led Demonstration and Discussion of Text

Kindergarten and First Grade

What is this book/part about, mainly? What did the author teach about that? (Figure RIT 2.2 provides a template.)

Second Grade

What is this part about? Work with students to identify a main idea and to record the details or examples. (Figure RIT 2.3 provides a template for summarizing.)

Third Grade

What is the main idea in this text (or part of the text)? What are the details the author uses to describe or support that? Work with students to record key details and examples. (Figures RIT 2.3 and RIT 2.4 provide templates for summarizing.)

Fourth and Fifth Grades

What is the main idea in this text (or part of the text)? Let's write that down and then summarize the details the author uses to describe or support that. Does the sequence matter or are we just describing some things that are related, but not in sequence? (Figures RIT 2.4 and RIT 2.5 provide templates.)

I Learn from Books!

Name: _____ Date: _____

Title: _____

Here is a picture of the topic of the book.

Here are some details to describe it.

© 2012 by Gretchen Owocki, from *The Common Core Lesson Book*, *K–5*. Portsmouth, NH: Heinemann.

A Main Idea and Its Parts

Name: _____ Date: _____

Title: _____

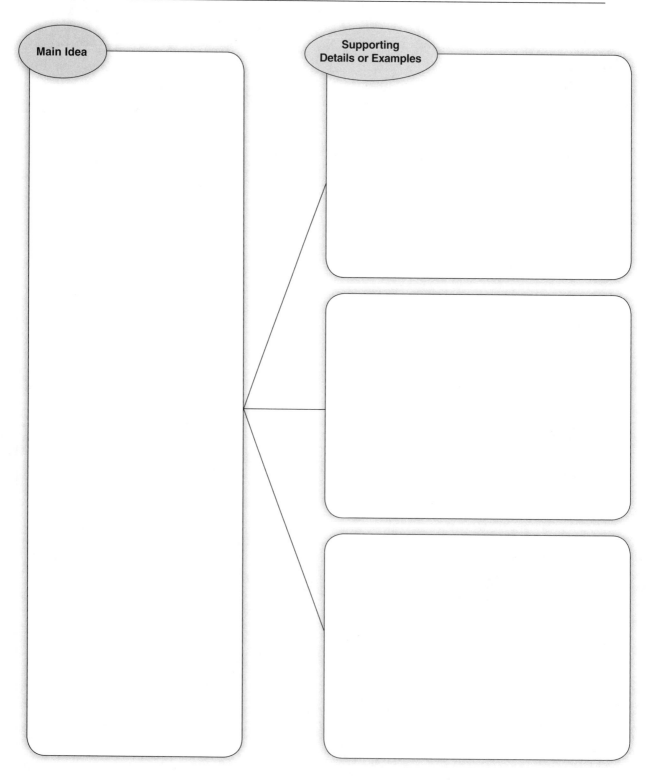

Main Idea

Supporting Details or Examples

Summarizing a Main Idea

Name: _____ Date: _____

Title: _____

In the shaded box, list a main idea. In the box below, record the key details or examples.

Summarizing Main Ideas

Name: _____ Date: _____

Title: _____

In the shaded boxes, list two main ideas. In the boxes below, record the key details or examples.

INTENSIFYING THE INSTRUCTION
Determining What's Important

Determining what is important to include in a summary is rarely easy, and there is rarely one "right" answer, but we can provide students with some support in developing concise summary statements that include key ideas and details.

1. To develop student awareness of determining what's important, select an informational text to use for demonstration. You can use this lesson several different times with different texts.

2. Because what's important depends on the purpose of the reading event, start by setting a goal. You might suggest, "We need to read this whole biography to understand what happened in this person's life" or "We need to figure out the main topic and be able to tell what the author taught about the topic" or "We just need to find the answer to our question."

3. Try to aim the students' attention at common nonfiction structures within the text, such as description, compare and contrast, or cause and effect. Considering the structure provides a mental frame for processing and summarizing the information.

4. Read the text aloud, demonstrating how to stop every so often to think through the ideas in relation to the purpose you have set. Following are some key questions to guide the demonstration process in relation to deciding what's important.

   - Why are we reading this? What is our purpose?
   - Let's describe the topic in one sentence.
   - What does the author teach or explain about the topic?
   - How does the author organize the ideas? Is this a description? Does it include cause and effect? Is there a timeline? A comparison? The author's way of organizing influences how we summarize.

   For English Learners

   Allow students to talk through the key ideas in their first language. This will support their development of content knowledge while they are developing their knowledge of the English language.

5. Provide follow-up lessons for small groups as needed.

INTENSIFYING THE INSTRUCTION
Summarizing

Helping students learn to attend to text structure can support their understanding of the concept of summary. The present lesson is focused on text structure.

1. To develop student awareness of summarizing, select a text to use for demonstration. Early on, look for text that has an easily identifiable structure (such as a description of an object, a list of objects that are described, or a comparison of two objects). More complex structures can be addressed after children have experience with summarizing using simple structures.

2. Read the text aloud, demonstrating how you take note of the way the text is organized. For example:

   - The author has described one object/event.
   - The author has described many different but related objects/events.
   - The author has written a story that takes place over time.
   - The author has written about the effects of _____.

3. Complete a written summary of key ideas by using the text's structure to guide the process. Figure RIT 5.3 (p. 227) provides visuals that may be sketched large and used to take notes. Demonstrate how to take notes, crossing off any less-important parts that you discover are not needed as the key content is being reviewed and discussed.

4. Students may use the visual to create an oral or written summary. Demonstrate both practices before expecting students to engage in this process independently or with peers.

For English Learners

Partnering an English learner with an experienced English speaker for structured activities such as writing or talking through a summary is a promising practice (Gersten et al. 2007). Regardless of whether English is the first language, you can partner students who both could benefit from intensified support with summarizing.

5. After demonstrating the process, team students up to read a short section of text together and retell the key ideas and details. Provide the graphic organizer or work with them to create their own diagram.

Collaborative Engagement

1. **Choose the literature and the reading context.** When choosing literature to support Reading Anchor 2, look for texts with content that is substantive enough for students to need to summarize and want to discuss. Text that is too simplistic or that contains concepts far beyond your students' grasp will not lead to meaningful use of summarization. You may read the text aloud to the whole class (providing at least one copy per group), or students may be arranged in groups according to different texts they are going to read together.

2. **Arrange for students to read or listen to the text.** Before the reading, let students know what they will be doing afterward. (See Figure RIT 2.8.) Be sure that the texts will be accessible to all of your students. If you are not reading the text aloud, provide support for any students who will be unable to read the text independently with success.

3. **Hold the meetings.** Arrange for the small groups to come together to discuss and summarize the text. Give students a guiding prompt or assignment (as in Figure RIT 2.8) to help them get their conversations going.

4. **Arrange a follow-up discussion.** When all groups are working on the same text, you may wish to organize for a whole-class discussion as a follow-up to the group activity.

READING ANCHOR 2:
Prompts to Support Student-Led Group Discussion of Text

- With teacher support, groups write the central topic in the center of a large piece of chart paper. Each student in the group then draws something the author taught or wrote about in relation to that topic.

- Groups write the topic of what they have read in the center of a large piece of chart paper. Working together, each student in the group selects one key paragraph or section and draws or writes a summary of the key information provided by that portion of the text. Students then discuss how their chosen portion relates to the main idea. They add to their work as new insights are generated.

- Students use a graphic organizer (an enlarged version of Figure RIT 2.3, RIT 2.4, or RIT 2.5) or create their own diagram to prepare a retelling. (Figure RIT 5.3 may be useful). After working as a group, students share the retelling with another group or the class.

Independent Application

Visual Summaries

To implement *visual summaries*, arrange for two or three students who have read the same text to reconstruct the content using sticky notes. They form a web for descriptive structures or a map for sequential structures. (See Figure RIT 5.3 for details.) Students may engage in this process after a whole-class or small-group read-aloud. When possible, pair English learners with native English speakers so that they can benefit from the low-risk context for identifying and discussing main ideas.

1. After the text has been read, students work together to write one sentence that captures the topic or the overall gist of what the author has taught or recounted. They write the sentence in the middle of a piece of paper.

2. Then, students use sticky notes to represent the key information the author taught in relation to the topic. Sticky notes are placed on the page in a meaningful way, according to the text structure. For example, if the author taught several facts about a single object or event, the notes might be placed around the topic sentence in a web to represent details of equal importance. They could draw spokes to show the connections. If some of the details are less important, they could draw a spoke extending from a spoke or use smaller sticky notes to represent those details. If the material was presented in time sequence, students might place the sticky notes in linear or clockwise order and use arrows to connect them. If the material was presented as cause and effect, they might draw arrows from cause to effect.

3. As students gain experience with visual summaries, follow-up lessons are provided based on observations of their performance.

Executive Summary

An executive summary is a short statement that captures the gist of an event and the reasons for its occurrence. To involve students in executive summary writing, assign a particular reading to groups or the whole class. Choose a news article or feature focused on a true event.

Try to choose a topic that will inspire conversation, such as a bear sighting in a neighborhood, the closing of a local factory, the capture of an elephant poacher, or a new scientific discovery. Using one side of a note card, students summarize the event as concisely as possible. On the other side, they make a statement about the event and the reasons it happened (Burke 1998). Students can bring the note cards to a small-group discussion or volunteers may be asked to share their thinking to get a whole-class discussion started.

Capture This!

Capture this! is a lesson frame for students to think through the most important information in a text by deciding the key parts to retell. Working alone, with a partner, or with a team, students use a graphic organizer (Figure RIT 2.9) to organize the content into what they think are the most important parts. Sticky notes are placed on the organizer and moved around until students find an order that seems meaningful and a set of statements that captures the key parts. If necessary, students may stack the notes, using more spaces than the four provided.

Capture This!

Name: _____ Date: _____

Title: _____

Use sticky notes to retell the key ideas in this text.

Choice of Media Summary

Before students read or listen to an informational text, let them know that they will be working either individually or in groups/teams of two to prepare a summary of the content. After the text has been read, students use different media available in the classroom or school to prepare a summary. Possibilities include:

- a bulleted-list summary created on the computer

- a bulleted-list summary created on a whiteboard

- a PowerPoint summary using one slide per big idea

- a web retelling using software such as Kidspiration

- a bulleted retelling prepared in a wiki environment

- a graphic organizer summary of their choosing (see Figure RIT 5.3 or Figures RIT 2.2 to RIT 2.5)

- an interactive graphic organizer from ReadWriteThink:

  - Compare and Contrast Map:
    www.readwritethink.org/files/resources/interactives/compcontrast/map/

  - Doodle Splash:
    www.readwritethink.org/files/resources/interactives/doodle/

  - Time Line:
    www.readwritethink.org/files/resources/interactives/timeline/

  - Webbing Tool
    http://interactives.mped.org/webbing127.aspx

  - Bio-Cube
    www.readwritethink.org/files/resources/interactives/bio_cube/

Depending on your goals, the summaries may be shared with the class. For example, if the whole class has read or listened to the same text, you could use the opportunity to discuss what should be included in the completed summaries. If the students have read different texts, the opportunity could be used to build content knowledge on a particular topic and encourage interest in reading new books.

Save the Last Word for Me

Save the last word for me (Short, Harste, and Burke 1996) is a lesson frame set up for students to identify key ideas in a text and then discuss them with peers.

1. Provide each student with three or four note cards. As students read, they write words, phrases, or sentences that are important to the meaning of the piece, recording a page number on each card. On the other side of the card, students write something they want to say or discuss about each item.

2. After the reading, each student places his or her cards in order of importance. Then, students meet in groups to share their cards. Starting from the top of the stack (round 1), each student reads aloud the word or quotation and the other students say why it is important to the piece. The student who recorded the quote then has the final word regarding why that word or segment was chosen. Students then move to round 2, using the second cards in their stacks.

Mapmakers

Mapmakers show the physical features of a setting, which can be used as a tool for retelling an event from history or for recounting key aspects of a biography. For example, students might create a map to show the path taken by the slave ship *Amistad* or the laboratory of Marie Curie. Maps can also show habitats, such as that of the Siberian tiger or the African elephant. After reading or listening, students act as mapmakers to create a physical map to be used as a tool for retelling key content.

Historians

Acting as *historians*, students use props and illustrations to retell true stories written about the recent or far past. The props provide concrete, visual information that students may draw on as they structure and restructure their retellings. For example, to retell *Mama: A True Story* (Jeanette Winter), the visual account of a hippopotamus separated from its mother during a natural disaster, two small hippopotamus props would suffice. To retell *Betsy Ross* (Alexandra Wallner) you might suggest a prop for Betsy, a colonial flag, a map showing England and the thirteen colonies, and perhaps some other small character figures to show other important people in the story.

To prepare for historian experiences, students may make/gather their own props or you can create them ahead of time. Keep the number of items manageable, with younger students using two to five props and older students using four to six props. In early childhood classrooms, the props may be made available during play or center time. Older students can meet in groups to prepare a retelling that could then be demonstrated for the class or for another group.

Depending on the technology you have available, older elementary students can be supported in creating new ways of retelling through word processing or PowerPoint tools, digital photography, clip-art montages, and literary "remixing," which involves pulling together multimodal cultural artifacts (music, art, oral language) to form new interpretations (Gainer and Lapp 2010; Knobel and Lankshear 2008; Zawilinski 2009).

Visual Retellings

Visual retellings offer a way for children to revisit and discuss a piece of text through drawing. Depending on the students' needs, they may create visuals of the following, adding captions or narrative as appropriate:

- an important event
- an important concept
- an important person
- an important object

Working in proximity with other students is probably enough to stimulate important discussion and learning, but if you wish, you may have students formally share their visuals with a group or the class.

Dramatic Retelling

After reviewing the key elements of a true story from the recent or far past, provide students with simple costumes and props for dramatizing a particular scene. Focusing on one scene can be more manageable than focusing on the whole story, and retelling even a short part of the story can be a key way for students to reflect on and demonstrate understandings about its content. In kindergarten classrooms, the costumes and props can be made available during play or center time. Older students can meet in groups to prepare a dramatic retelling that is then demonstrated for the class.

English Language Arts Standards **Reading: Informational Text** **ANCHOR 3**

Reading Anchor 3: Analyze how and why individuals, events, and ideas develop and interact over the course of a text.

K	First	Second	Third	Fourth	Fifth
With prompting and support, describe the connection between two individuals, events, ideas, or pieces of information in a text.	Describe the connection between two individuals, events, ideas, or pieces of information in a text.	Describe the connection between a series of historical events, scientific ideas or concepts, or steps in technical procedures in a text.	Describe the relationship between a series of historical events, scientific ideas or concepts, or steps in technical procedures in a text, using language that pertains to time, sequence, and cause-effect.	Explain events, procedures, ideas, or concepts in a historical, scientific, or technical text, including what happened and why, based on specific information in the text.	Explain the relationships or interactions between two or more individuals, events, ideas, or concepts in a historical, scientific, or technical text based on specific information in the text.

Decision Tree for
Reading: Informational Text ANCHOR 3

Do my students need focused instruction in relation to Reading Anchor 3?

Anchor 3 requires that students *analyze connections and relationships among individuals, ideas, or events* described within a text. (Refer to your grade-level standards for specific details.)

When some or all of your students could use support in this area, it is recommended that you start the process by implementing three types of instruction in sequence over the course of 191 a week:

| **Demonstration**
Page 191 | **Collaborative Engagement**
Page 201 | **Independent Application**
Page 203 |

The initial demonstration requires just one session (to be repeated as needed), leaving one or two days for collaborative engagement and one or two days to begin the independent applications, which become ongoing as you choose. If you find during any phase of the instruction that some or all of your students could use more intensified support, it is recommended that you move to the lessons for intensifying the instruction.

Do my students need intensified support with building background knowledge in relation to the text being read?

Analyzing connections and relationships within a text can be difficult without the relevant background knowledge. Students who can benefit from background-lessons are those who seem to have difficulty comprehending due to low vocabulary or conceptual knowledge in relation to the topic being studied. See page 198.

Do my students need intensified support with monitoring connections and relationships?

Monitoring is a comprehension strategy that involves keeping close track of meaning across the pages of a text. Students who can benefit from individualized support with monitoring are often those who provide incomplete information as they describe connections and relationships in text. See page 200.

Demonstration

Anchor 3 requires that students *analyze connections and relationships among individuals, ideas, or events* described within a text. With analysis as the goal, this standard brings students beyond reading closely and summarizing (the focus of Anchors 1 and 2); it is about also considering the hows and whys that bring depth to our understanding.

Consider an example. Closely reading to summarize a set of historic events might in itself be important, but such an experience could be deepened through consideration of the causal connections and relationships. Let's say students are reading about key events in Sioux history in the 1800s. Understanding the key events is important, but considering aspects such as the relationships among loss of hunting grounds, food shortages, and a call for government support would deepen understanding. With focused analysis, the child sees through a new lens and comes to a deeper level of internalization and understanding.

Understanding and explaining connections and relationships in text often requires that students have background knowledge on the topic at hand. Therefore, building and activating background knowledge are important parts of the lessons provided in relation to Anchor 3. Another competency needed for analysis is holding meaning across the pages of a text. To see the big picture typically requires reading the whole piece or section and putting together the meaningful pieces. The present lesson is designed with these goals in mind and may be implemented as many times as needed, using a different text each time. You will need just one text per lesson.

1. **Choose the text.** Select a piece of content-area literature that warrants careful attention to connections and relationships among individuals, ideas, or events. Following are some examples of what students analyze:

   - an important connection between two individuals; for example:

     - members of a family

     - members of a neighborhood or community

     - a consumer and a producer of a good or service

     - an elected official or lawmaker and a citizen

   - critical relationships in the field of science; for example:

     - the relationship between force and motion

     - the connection between magnetic objects and other objects

     - how a substance changes when it is mixed, cooled, or heated

     - the feeding relationships within a food chain

- critical consequences that have occurred from human actions; for example:

    - the consequence of not following a rule or abiding by a law

    - the relationship between heavy industry and pollution

    - the sequence of events leading to the need for rain forest preservation

    - the relationship between land use and erosion

- the sequence of events leading to a key event in history; for example:

    - the Atlanta bus boycott

    - school desegregation

    - the Battle of Little Bighorn

    - the Declaration of Independence

2. **Introduce the text and the concept.** Introduce the text and any content or vocabulary that might help students move meaningfully into the material. Let students know that one way to explore and understand the content of a text is to think about the important connections within. (How does one event influence another? What are the steps in this process or situation?) Preview the text by turning through and discussing key pages, letting students know the connections you want them to consider. Use this opportunity to help students begin to see the "whole picture" in preparation for developing detailed understandings about the parts. Use the preview to activate or build background knowledge on the topic.

3. **Demonstrate and discuss the concept.** Read the text aloud, using a focused set of prompts (with a graphic organizer if desired) to show students how you consider and talk through a set of key connections or relationships. Figure RIT 3.1 offers a starter set of prompts and organizers to use with informational text.

READING ANCHOR 3:
Prompts to Support Teacher-Led
Demonstration and Discussion of Text

Kindergarten and First Grade

Let's describe the connections between these two (individuals, events, ideas, pieces of information) in our book. (Figure RIT 3.2 provides a template to enlarge. Use the first column to describe one individual/event/idea and then use the second to describe the connecting individual/event/idea.)

Second Grade

Let's describe the parts of this (event, concept, set of procedures). How does one part influence the next? (Figures RIT 3.3 and RIT 3.4 provide templates to enlarge. If students will be working independently with the templates, show them how to write on sticky notes instead of writing directly on the organizers. This allows students to revise their ideas until they have worked the material into a logical sequence.)

Third, Fourth, and Fifth Grades

Let's take some notes that will help us describe/explain the parts of this (event, concept, set of procedures). (Figures RIT 3.3 to RIT 3.5 provide templates to enlarge. If students will be working independently with the templates, show them how to write on sticky notes instead of writing directly on the organizers. This allows students to revise their ideas until they have worked the material into a logical sequence.)

As we write, we will use language to help us show the connections between events and to help show why certain events occurred.

I Can Describe Connections!

Name: _____ Date: _____

Title: _____

Cause-and-Effect Chain

Name: _____ Date: _____

Title: _____

Cause-and-Effect Web

Name: _____ Date: _____

Title: _____

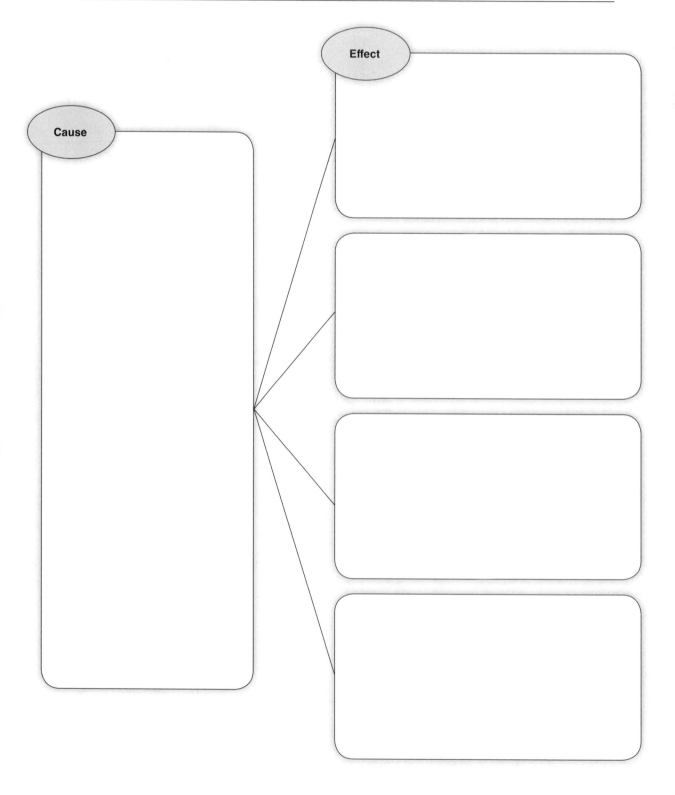

Important Events, Ideas, and Processes

Name: _____ Date: _____

Title: _____

INTENSIFYING THE INSTRUCTION
Building Background Knowledge

Describing and explaining connections and relationships within a text can be difficult to do without the relevant background knowledge. Activating and building background knowledge before reading can help readers connect with the material and see the connections within.

English learners in particular may benefit from this lesson if they do not have some of the "mainstream" cultural knowledge that many other students are likely to draw from as they read. For example, a general understanding of concepts such as "pilgrim" or "football" may be unfamiliar to new immigrants (Tompkins 2011).

We can increase comprehension of important content material by taking measures to develop background knowledge. The following strategies may be used with the whole class or small groups.

- **Reviews.** When students are starting a new text, review previously read material by turning back through the pages and discussing what was learned.

- **Key questions.** Before reading, write a key question on the board and discuss possible answers. For example, What is a food chain? What is the *Declaration of Independence?*

- **Prereading webs.** Before reading, work with students to create a web that will help activate and build content knowledge in relation to the piece. Write the topic that will be read in the center, and then ask students, "What do you know about _____?" Act as scribe, recording student ideas and helping them to make connections between concepts.

- **Book browsing.** Have available several books focused on the key topic to be read. Allow students time for browsing and talking about the material.

- **Previewing.** Before reading, walk students through a detailed preview of the key features of the text (such as the table of contents, subheads, illustrations, and the glossary), working to build understandings about content and vocabulary as you go. Focus on identifying possible connections and relationships.

- **Read-alouds.** Before having students read an important text, read a section aloud. Discuss the content with your students, taking time to explain key concepts and helping them make connections between what they know and the new material. Then have students reread what you have read before finishing reading the text on their own.

INTENSIFYING THE INSTRUCTION
Building Background Knowledge

- **Teacher Web searches.** As your students observe, do an Internet search for information related to the topic students will be reading about. Set a purpose that goes beyond searching for a quick fact. For example, you might seek information on the mechanism that makes hot air balloons stay aloft or about the difference between chemical changes and physical changes in science. Allow students to observe and listen to you talk and reason through the material.

- **Student Web searches.** Allow students to do an Internet search for information related to the topic they will be reading about. Arrange for them to take notes or talk with a peer in relation to a specific purpose or question.

- **Minilessons.** Provide a minilesson on the topic before students read, drawing attention to key connections and relationships they will encounter. When appropriate, use manipulatives, photographs, hands-on material, and hands-on experiences.

- **Real experiences.** If you have content that lends itself to hands-on experiences, implement the experiences before reading. For example, before reading the story of Betsy Ross, show a colonial flag; before reading about bacteria, use microscopes or show slides of cells; before reading about skin, examine it using magnifying glasses.

- **Stories.** Tell the students a story in relation to the topic they will be reading about. For example, you might tell what you know about the story of Ruby Bridges before reading the book with your students, or you might tell a story that is connected to what Ruby Bridges experienced that will help students understand the content.

- **Reciprocal teaching.** After the whole class reads or listens to a key text once, each student or group rereads a short section and presents it to a larger subset of the class. The presentation may involve creating a summary, illustration, or diagram.

- **Transparency lessons.** Divide students into five groups and give a blank transparency to each. Before reading, photocopy five key sections of the text onto a transparency. Have groups read their sections and use dry-erase markers to highlight what they think might be important words, phrases, and sentences. Give all groups 3 to 5 minutes to "teach" the class what they have discovered. Transparency lessons may be used after the text is read as well.

INTENSIFYING THE INSTRUCTION
Monitoring

Monitoring is a comprehension strategy that involves keeping close track of meaning across the pages of a text.

1. To develop student awareness of monitoring in relation to Reading Anchor 3, select a text that features individuals, events, or ideas that are important to discuss in terms of their connections and relationships. Each participating student should have access to a copy of the text.

2. Introduce the text and let the students know that they will be reading softly or silently and then responding to some key questions or prompts. Let them know the questions/prompts beforehand. For example:

   - How do these individuals/events/ ideas connect with or influence one another?

   - Let's rethink this part in the order (sequence) in which it is described.

   - What caused this change or event? What are the effects?

3. Guide students to read short sections of the text in order to respond to the question at hand. You may find that graphic organizers (such as Figures RIT 3.2 to RIT 3.5) can be helpful in this process.

4. After working closely with students to read and respond to the prompt, team up students to read a passage together and to respond to the same or similar prompt more independently.

For English Learners

Be sure to support students in building meaning across the pages of text even in the earliest phases of English language development. This may require that you work in small groups to allow students the time and support to respond to the text. In relation to Anchor 3, work toward a discussion routine that involves extended explanation and description of events (rather than allowing for brief or one-word answers). This may be fostered by continually prompting with "And then what happened? Why do you think so?" (Short and Echevarria 2005).

5. Continue instruction with students who have not yet developed effective monitoring.

Collaborative Engagement

1. **Choose the literature and the reading context.** Decide on a piece of literature that can be read aloud to all participating students and then discussed in small groups. Provide at least one copy per group. Although early on you may want to do the reading with your students so that you can provide support with the in-depth analysis required by Reading Anchor 3, later, when students have more experience, they may be asked to read the text independently.

2. **Arrange for students to read or listen to the text.** Before reading, students should preview the material with teacher support that helps them begin to consider the key connections or relationships among the individuals, events, or ideas. They should also know what they will be doing afterward. (See Figure RIT 3.8.)

3. **Hold the meetings.** Arrange for students to come together after the reading to discuss key aspects of the text. Give students key prompts (as in Figure RIT 3.8) to help them focus on the key ideas to consider in preparation for their discussions.

4. **Arrange for a follow-up discussion.** When all groups are working on the same text, organize for a whole-class discussion as a follow-up to the group activity.

READING ANCHOR 3:
Prompts to Support Student-Led Group Discussion of Text

Kindergarten and First Grade

Students work together to draw or write about a connection between two (individuals, events, ideas, pieces of information) in a text. Before sending them off to work together, help them generate ideas regarding the connections they might explore. (Figure RIT 3.2 provides a template to enlarge.)

Students create a diagram to show important changes that occurred over the course of the text. For example, you can ask them to show what happened in the beginning, middle, and end, and to use arrows to show the connections.

Second Grade

Students work together to describe the parts of an event, concept, or set of procedures. Before sending them off to work together, support them in generating ideas regarding the connections they might explore. (Figures RIT 3.3 and RIT 3.4 provide templates to enlarge. If students will be working independently with the templates, show them how to write on sticky notes instead of writing directly on the organizers. This allows students to revise their ideas until they have worked the material into a logical sequence.)

Students create a diagram to show important changes that occurred over the course of the text. They can use numbers or arrows to show the order or key connections.

Third, Fourth, and Fifth Grades

Students work together to describe in writing the parts of an event, concept, or set of procedures they have read about. (Figures RIT 3.3 to RIT 3.5 provide templates to enlarge. If students will be working independently with the templates, show them how to write on sticky notes instead of writing directly on the organizers. This allows students to revise their ideas until they have worked the material into a logical sequence.) As they write, they are to use terms that help show the connections and relationships among events.

Students create a diagram to show important changes that occurred over the course of the text. Encourage them to use arrows, numbers, and placement on the page to show key connections and relationships.

Independent Application

Preview, Overview, Review

Preview, overview, review (Goodman, Watson, and Burke 2005) is a small-group or whole-class experience designed to support students in browsing a topic before reading the assigned material. The initial browsing helps students develop some language and confidence that will facilitate more extensive discussion of key connections and relationships appearing in the focus text. This type of experience is especially useful for English learners because it develops a familiarity with the language that will be used in the text.

1. Set up a browsing table with a variety of material related to the topic. Materials may include books, articles, websites, and hands-on manipulatives. In the interest of Reading Anchor 3, you can let students know the connections or relationships they will be reading about in the focus text—for example, "We're going to be reading about the causes and effects of deforestation, and browsing this set of materials will help you get the background knowledge you'll need."

2. Provide scheduled times for students to examine the materials in small groups.

3. When students have had a chance to browse the materials, place them in groups of two or three. Ask them to create lists that indicate what they know about the topic so far.

4. Guide the students to organize the lists into categories by coming up with headings and listing appropriate items beneath or by creating a web with spokes to indicate subtopics.

5. Hold a whole-class meeting in which students share their lists with the class. As the students share their lists, make a web that includes all of the contributions and shows connections among the ideas. Such experiences build the background necessary for analyzing complex connections and relationships in informational text.

Mental Mapping

Mental mapping involves students in simply surveying the key features of a text, including the title, subheads, key words, illustrations, and captions, to create a mental frame for holding together and analyzing the connections among the ideas. Set students up for mental mapping by asking them to turn through the pages of the book they are about to read and use the text's features to predict what they will read. Capturing the structure of a text early on in the reading facilitates comprehension (Dymock and Nicholson 2010) and should regularly be encouraged to support student attention to key connections and relationships.

Getting the Picture

Getting the picture is a way of encouraging students to study illustrations and analyze the details in ways that will enhance their construction of meaning across the pages. The experience may occur before or after reading. For English learners, implementing the experience before reading will serve the important function of familiarizing them with the vocabulary of the text.

1. Guide your students to construct a key set of questions to ask in relation to informational text illustrations. Post the list somewhere in the classroom. The following questions illustrate the type that could be asked in relation to Reading Anchor 3:

   Grades K–1:

   • What information do the illustrations provide?

   • How do the illustrations tell this story?

   • What do the illustrations tell about this sequence of events?

   Grades 1–5:

   • What information do the illustrations give about changes over time?

   • What do the illustrations show about how one (individual, event, idea) impacts another?

2. Assign students to pair up and discuss their interpretations using one or all of the questions you have constructed together.

3. Allow the students to share their observations with the class.

Technical Writers

After reading a text involving the implementation of a set of procedures, steps, or tactics, students describe the connections and relationships, based on specific information in the text. For example, in science, students might list the written procedures they followed as they took a "touch test" to see which parts of their skin are more sensitive than others, or they might bullet out what they learned about the process of recycling manufactured materials. In math, they might explain how a set of data was collected or a process of solving a problem. As you conference with your students about their writing, work specifically with them to effectively use language that pertains to time, sequence, and cause and effect.

Historians

As students read informational text, they create a timeline that includes the key concepts or events, documenting and pulling together the information in the style of a historian. For example, they might plot key events in the lives of famous individuals such as Betsy Ross or Martin Luther King; or they might plot key events in history, such as the phases of the Shackleton expedition, the events leading to the Declaration of Independence, or the gradual pollution of a body of water. Students use the timelines to explain and describe what happened and why.

Connection Charts

Students use *connection charts* to describe and explain the connection between two or more individuals, events, pieces of information, or ideas. For example:

Text: *Almost Gone,* by Steve Jenkins			
	Yangtze River Dolphin	**Miami Blue Butterfly**	**Javan Rhinoceros**	**Connection**
Why is the population of animals dwindling?	Pollution, boat traffic, construction	Development, collectors, pesticides	Farming, logging, poachers	Human encroachment on habitat

Text: *Throw Your Tooth on the Roof,* by Sally Beeler			
	Argentina	**Brazil**	**Columbia**	**Connection**
What do kids do when a tooth falls out?	Put in glass of water.	Put outside.	Put under pillow.	Teeth are placed somewhere special.
What happens next?	El Ratoncito leaves coins or candy.	St. John brings a healthy new tooth.	El Raton Miguelito leaves money.	Teeth are replaced with something.

When using connection charts, guide students in the development of the categories, and then allow them to work in pairs or teams to fill in the information. Connection charts work well with books in which the author has used a descriptive structure to address several similar concepts (customs from different countries, different family celebrations, endangered species, extinct species, different types of leaves or trees).

English Language Arts Standards Reading: Informational Text ANCHOR 4

Reading Anchor 4: Interpret words and phrases as they are used in a text, including determining technical, connotative, and figurative meanings, and analyze how specific word choices shape meaning or tone.

K	First	Second	Third	Fourth	Fifth
With prompting and support, ask and answer questions about unknown words in a text.	Ask and answer questions to help determine or clarify the meaning of words or phrases in a text.	Determine the meaning of words and phrases in a text relevant to a grade 2 topic or subject area.	Determine the meaning of general academic and domain-specific words and phrases in a text relevant to a grade 3 topic or subject area.	Determine the meaning of general academic and domain-specific words or phrases in a text relevant to a grade 4 topic or subject area.	Determine the meaning of general academic and domain-specific words and phrases in a text relevant to a grade 5 topic or subject area.

Decision Tree for
Reading: Informational Text ANCHOR 4

Do my students need focused instruction in relation to Reading Anchor 4?

Reading Anchor 4 requires that students *determine the meaning of key words and phrases in text.* (Refer to your grade-level standards for specific details.)

When some or all of your students could use support in this area, it is recommended that you start the process by implementing three types of instruction in sequence over the course of about a week:

Demonstration	**Collaborative Engagement**	**Independent Application**
Page 208	**Page 214**	**Page 216**

The initial demonstration requires just one session (to be repeated as needed), leaving one or two days for collaborative engagement and one or two days to begin the independent applications, which become ongoing as you choose. If you find during any phase of the instruction that some or all of your students could use more intensified support, it is recommended that you consider the lessons for intensifying the instruction.

Do my students need intensified support with vocabulary-learning strategies?

Students who do not have a strong repertoire of strategies for seeking the meaning of unfamiliar words can benefit from vocabulary-learning strategy lessons. We see this need in students who do not take action in relation to critical words even though they do not know their meaning. See page 212.

Do my students need intensified support to develop new vocabulary?

Vocabulary studies are frameworks for studying words within the wider context in which they appear. Any student who has not yet developed key conceptual knowledge in relation to a topic being studied can benefit from intensified vocabulary support. English language learners who are still developing their academic vocabulary in the new language, regardless of their amount of prior knowledge in relation to the topic, can also benefit. See page 213.

Demonstration

Anchor 4 requires that students *determine the meanings of key words and phrases* in text, with a focus on academic or domain-specific vocabulary. It is widely recommended that instruction related to vocabulary be steeped in an effort to develop in students a word consciousness—an awareness of and interest in learning new words—because ultimately students are the ones who must be willing to take action or initiative when they come to unfamiliar words.

Read-alouds are an important source of development in relation to vocabulary because books are full of words that might not be used in ordinary conversation and because they provide a rich context for understanding and investigating word meanings (Yopp and Yopp 2007). Research shows that when children experience repeated read-alouds, accompanied by direct attention to words, they can show significant growth in vocabulary (Graves and Watts-Taffe 2008). Research also suggests that children benefit from exposure to new words in many contexts and that their exposure should involve engagement in meaningful discussion (Caldwell and Leslie 2009). "Connecting words to literature, the world, and life experiences helps children to make the necessary connections needed to make the new word theirs" (Strickland 2005, 62).

The present lesson is designed to support students in developing domain-specific vocabulary as well as word consciousness. It may be implemented several times over the course of the year, using different texts each time. Before teaching the lesson, decide whether you wish to use it as a frame for creating or adding to a word wall. Developing your word walls in connection with literature will provide a meaningful context for vocabulary development.

1. **Choose the text.** Choose a text that is related in an important way to your content-area curriculum. You may use a textbook, a trade book, a magazine, a newspaper, or information from the Internet. The text should provide a meaningful context for building content knowledge by discussing the vocabulary that is central to it.

2. **Introduce the text and the concept.** Let students know that you will be reading the text aloud and then showing them some words you found to be interesting, confusing, or particularly important- and that you will want them to help you interpret their meanings. As part of your introduction, demonstrate a preview of the text, focusing on features connected to the words you have chosen, such as subheads, captions, and bolded font.

3. **Demonstrate and discuss the concept.** Read through the text or section, pausing to discuss key words and phrases of interest. Also, encourage students to identify words they feel should be discussed. Then back up and go through the text a second time to discuss the words in more detail and decide which might be appropriate for a word wall. To prepare words for the word wall, write a small, carefully selected set of words from the lesson on note cards. You can write a dictionary or child-constructed definition on the back. Keep the list short in order to focus on depth. Long word lists for any one lesson are not recommended (Gersten et al. 2007). Figure RIT 4.1 offers a starter set of prompts.

Figure RIT **4.1**

READING ANCHOR 4:
Prompts to Support Teacher-Led Modeling and Discussion

Kindergarten and First Grade

We are going to look back through the text to talk about some of the interesting words.

I noticed _____. What do you think it means? I think it means _____ because _____.

Did you have any questions about words? Let's listen again. . . .

Figure RIT 4.2 offers a template for students to record words and their meanings.

Second Through Fifth Grades

We are going to look back through the text to talk about some of the interesting words.

I noticed _____. What do you think it means? I think it means _____ because _____.

Did you have any questions about words? Let's listen again. . . . What questions do you have about the words in this text? What are some ways we could answer these questions?

- Use our own logic?
- Use the surrounding context?
- Look for meaningful parts?
- Ask someone?
- Use a dictionary?

Figure RIT 4.3 offers a template for students to record words and their meanings.

I Learn About Important Words When I Read!

Name: _____ Date: _____

Title: _____

Write the word.

Draw a picture to show what the word means.

Words Worth Noticing

Name: _____ Date: _____

Title: _____

Word	Meaning	Quick Sketch

INTENSIFYING THE INSTRUCTION
Vocabulary-Learning Strategies

The vocabulary-learning lesson is for students who do not have a strong repertoire of strategies for dealing with unfamiliar words. You may wish to occasionally use this lesson as a refresher for the whole class.

1. To develop student awareness of vocabulary-learning strategies, select a text for modeling that contains vocabulary you know will challenge the participating students. Each student should have access to a copy of the text.

2. Read a portion of the text, demonstrating your thinking processes for dealing with vocabulary that you think may be new or not fully familiar to your students. You may wish to post the process on a permanent chart:

   - Is this a word I should try to understand or is it not important here?
   - Can I use my own logic to figure out what it means?
   - Do the surrounding sentences provide any clues to the meaning?
   - Do I recognize any of the word parts?
   - Is there someone I could ask?
   - Should I check the dictionary or thesaurus? (It is recommended that you teach students to use online tools if they are available.)

3. After modeling, team students up to read and discuss passages of the text together, identifying unfamiliar words and discussing the best strategies for determining their meanings. Students can use highlighting tape or they can document words on sticky notes or note cards. Pull the students back together to discuss the processes they tried.

4. Continue instruction with students who have not yet developed effective strategies for independently learning new words.

Figure RIT 4.5

INTENSIFYING THE INSTRUCTION
Vocabulary Studies

To implement a vocabulary study, work with students to select a word that is critical to understanding the key concepts in a text, and use one of the graphic organizers featured in Part 1 (Figures RL 4.6 to RL 4.10) to guide students to explore it from a variety of angles. The organizers are examples of materials you may use, but ideally, you will create one on your own so that you can tailor the parts to help students home in on key aspects of the particular words you are studying.

As you develop your instruction and create your materials, take into consideration the following three guidelines for effective vocabulary instruction (synthesized from research on vocabulary instruction reviewed by Jitendra et al. 2004).

1. Ensure that students read often.

2. Select words students will need to know to deeply comprehend the material they are reading.

3. Focus not on a casually chosen set of words, but on a key word with multiple connections to other words in the text.

For English Learners

English learners benefit when teachers do the following (Echevarria 2006):

- Write the new vocabulary word so that students have a visual reference.
- Model the pronunciation of the word.
- Repeat the word numerous times, in a variety of contexts.
- Provide planned opportunities for students to use the word in context.
- Emphasize the word during reading experiences.
- Provide opportunities for review and practice.
- Provide opportunities to work with peers and small groups so that genuine dialogue may occur.

Collaborative Engagement

1. **Choose the literature and the reading context.** Either select a text or section to read aloud to the whole class or plan for students to read different texts together in groups. If students are to do the reading, the chosen text need not be the same across groups. You can differentiate by choosing the literature based on student interest or on text difficulty.

2. **Arrange for students to read or listen to the text.** Before the reading, let students know what they will be doing afterward. (See Figure RIT 4.6.) Note: For some of the collaborative engagements, students complete the reading after the group initially meets.

3. **Hold the meetings.** Arrange for students to come together to discuss key words and phrases from the text. Figure RIT 4.6 offers a set of starter prompts.

4. **Arrange a follow-up discussion.** When all groups are working on the same text, or the same concept, organize for a whole-class discussion as a follow-up to the small-group activity.

Figure RIT 4.6

READING ANCHOR 4:
Prompts to Support Student-Led Group Discussion of Text

Word Illustrations (Grades K–5)

As a group, students choose three key words or phrases from the text or theme of study and work as a team to create a visual representation of each. (Or the teacher can choose the words/phrases and post them for the class.)

Graphic Organizers (Grades K–5)

Groups are given a vocabulary-related graphic organizer to enlarge and complete as a team. Use organizers you have modeled with the whole class, as in Figures RIT 4.2 and Part 1 RL 4.6 to 4.10. Students may focus on a word of their choosing or one you have chosen. After they gain experience with organizers, allow students to create their own.

Vocabulary Sorts (Grades K–5)

Students are given a set of pictures, words, or phrases (prewritten on note cards or sticky notes) to sort. The cards should be created to represent important concepts in the text or thematic unit. Students place the cards in categories in any way that makes sense and develop a title for each category. The words are then visually displayed in a meaningful format, such as a chart or web.

Parts Sorts (Grades 2–5)

Students are given a set of words, some of which are selected from the book or content they are studying. They sort the words into categories based on parts the words have in common, such as prefixes, root words, or suffixes (*replay, redo, reassemble; interact, international*). They discuss the meanings of the parts and report back to the class.

Comparing Word Meaning (Grades 2–5)

Keep a collection of words the class has studied within a content-area topic on small note cards. Pull two random words from the pile for each group and ask students to discuss or make a list showing how the two words are alike or how they connect (Caldwell and Leslie 2009).

Knowledge Rating Charts (Grades 2–5)

Before reading or listening, students individually rate their knowledge in relation to a teacher-chosen set of words. (See following chart for an example). They discuss their ratings with peers and share knowledge of words they know well.

While reading, they seek new meanings by using background knowledge, context clues, more information from peers, and the dictionary.

After reading, the words are discussed again and rated again on the chart, using a different-color pen.

Word	Know it Well	Have Some Knowledge of It	Don't Know It

Independent Application

Independent Reading

A well-documented benefit of independent reading is that it is an important source of vocabulary growth (Nagy, Anderson, and Herman 1987). Encountering words within the meaningful context of a written text helps students deduce the meaning of new words and extend understandings of those that are already familiar. To specifically encourage vocabulary development during *independent reading*, try the following:

- Create bins of book choices based on important topics and themes in your curriculum. The more students read on particular topics, the deeper vocabulary knowledge they can build on that topic.

- Be sure that all students have books they can read with understanding. Books that are too easy can cause boredom and stagnation, and books that are too hard can cause frustration and lead to little time spent actually reading.

- Let students know that after reading they will have time to respond through writing or talk. You might allow students 1 minute to review what they have read and informally prepare to discuss one interesting or important word with a peer. Interactive journals (see below) may be used for this purpose. Or you can give students note cards and ask them to record the word on one side and a sentence or definition on the other. The cards can be kept together on a key ring as a personal dictionary for a unit of study.

Interactive Journals

Interactive journals are notebooks in which students record interesting ideas from their reading and explore them with a partner. The journals may be used any time two or more students are reading the same text. In support of Reading Anchor 4, interactive journals can be used as a tool for recording words and phrases that have special meaning in relation to the content being read and for organizing conversation around these words and phrases. You can ask students to reserve a section of the journal for this purpose.

1. Instruct students to decide on a selected amount of text to read. As they read, they are to choose one or two key words or phrases to record.

2. After recording their words or phrases, students then exchange journals. To respond, peers write what they think the word means. They then discuss any differing points of view or understandings.

Stop-and-Chats

*Stop-and-chat*s provide a useful forum for setting up students to read with a specific purpose in mind and fostering conversations related to that purpose. Two or three students who are reading the same text can work together.

1. Students place a marker at an agreed-upon stopping point. As they read, they use a sticky note to write down unfamiliar words or phrases. Students need not mark every applicable word or phrase they encounter. It is often the case that just one or two key choices will provide enough substance to sustain a rich conversation.

2. Upon reaching the stopping point, students discuss the meaning of their documented words and then place the marker at the next agreed-upon stopping point

3. As a possible follow-up, the words may be revisited through whole- or small-group discussion with the teacher.

Word Wonder Readings

Word wonder readings are sessions organized for students to revisit text with the wonder of words in mind. After students have read or listened to an informational text at least once, they go back into the text to look closely for particularly *interesting* uses of language or uses of language that are particularly *important* to the content they are studying.

1. Prepare students for word wonder by telling them you would like them to read (or listen) closely and to think about the words that stand out as interesting or important.

2. Students use highlighting tape or an erasable highlighter to mark one to three words or phrases that stand out for them. Or they can write the words on a sticky note.

3. Students talk with a partner about the words they marked/wrote, telling why they think they are important to the piece.

Dictionary Entries

We know that simply reading or copying definitions is not a useful strategy for developing word knowledge or comprehension. Students develop vocabulary as a *concept*, not a word. They need to experience a word many times and in many contexts to fully understand its meaning. Still, dictionaries serve important functions, and students need to learn to use them. Maintaining a collection of words that have been studied in their appropriate contexts—through the creation of a personal dictionary—can be enriching and empowering.

1. Teach your students to read and write dictionary entries by preselecting three or four words from their content-area reading and then showing them the professionally constructed definitions in a children's dictionary, including the illustrative sentences and any lists of related words that are included.

2. Arrange for students to use what you have shown them to build their own dictionaries over the course of the school year. To facilitate this process, have available a key ring for each student and a large stack of note cards with a hole punched in one corner. This allows students to add words in alphabetic order at any time. Keeping the entries meaningful and limited to just a few key words per week will sustain engagement over the course of the year.

Encyclopedia Entries

Find an online encyclopedia entry for a word that is key to a topic your class is studying. Show students the entry, focusing on the content and how it is set up. Let students know that they will be creating a class encyclopedia on a specific topic, with each student or team writing a different entry. Give guidelines for the project. The following is an example from a third-grade classroom:

-   Choose one of the following weather conditions and title your entry using bold font: rain, snow, hail, thunder, lightning, tornado, hurricane, high wind, cloud, precipitation.

-   Use a resource to provide a one-sentence definition.

-   Explain the key characteristics of your condition. Use 100–150 words.

-   Find or draw a picture of your condition.

Illustrated Definitions

Each student chooses a key word or phrase from a text the class is reading together, writes it in large print on a piece of paper, and creates an illustration to help show the meaning. As an option, students may be asked to write the word in a sentence or write a definition using their own wording. To help students choose appropriate words, you can list several possibilities, having the students choose just one. Compile the pages into a book and share it with the class.

Number One Word!

Whether they are reading independently, with a group, or with the whole class, students use highlighting tape to mark what they feel is the single most important (number one) word in a designated section of text or in the whole text. You can teach students to choose a word that signifies either an important concept worth considering or one that best signifies what the piece is about. After the students have chosen their words, allow time for small-group or whole-class discussion, asking students to articulate the reasons for their choices.

Ten Important Words

Ten important words (Yopp and Yopp 2003, 2007) involves students in closely reading a text to note the key ideas and then selecting the most important words in relation to those ideas.

1. After an initial read, students reread to identify the ten (or fewer depending on the length of the piece) words they believe to be most important to the content. Each word is written on a separate sticky note.

2. The teacher guides the class in using the sticky notes to construct a bar graph, making columns of words to see which words were chosen by most students.

3. With teacher guidance, the students discuss why certain words were deemed by many to be important to the text and what these words contribute to the content.

4. Each student writes a one-sentence summary of the content. This often results in use of the posted words, offering yet another opportunity for considering and discussing their meanings.

Word Clouds

A *word cloud* (Dalton and Grisham 2011) is a computer-generated cluster of words created from a text of your choice. Students can use word cloud activities to activate and build background knowledge on a topic and to reflect on the key words used in a text.

To get started, use www.wordle.net to generate a word cloud from a text your students will be reading or listening to. You will need to type in or copy and paste part (or all) of the text. If you are working with longer text, typing in about one hundred words or more from the beginning works well. Trade books, textbooks, or online articles may be used. The application will generate a "word cloud," with the words used most often standing out most prominently. If you make five or six copies of the word cloud, students can work in groups to discuss the clouds. Dalton and Grisham (2011) suggest prompts including the following:

Prereading Prompts

- What does the word cloud suggest this piece is about?

- What seem to be the most important words?

- How do these words go together?

Postreading Prompts

- Do you think the word cloud captured what was most important to learn?

Focused Word Studies

Focused word studies are independent projects designed to support students' vocabulary development in relation to a key content-area topic.

Kindergarten: Students choose three words from the word wall and draw a picture that helps show what each word means. (*Note:* The word wall should be of the type that focuses on vocabulary and meanings of words in the content areas you are studying rather than the type that is focused on teaching students to read and write commonly used words.)

Grade 1: Students choose a book from a set selected by the teacher. They read the text or a section of it a few times to determine three key words or phrases for study. They record the words or phrases and create an illustration for each.

Grade 2: Students choose a text from a set selected by the teacher. The choices may include books or magazine articles. Students read the text or a section of it a few times to determine three key words or phrases for study. They record the words or phrases and create an illustration for each. They write a definition in their own words.

Grade 3: Students choose a text from a set selected by the teacher. The choices may include books, magazine articles, or other informational texts. Students read the text or a section of it a few times to determine three key words or phrases for study. They record the words or phrases and create an illustration for each. They use a dictionary to find a formal definition of each word, which they rewrite into their own words.

Grade 4: Students choose a text from a set selected by the teacher. The choices may include books, magazine articles, information from the Internet, or other informational texts. Students read the text or a section of it a few times to determine three key words or phrases for study. They record the words or phrases and create an illustration for each. They choose one of the words and use a graphic organizer (such as Figures RL 4.6 to RL 4.10 in Part 1) to fully describe it. Dictionaries and the chosen text may be used as resources.

Grade 5: Students choose a text from a set selected by the teacher. The choices may include books, magazine articles, information from the Internet, newspaper articles, or other informational texts. Students read the text or a section of it a few times to determine three key words or phrases for study. They record the words or phrases and create an illustration for each. They choose one of the words and use a graphic organizer (such as Figures RL 4.6 to RL 4.10 in Part 1) to fully describe it or they create their own graphic organizer to suit this purpose. Dictionaries and the chosen text may be used as resources.

English Language Arts Standards Reading: Informational Text ANCHOR 5

Reading Anchor 5: Analyze the structure of texts, including how specific sentences, paragraphs, and larger portions of the text (e.g., a section, chapter, scene, or stanza) relate to each other and the whole.

K	First	Second	Third	Fourth	Fifth
Identify the front cover, back cover, and title page of a book.	Know and use various text features (e.g., headings, tables of contents, glossaries, electronic menus, icons) to locate key facts or information in a text.	Know and use various text features (e.g., captions, bold print, subheadings, glossaries, indexes, electronic menus, icons) to locate key facts or information in a text efficiently.	Use text features and search tools (e.g., key words, sidebars, hyperlinks) to locate information relevant to a given topic efficiently.	Describe the overall structure (e.g., chronology, comparison, cause-effect, problem-solution) of events, ideas, concepts, or information in a text or part of a text.	Compare and contrast the overall structure (e.g., chronology, comparison, cause-effect, problem-solution) of events, ideas, concepts, or information in two or more texts.

Decision Tree for
Reading: Informational Text ANCHOR 5

Do my students need focused instruction in relation to Reading Anchor 5?

Anchor 5 is aimed at helping students learn to *use text structure to support meaning making*. (Refer to your grade-level standards for specific details.)

When some or all of your students could use support in this area, it is recommended that you start the process by implementing three types of instruction in sequence over the course of about a week:

Demonstration	**Collaborative Engagement**	**Independent Application**
Page 224	**Page 230**	**Page 231**

The initial demonstration requires just one session (to be repeated as needed), leaving one or two days for collaborative engagement and one or two days to begin the independent applications, which become ongoing as you choose. If you find during any phase of the instruction that some or all of your students could use more intensified support, it is recommended that you move to the lessons for intensifying the instruction.

Do my students need intensified support using surface features to support meaning making?

Using surface features helps students locate key information in a text. Students who have difficulty locating information or who seem to have difficulty holding meaning across the pages of a text can benefit from support with previewing the surface features. See page 228.

Do my students need intensified support using internal structures to support meaning making?

Effective readers use their knowledge of text structure as a mental frame for both comprehending and retelling. Students who do not retell accurately, concisely, and with a logical sequence can generally benefit from intensified support in this area. See page 229.

Demonstration

Anchor 5 is aimed at helping students learn to *use text structure to support meaning making*. Text structure includes *surface features* that are easy to see, such as headings, tables of contents, indexes, and glossaries, as well as *internal structures* that are not as transparent, such as a cause-effect or problem-solution approach to the narrative.

Nearly all of the informational text that students read falls into two categories of internal structure: *descriptive* and *sequential*. (See Figure RIT 5.3.) The most frequent descriptive structures are *lists* (the author presents a set of items or attributes), *webs* (the attributes of an object are described), and *matrices* (the attributes of more than one object or type of object are described.) Common sequential structures are *strings* (step-by-step descriptions or instructions), *cause-effect* (one event leads to others), and *problem-solution* (the author poses a problem or question that is followed by a solution or answer; Dymock and Nicholson 2010).

Both types of structure are important for making meaning. Having an understanding of the surface features allows readers to find information quickly and efficiently. If students know about tables of contents, headings, indexes, and online features such as hyperlinks and sidebars, they can quickly home in on the information they need. Having a sense of the internal structure—or how the narrative itself is organized—can do two important things: It can support students in holding meaning across the pages of a text, and it can support them in pulling together all of the critical pieces of information. (See sidebar for information on common structures.) Teacher-led instruction toward Anchor 5 builds a common language for discussing and analyzing text structure in ways that contribute to meaning making.

1. **Choose the text.** Any text from the content areas you are studying can be used to help students develop understandings about using structure, but over time, work to ensure variety in terms of the structural elements that are represented. To give students a broad range of experience navigating surface features, we should use both print and online material. Online material has a surface structure that is different from books and magazines and should be included in the instructional process. Figures RIT 5.2 and RIT 5.3 feature a set of structural features that are of value to teach in K–5 settings. You will need just one text per lesson.

2. **Introduce the text and the concept.** As with any informational reading, be clear with your purpose. For example, say something like, "Let's see if this book can help us learn about the differences between amphibians and reptiles" or "We need to find out all we can about the natural resources found in our state." Show the students the surface features you use to help get a feel for the overall content

or that help you to locate the section you plan to read, making your use of these features explicit.

3. **Demonstrate and discuss the concept.** As you read through the text, demonstrate how you attend to text features, including those designated as appropriate for exploration at your grade level (see the grade-level standards), moving beyond your grade level as it is useful within the reading event. (Figure RIT 5.1 offers a starter set of prompts.)

Figure RIT **5.1**

READING ANCHOR 5:
Prompts to Support Teacher-Led Modeling and Discussion of Text

Kindergarten

Let's look at the information provided by the front cover (show title and author). What does the cover tell us?

Let's look at the title page. Let's talk about what is here.

Let's look at the back cover. Sometimes, extra information is provided here.

Let's look inside. Look at where the author put the writing (refer to structural elements such as titles, captions, labels, and so on). How does this help us? What looks like writing you have seen before? Which parts are different?

First, Second, and Third Grades

Let's preview all the features of this book (or website). What features do you see? What are they for? How do they help us?

Fourth and Fifth Grades

Let's see if we can tell how this author has organized the information with this section. First, let's think about whether this is information *with* a sequence that matters or *without*. Then we can dig in further to think about how the information is organized. (Use Figure RIT 5.3 as a guide.) *Important:* What matters is not that students identify the "right" structure, but that they identify a structure that allows them to hold the information in their minds and organize it for retelling or rethinking.

Some Important Surface Features

Organizational Features

- **Table of contents.** Provides an overview of what the text contains and where it might be located.

- **Headings.** Provide information about key topics in a text and the order in which they are presented.

- **Subheads.** Provide information about the key topics in a section of text and the order in which they are presented.

- **Index.** Shows the topics addressed in the text; is organized alphabetically so that the reader may quickly locate information.

Informational Features

- **Diagrams.** Used to show relationships among concepts.

- **Charts and graphs.** Used to summarize and compare information.

- **Maps.** Used when location is relevant to understand.

- **Illustrations.** Provide a visual interpretation of the way something looks.

- **Captions.** Describe what is happening in the illustration.

- **Labels.** Provide information about parts of the illustration.

- **Bold, italics, colored print.** Used to signify important words or concepts, and made to stand out for quick location. Often, such words are found in the glossary.

- **Glossary.** Provides definitions for key words in the text.

Features Unique to the Electronic Environment

- **Electronic menu.** Consists of a series of titles that link the reader to the desired information.

- **Electronic sidebar.** Contains hyperlinks that provide new information.

- **Icons.** Images that can be "clicked" in the electronic environment to link the reader to the desired information.

- **Search terms (key words).** Used to narrow down and locate key information in the Internet or on a website.

- **Hyperlinks.** Move the reader to a new page within the website, or to another website.

Some Important Internal Structures

DESCRIPTIVE STRUCTURES

- **List.** The author lists a set of items or attributes.

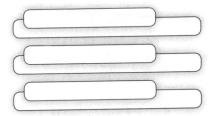

- **Web.** The author describes the attributes of an object.

- **Matrix.** The author describes the attributes of more than one object (used for comparison).

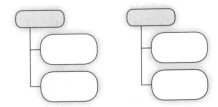

SEQUENTIAL STRUCTURES

- **String.** The author provides a chronological description or step-by-step instructions.

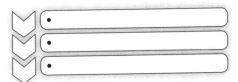

- **Cause-effect.** The author presents one event that leads to others.

- **Problem-solution.** The author presents a problem or question that is followed by a solution or answer.

Structures are identified by Dymock and Nicholson 2010; organizers are adapted from their work.

INTENSIFYING THE INSTRUCTION
Previewing Surface Features

Previewing is a comprehension strategy that involves using surface features to locate key information in a text. Students who have difficulty locating information or who seem to have difficulty holding meaning across the pages of a text can benefit from support with previewing.

1. Choose a feature-rich informational text for demonstration, and have a copy available for each student or student team.

2. Set a purpose for the reading. For example, "I am interested in learning something specific about leaves. I want to know how leaves change color." In light of this purpose, show students the relevant surface features (such as tables of contents, index, and chapter headers) you can use to find your information. Identify the section you might read in light of your purpose.

3. Go to the section, and if there are subheads, use them to predict what the author addresses under each. You may read the section at this point, or continue with the previewing lesson.

4. To continue with the previewing lesson, have students look for specific information as you observe and provide support. For example, "Now you see if you can find the section that tells why leaves fall from trees." Ask the students to turn through the pages and note any special surface features that could help them locate relevant information. Then have them closely review and make predictions based on subheads and other features within that section, as you have demonstrated.

5. Have students report their strategies back to the whole group and remind them that previewing before reading can help them be more efficient and better understand the text.

Figure RIT 5.5

INTENSIFYING THE INSTRUCTION
Identifying Internal Structures

Effective readers use their knowledge of text structure as a mental frame for both comprehending and retelling or summarizing. Students who do not retell accurately, concisely, and with a logical sequence can generally benefit from intensified support in this area.

1. Choose an informational text for demonstration, and have a copy available for each student or student team. Also have available chart paper and a copy or enlarged replication of the graphic organizers from Figure RIT 5.3.

2. Meeting with a group or the whole class, set a purpose for the reading. For example, "I am interested in learning something specific about leaves. I want to know why leaves change color." In light of this purpose, show students the relevant surface features of the book (such as tables of contents, index, chapter headers, and subheads), and demonstrate how you use them to identify and locate the section you want to read.

3. Let students know that as they read the chosen section, you want them to think about the organization of the text. Show them the possibilities from Figure RIT 5.3 and ask them to predict the structure the author might use to address the question of how leaves change color: descriptive or sequential. Let them know that they will use the author's chosen structure to help retell or summarize the content.

4. Guide them to match the content to one of the structures. Let them know that there is rarely a "perfect" match and that they can choose the one they think fits best and adapt the organizer if necessary.

5. Have students use the chosen graphic organizer to retell the content. They can be asked to do this orally or in writing. Provide follow-up instruction as needed.

Collaborative Engagement

READING ANCHOR 5:
Prompts to Support Student-Led Group Discussion of Text

Kindergarten

- Gather a bin of feature-rich books for each group. Allow students time to browse and discuss the features, bringing the class together afterward to discuss the interesting features they noticed.

- Students sit together as they each design the front and back cover of a book. They may do this on one sheet of paper "just for fun" or they may be instructed to create a cover based on a real book. As students work, they are encouraged to talk about what they are drawing and writing.

First, Second, and Third Grades

- Give each group a bin of about a dozen informational books. The task for each group is to list the different types of features in the books and to identify the purpose for each. Along with naming the features and recording their purpose, students should record page numbers. Each group can share a set number of features with the class.

Fourth and Fifth Grades

- After reading a section of text, students reread together to determine the internal structure using the strategies you have demonstrated (see Figures RIT 5.1 and RIT 5.3). After they have determined the structure, they should draw a large diagram that helps show it. (They may use or adapt a diagram from Figure RIT 5.3.) The diagram is filled in and used to summarize.

- Give students a passage from a sequential text that has been cut into parts. Students read the parts and place them in logical order. (This may occur before or after the text has been read. The whole text need not be used.) Ask students to determine the structure (string; cause-effect; problem-solution) and to be prepared to provide a rationale for their decision. (See Figure RIT 5.3.)

- Give students a short passage from a descriptive text and ask them to decide whether the information could fit best into a list, web, or matrix. (See Figure RIT 5.3.)

Independent Application

Browsing Bins

Provide your students with the resources necessary to develop familiarity with different text features and structures by organizing bins of informational texts and access to key websites. Include books and websites with varied features so that students gain familiarity with all types, and be sure the information is related to the key content you are studying.

To help students maintain focus, you can ask that they record ideas or findings in a response journal (see page 165). Or information can be recorded on individual sticky notes or chart paper and then discussed after the browsing session. As another option, ask students to team up after reading and list on sticky notes all the text features they found in their books. They can then use their collaborative lists to generate a class list of text features and their purposes (as in Figure RIT 5.2).

Page Design

After students have examined different text features and structures through demonstration, collaborative engagements, and independent reading experiences, allow them to create their own informational text page designs. Designing a single page for a class-created text is a manageable way for students to explore different features and their purposes.

1. Students will need support in choosing a topic. Model how to create a list of possibilities within a given theme and then home in on one that you know and care about. For example, if you are studying what plants need to grow, students might choose a particular plant to focus on. Whatever topics are chosen, you will want to require that students can find reading material (at least one book or article) in relation to the topic so that they can use reading for information as part of the writing process.

2. Model how to collect and organize your ideas for writing. If your students are ready, show them how to choose one of the graphic organizers (Figure RIT 5.3) to collect and organize ideas. Or just show them how you jot down a list of the ideas to include, and then think about how to organize them. And show students how you could use a variety of text features (as in Figure RIT 5.2) to present your information.

3. Allow students time for planning and reading. When students are still in the planning phase, support them in using resources such as books, magazines, and Web information to create their content.

4. Allow students time to prepare their pages and compile the pieces into a class book.

Book Design

After students have worked with different text structures and features through demonstration and collaborative engagements, allow them to create their own books. Before creating a book, you may also wish to work with them to design a single page for a class-created text (see Page Design above). This will help them develop some of the necessary skills for creating an effective book of their own.

1. Students will need support in choosing a topic. You can ask them to choose a key focus from within a thematic area you have been studying as a class. Model how to create a list of possibilities and then home in on one that you know and care a lot about. You may wish to give a set of choices. For example, whether you are studying important people in history, how we use shapes to describe the physical world, simple mechanical devices, or the effects that organisms have on one another, you can offer several choices within the theme area and let students choose just one. Whatever topics are chosen, you will want to ensure that students can find reading material (at least one book or article) in relation to the topic so that they can use reading for information as part of the writing process.

2. Model how to collect and organize your ideas for writing. If your students are ready for structured informational writing, you can show them how to choose one of the graphic organizers (Figure RIT 5.3) to collect and organize ideas. Or just show them how you jot down a list of the ideas you would like to include, and then think about how to organize the ideas onto separate pages and/or into separate sections with appropriate subheads. As you plan, show students how you could use a variety of text features (as in Figure RIT 5.2) to present your information.

3. Allow students planning time. Use this time to be sure they have appropriate resources available and to see that they are planning to include varied text features appropriately.

4. Allow students time to prepare and share their books.

Website Browsing

Website browsing offers opportunities for students to study the design of Web pages and learn how to navigate through the information available on a site. If you have a computer lab or even one computer with a projector, you can help students develop skill at finding and interpreting information online by coming up with a question and then using features such as menus, icons, sidebars, links, and key words to answer it. Be sure to show students how to choose key words. Discuss the terms you choose and why, and allow them to explore the results of trying out their own different combinations of words. Following are some sites with easy-to-use, kid-friendly features:

http://kids.nationalgeographic.com/kids/
www.pbskids.org
www.wordcentral.com
http://kids.yahoo.com/

Accessing information on the Internet requires special skills and strategies that are unique to the online environment. For children to be successful with online literacy, they must learn to quickly find, evaluate, use, and communicate information using digital technologies (Leu et al. 2004).

Website Design

Website design involves students in thinking through key information on a topic and how it might be best presented in an online environment. After students have gained experience viewing and browsing websites with your guidance, they can create their own site designs based on a content-area topic. Depending on the technology you have available, they may be able to work on an actual site, but even without specific tools available, thinking through the design can support their development of both content knowledge and technology skill.

Figures RIT 5.7 and RIT 5.8 show a basic design that could be used or adapted for a science topic. At the top of the page, students fill in information for screen 1, which functions as a home page, by writing or typing the topic and the menu choices that would serve as hyperlinks to another screen. At the bottom of the page, they show what the linked screens would contain. Each link contains a space for a definition and example that would be filled in by the student. Students could decide to hyperlink these pages (usually signified by blue font and an underline) to another page or to a website. For example, they might send the reader to an online dictionary for the definition.

Students should be encouraged to consider the audience for their pages. Is it other members of the class? Or is it perhaps younger students? Along with content and structure, students can consider what colors and fonts and visual images might appeal to their audience.

Home Page/Links Page (2 menu items)

Name: _____ Date: _____

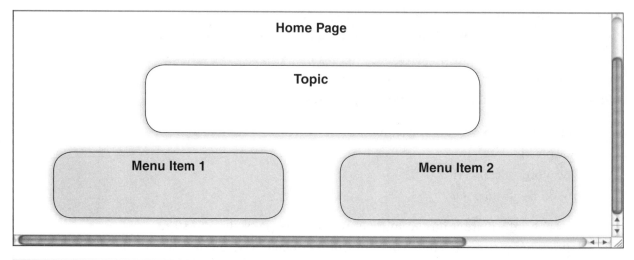

Home Page

Topic

Menu Item 1   **Menu Item 2**

Links Page

or

Menu Item 1

Definition

Example

Menu Item 2

Definition

Example

Figure RIT 5.8

Home Page/Links Page (4 menu items)

Name: _____ Date: _____

Home Page

Topic

| Menu Item 1 | Menu Item 2 | Menu Item 3 | Menu Item 4 |

Links Page

or

Menu Item 1

Definition

Example

Menu Item 2

Definition

Example

or

Menu Item 3

Definition

Example

Menu Item 4

Definition

Example

Writing in Structure

Writing in structure involves identifying the structure of a text and using a graphic organizer to summarize it. Start with a text the whole class has read or listened to, choosing an important section to summarize. Guide students to choose the best-matched organizer from Figure RIT 5.3, or to develop their own. They should write out only the key content. After working with the students through several texts, provide opportunities for them to write in structure independently or in teams.

Collaborative Sequencing

Collaborative sequencing is a whole-class effort involving putting together the pieces of an informational text. After reading or listening to a text read aloud, each student is given one-quarter of a piece of paper or an extra-large sticky note to sketch one key part and write one rich and detailed sentence about that part.

If working with a sequential structure, students then determine where the event falls best: the beginning, middle, or end. The class then meets in three groups (whose membership is based on who has drawn parts from the beginning, middle, and end) to determine an order for each piece within that group. Finally, the class works together to read the whole retelling and revise the placement of the pieces as necessary.

If working with a descriptive structure, the class works together to create a web or matrix that contains all of the ideas. The class then stands in a circle around the room and reads the combined pieces in sequence.

English Language Arts Standards Reading: Informational Text ANCHOR 6

Reading Anchor 6: Assess how point of view or purpose shapes the content and style of a text.

K	First	Second	Third	Fourth	Fifth
Name the author and illustrator of a text and define the role of each in presenting the ideas or information in a text.	Distinguish between information provided by pictures or other illustrations and information provided by the words in a text.	Identify the main purpose of a text, including what the author wants to answer, explain, or describe.	Distinguish their own point of view from that of the author of a text.	Compare and contrast a firsthand and secondhand account of the same event or topic; describe the differences in focus and the information provided.	Analyze multiple accounts of the same event or topic, noting important similarities and differences in the point of view they represent.

Decision Tree for
Reading: Informational Text ANCHOR 6

Do my students need focused instruction in relation to Reading Anchor 6?

Anchor 6 is aimed at helping students *consider the ways in which purpose and point of view affect content and style.* (Refer to your grade-level standards for specific details.)

When some or all of your students could use support in this area, it is recommended that you start the process by implementing three types of instruction in sequence over the course of about a week:

Demonstration	**Collaborative Engagement**	**Independent Application**
Page 239	**Page 248**	**Page 251**

The initial demonstration requires just one session (to be repeated as needed), leaving one or two days for collaborative engagement and one or two days to begin the independent applications, which become ongoing as you choose. If you find during any phase of the instruction that some or all of your students could use more intensified support, it is recommended that you consider the lesson for intensifying the instruction.

Do my students need intensified support with evaluating text?

Evaluating is a comprehension strategy that involves considering author intents and viewpoints and how they influence what is included in a text. Students who rarely show critical thinking about text, or who seem hesitant to express their own viewpoints, can benefit from support with evaluation. See page 247.

Demonstration

Anchor 6 requires that students *consider the ways in which an author's purpose and point of view affect content and style.* The goal is for students to explore the notion that texts are created for particular purposes and written from particular points of view. We "see" the information under the influence of the person who is sharing it. For example, a farmer telling the story of a groundhog tunneling under the barn might focus on the cost of damage and possible solutions. We might note a tone of frustration. A biologist telling the same story might focus on what makes an ideal habitat and might take a more matter-of-fact tone. Considering point of view helps students evaluate text and think critically about its content.

The present lesson is designed to help K–5 students consider point of view in relation to various texts and to build a common language for conversation and group activity in relation to this standard. This lesson may be implemented several times, using a different text each time.

1. **Choose the text.** Choose a text or text set that will lead to interesting discussions about point of view. Figure RIT 6.2 features a recommended starter list.

2. **Introduce the text and the concept.** Let students know that you would like to discuss the author's point of view regarding the content at hand and that they will later be expected to follow up with an activity in a small group. After you have read more than one text on the issue, you can begin to make point-of-view comparisons across texts.

3. **Demonstrate and discuss the concept.** Read the text aloud, pausing at points during and after the reading to show the students how you think about point of view. Figure RIT 6.1 offers a starter set of prompts designed to support student development in relation to Reading Anchor 6.

READING ANCHOR 6:
Prompts to Support Teacher-Led Modeling and Discussion

Kindergarten and First Grade

Who is the author of this text? Who is the illustrator? Let's discuss what the author taught. Let's discuss what the illustrator taught. (Figure RIT 6.3 provides a template for response.)

Second Grade

Let's discuss why we think the author wrote this text. What does the author want to answer/explain/describe? How do you think the author feels about this topic/issue? (Figure RIT 6.4 provides a template for response.)

Third Grade

Let's discuss why we think the author wrote this text. How do you think the author feels about this topic/issue? Do you feel the same? Let's discuss how our points of view are similar or different. (Figure RIT 6.5 provides a template for response.)

Fourth Grade

Let's discuss why we think the author wrote this text. What do we think the author feels about this topic/issue?

We have a firsthand and a secondhand account to compare. How are they similar and different in their focus? (Figure RIT 6.6 provides a template for response.)

Fifth Grade

Let's discuss why we think the author wrote this text. What do you think the author thinks/feels about this issue?

We have two accounts to compare. How are they similar and different in terms of the point of view presented? (Figure RIT 6.6 provides a template for response.)

Figure RIT 6.2

Recommended Informational Text for Teaching Point of View in Grades K–5		
Grade	**Standards**	**Recommended Texts**
K	Name the author and illustrator of a text and define the role of each in presenting the ideas or information in a text.	• *Actual Size*, by Steve Jenkins • *Mama*, by Jeanette Winter • *It's a Good Thing There Are Insects*, by Allan Fowler • *What Boo and I Do*, by Laura Williams • *Two Eyes, a Nose, and a Mouth*, by Roberta Intrater
1	Distinguish between information provided by pictures or other illustrations and information provided by the words in a text.	• *Almost Gone: The World's Rarest Animals*, by Steve Jenkins • *Just for Elephants*, by Carol Buckley • *Autumn Leaves*, by Ken Robbins • *Ibis: A True Whale Story*, by John Himmelman • *Oil Spill!* by Melvin Berger
2	Identify the main purpose of a text, including what the author wants to answer, explain, or describe.	• *Martin Luther King and the March on Washington*, by Frances Ruffin • *A Weed Is a Flower: The Life of George Washington Carver*, by Aliki • *If the World Were a Village: A Book About the World's People*, by David Smith • *Throw Your Tooth on the Roof*, by Selby Beeler • *The Story of Ruby Bridges*, by Robert Coles
3	Distinguish their own point of view from that of the author of a text.	• *Passage to Freedom: The Sugihara Story*, by Ken Mochizuki • *Encounter*, by Jane Yolen • *Letting Swift River Go*, by Jane Yolen • *If a Bus Could Talk: The Story of Rosa Parks*, by Faith Ringgold • *Faithful Elephants*, by Yukio Tsuchiya
4	Compare and contrast a firsthand and secondhand account of the same event or topic; describe the differences in focus and the information provided.	**The Story of Ruby Bridges** • *The Story of Ruby Bridges*, by Robert Coles • *Ruby Bridges*, by Ruby Bridges and Grace Maccarone • *The Education of Ruby Nell*, by Ruby Bridges Hall, www.rubybridges.com/story.htm • *Ruby Bridges the Movie Part 1/9* (10 minutes 22 seconds), www.youtube.com/watch?v=klj5fgaKzIk&feature=related **The Story of the Fourteen Cows** • *14 Cows for America*, by Carmen Agra Deedy • *Cows: Cows and the Maasai* by Peachtree Publishers, http://14cowsforamerica.com/cows_complete.pdf • "Where 9/11 News Is Late, But Aid Is Swift," by Marc Lacey, www.nytimes.com/2002/06/03/international/africa/03KENY.html **The Story of Chiune Sugihara** • *Passage to Freedom: The Sugihara Story*, by Ken Mochizuki • *One More Border: The True Story of One Family's Escape from War-Torn Europe*, by William Kaplan and Shelley Tanaka • *About Chiune Sugihara*, www.visasforlife.org/sugihara.html • *Chiune and Yukiko Sugihara*, www.jewishvirtuallibrary.org/jsource/Holocaust/sugihara.html • Chiune (Sempo) Sugihara, www.ushmm.org/wlc/en/article.php?ModuleId=10005594

(continues)

\multicolumn{3}{l}{**Recommended Informational Text for Teaching Point of View in Grades K–5**}
Grade	**Standards**	**Recommended Texts**
5	Analyze multiple accounts of the same event or topic, noting important similarities and differences in the point of view they represent.	**Colonization** • *A Picture Book of Christopher Columbus*, by David Adler • *Encounter*, by Jane Yolen • *Examining the Reputation of Christopher Columbus*, by Jack Weatherford, www.hartford-hwp.com/Taino/docs/columbus.html **English Only** • *Home to Medicine Mountain*, by Santiago Chiori • *Cheyenne Again*, by Eve Bunting • Debate Rages on Over English Only Policies, www.youtube.com/watch?v=cHVRDay8UEk&feature=fvsr • Debate on Spanish Speakers Refusing to Learn English! www.youtube.com/watch?v=-S55FSjZHn8&feature=related **Global Warming** • Global warming articles (Whyfiles), http://whyfiles.org (search global warming) • Global warming website (Environmental Protection Agency), www.epa.gov/climatechange/kids/ • *Global Warming* (Thinkquest), http://library.thinkquest.org/CR0215471/global_warming.htm www.clean-air-kids.org.uk/globalwarming.html

Figure RIT **6.3**

Author and Illustrator

Name: _____ Date: _____

Title: _____

What the Author Taught

What the Illustrator Taught

Considering Author Point of View

Name: _____ Date: _____

Title: _____

Who wrote this text?

What did the author want to teach or explain?

How do you think the author feels about this topic/issue?

READING: INFORMATIONAL TEXT

Considering Different Points of View

Name: _____ Date: _____

Title: _____

Who is the author?

How do you think the author feels about this topic/issue?

How do you feel about this topic/issue?

Compare and Contrast Points of View

Name: _____ Date: _____

Title: _____

List the authors or websites at the bottom and then record differences in focus or point of view.

Figure RIT 6.7

INTENSIFYING THE INSTRUCTION
Evaluating

Evaluating is a comprehension strategy that involves considering author intents and viewpoints and how they might influence what is in a text. Students who rarely show critical thinking or who seem hesitant to identify authors' viewpoints or express agreement/disagreement with such viewpoints can benefit from support with evaluation. The lesson may be used with the whole class, or with students receiving small-group or intervention-based instruction.

1. Choose a text for discussion. (This may be a text you have already read or viewed with the class, or one you choose to read/view solely for the purposes of this lesson.) Figure RIT 6.2 provides a starter list of recommended informational text for teaching point of view. Let students know that you want to talk with them about the author's purpose or point of view.

2. During or after reading, use questions such as the following to support students in evaluating the text and thinking critically about the impact that the author's point of view has on content and style. Demonstrate your own thinking in relation to answering the questions as well as allowing time for student discussion.

- What topic did the author write about?
- What did the author teach about that?
- What evidence or examples did the author provide?
- What do we know about the author?
- How do you think that makes a difference in what this author has to say?
- How do you think the author feels about the topic? How can you tell?
- Do you agree with this author's views?
- Do you think that people or issues are fairly portrayed in this text? Why?
- Are people from parallel cultures (boys/girls, men/women, people of color) presented realistically or in stereotypical roles?
- How does this information compare with other accounts you have encountered?
- How could you use the information in this text?

Collaborative Engagement

1. **Choose the literature and the reading context.** You may use text that has been read aloud to the whole class (providing at least one copy per group) or students may be arranged in groups to read different texts. For kindergarten and first-grade students, choose literature that will allow for consideration of the important role that both the author and illustrator take in creating a book. For grades 2 through 5, with the focus moving to author point of view, look for texts with issues that will inspire discussion about the author's perspective on issues. Figure RIT 6.2 features a recommended starter list.

2. **Arrange for students to read or listen to the text.** Before the reading, let students know what they will be doing afterward. (See Figure RIT 6.8.) If students are doing the reading, provide support for those who cannot read the material independently with success.

3. **Hold the meetings.** Arrange for students to come together after the reading (or before, depending on the group assignment) to discuss point of view. Give students key prompts (as in Figure RIT 6.8) to help focus their discussions.

4. **Arrange for a follow-up discussion.** When all groups are working on the same text or text set, organize for a whole-class discussion as a follow-up to the group activity.

Figure RIT 6.8

READING ANCHOR 6:
Prompts to Support Student-Led Group Discussion of Text

Kindergarten and First Grade

- Give each group a large piece of chart paper with a line drawn down the middle. Write *Author* at the head of one column and *Illustrator* at the head of the other. Each group member draws something the author taught in one column and something the illustrator taught in the other column. (Figure RIT 6.3 provides a template that may be used if students will eventually be doing this project independently.)

Second Grade

- Students work as a group to record a response to the following questions.

  - Why do you think the author wrote this text?
  - What did the author want to explain?
  - How do you think the author feels about the topic?

Figure RIT 6.4 provides a template that may be used if students will eventually be doing this project independently.

Third Grade

- Students work with their group to record a response to the following questions:

  - Why do you think the author wrote this text?
  - How do you think the author feels about the topic/this issue?
  - Do you feel the same? Why or why not?

Figure RIT 6.5 provides a template that may be used if students will eventually be doing this project independently.

- Before reading, students draw a picture or map related to the topic being considered (for example, the uses of a cow in the world), and then they draw an updated picture or map after reading. This experience shows students how perspective changes after reading something.

(continues)

Fourth Grade

- Students work with their group to compare and contrast the *focus* taken in firsthand and secondhand accounts addressing the same topic. Figure RIT 6.2 provides some suggested literature for getting started. For each text, the group records a response to the following questions:

  - Why do you think the author created this text?
  - How do you think the author feels about the topic?
  - What was the author's focus in relation to this topic?
  - What special insights does this author offer?
  - Who do you think should read or view this text? Tell why.

  Figure RIT 6.6 provides a template that may be used if students will eventually be doing this project independently.

- Before reading, students draw a picture or map of what something looks like (for example, Christopher Columbus' entry into the new world), and then they draw an updated picture or map after reading. This experience shows students how perspective changes after reading something.

Fifth Grade

- Students work with their group to compare and contrast the point of view presented in different informational texts addressing the same topic. Figure RIT 6.2 provides some suggested literature for getting started.

  - Why do you think the author wrote this text?
  - How do you think the author feels about the topic?
  - What was the author's point of view in relation to this topic?
  - What special insights can this author offer?
  - Who do you think should read this text? Tell why.
  - Do you think that people are fairly portrayed in this book? Why or why not?

  Figure RIT 6.6 provides a template.

- Students draw a picture or map of what something looks like before reading (for example, United States Expansion or the relationship between a proton, neutron, and electron), and then they draw an updated picture or map of what it looks like after reading. This experience shows students how perspective changes after reading something.

Independent Application

Point-of-View Illustrations

Point-of-view illustrations are student-created drawings that illustrate the author's perspective on an issue. The purpose is to support students in learning to assess the ways in which point of view can be communicated through illustration.

> **Kindergarten:** Students draw a picture of an individual at a particular point in time, using details from the author to guide the illustration. Students should "show what the person was thinking" or "show what the author wants us to understand."

> **First Grade:** Students draw a picture of an individual at a particular point in time, using details from the author to guide the illustration. Students should "show what the person was thinking" or "show what the author wants us to understand." After drawing, students use thought bubbles to write what the individual is thinking.

> **Second, Third, Fourth, and Fifth Grades:** Students draw pictures of individuals from the probable perspectives of other individuals. For example a "Sioux leader" during the time of U.S. expansion depicts a "government leader." A "settler" depicts a "Sioux adult."

Book Talks

Book talks put students in a frame of mind for carefully evaluating texts and their illustrations and can be specifically aimed at encouraging students to identify and explore point of view. Figures RIT 6.9 to 6.11 provide planning forms. Show students what you expect in a book talk by choosing a form and using it to demonstrate what to include. Then, demonstrate how to use the form to give an oral book talk. Finally, arrange for individuals or teams to prepare and give book talks.

Book Talk Planning Form, K–1

Name: _____ Date: _____

Title: _____

Draw a picture that shows something the author taught. Tell the class about the picture.

Find a page that shows a lot about what the author taught. Mark it with a sticky note and explain it during your book talk.

Book Talk Planning Form, Grades 1–2

Name: _____ Date: _____

Title: _____

Write an opening that will enthrall your listeners.

Tell why you think the author wrote this book.

Tell what the author did well to meet the purpose.

Tell what the illustrator did well to meet the purpose.

Write a closing line to pull everything together.

Book Talk Planning Form, Grades 3–5

Name: _____ Date: _____

Title: _____

Write an opening that will enthrall your listeners.

Tell why you think the author wrote this book.

Tell why this is a book worth reading.

Tell what other points of view might be interesting to consider now that you have read this book.

Write a closing statement to wrap up your talk.

READING: INFORMATIONAL TEXT

Book Reviews

Book reviews provide an excellent forum for encouraging students to evaluate point of view. To get started, locate several professional reviews and read them with your students. (Choose reviews from familiar books.) You can often find reviews on the back covers of books, and Amazon's website (www.amazon.com) has professionally constructed reviews of many children's books. Demonstrate how to write a review, or write a review together as a class. You may brainstorm a set of questions to answer, or you may provide a set of possibilities, allowing students to choose the ones that best match the topic and content. Here are some examples:

- What topic did the author write about?

- What was the author's focus in relation to this topic?

- Who should read this? Why?

- How would the illustrations help a reader understand this text?

- How do you think the author feels about the topic? How can you tell?

- Do you think most readers would agree with this author's views? Why?

- What perspectives are *not* addressed?

- Is this a firsthand or secondhand account?

- How does this compare with other accounts you have read?

- What do we know about the author? How might being (in a wheelchair, a woman, Native American) make a difference in what this author has to say?

- What special insights can this author offer?

- Do you think that people are fairly portrayed in this book? Why?

- Are people from parallel cultures (boys/girls, men/women, people of color) presented realistically or in stereotypical roles?

- How can you use this information?

Blogs

A *blog* is a public forum for expressing ideas and viewpoints that can serve numerous functions in the upper elementary classroom. If you have never tried blogging as a teaching tool, don't let concerns about technology steer you away. Blog set-up is easy to do. Edublogs (http://edublogs.org/) offers a free system that is set up for educational purposes only and includes easy-to-follow guidelines for implementing the entire process. Your blogs can be set for complete privacy (such as allowing only the teacher to log in, or only the teacher and students, or only the teacher and other teachers in the school). Before getting started, check with your administration to learn about any existing tools or policies your school may have to guide the process.

In relation to Reading Anchor 6, students might do the following after reading articles or viewing news features on a topic:

- Work in small groups to write a point-of-view statement in relation to the topic. The statement should show understanding of more than one perspective on the issue. ("Some people believe English should the only language spoken in United States schools. Others believe. . . .") Students post the statement for comments from classmates. Each group then posts comments to other groups.

- Work in small groups to create a survey on a topic (two to four questions). Post the survey, allowing participants or groups to express their point of view on the issue.

- Work in small groups to pose a question and lead a discussion on an issue. For example, "What do you think kids can do about global warming?" Other groups develop and post responses.

Blogging in a classroom setting allows students to share their perspectives in a safe learning environment, develop skills for critical literacy, and gain experience in using technology as a tool for learning and communication.

Letters from Authors

Letters from authors are written after students read or listen to an informational text. Students consider the point of view of the author and compose a letter *as* the author, telling the class the reason for writing the piece. Students discuss their rationales in small groups or with the whole class.

Informational Interviews

In *informational interviews*, you or your students write three to six interview questions for the author to answer, and then students take on the persona of the author to write responses to the questions. For example: "Why did you write this book?"; "Why do you want people to know about this topic?"; "What is your background in relation to the topic?"; "What do you know about (present a point of view or focus different from what the author has presented)?"

As an alternative, students may answer interview questions from the persona of people or animals in the text they are reading. For example, in social studies, students might "be" Ruby Bridges or an individual who protested her attending a desegregated school. In science, they might be a rain forest logger, the owner of a logging company, or a rain forest animal losing its habitat. Allow time for performance, as the responses to questions inspire reflection on multiple points of view and often generate lots of discussion.

Narrated Illustrations

Narrated illustrations are written as first-person accounts of what is happening in an illustration from the probable perspective of the author. After reading or listening, students choose an illustration and write a description of what is happening. Giving students one or two stems can help them write in a focused way. For example:

- This illustration in my book shows . . .
- I wanted to write this book to help people understand . . .

Students may also be encouraged to write from the perspective of individuals they are reading about. For example, using a picture of Ruby Bridges walking into her all-white school, students might write from the following prompts: How might Ruby Bridges describe her walk into the all-white school on the first day? How would the marshals who were escorting her describe the situation? How would the protestors describe it? How would her mother describe it? To compare two different perspectives, students can narrate the illustration from two perspectives. Engaging students in narrated illustrations provides a structured medium for considering different points of view.

Perspective Writing

Perspective writing provides a medium for students to identify and consider the point of view of a text author as well as different points of view not explicitly addressed.

1. After reading or listening to a text related to the social studies or science curriculum, students identify who is telling the story.

2. Students choose a paragraph or page and rewrite it to show a *different* point of view than the one presented. For example, in *Almost Gone*, Steve Jenkins presents information about a series of animals that are almost extinct. For each, he gives the reason for decline in population, such as logging or hunting. In perspective writing,

students consider the issue from the perspective of someone who is involved. For example, they could write from the point of view of a logger or hunter, or even one of the almost-extinct species.

3. Allow students to share their pieces with the whole class, a small group, or a partner. Use this opportunity to emphasize the concept that the point of view that is presented is influenced by who is telling the story.

Journalists

Acting as *journalists*, students create a newspaper focused on the content they are studying in social studies or science. For example, in "Expansion Times," students could write an article as a pioneer/settler child, as a Native American child being resettled, as a participant in Ghost Dance, as a member of the Donner party, as a wagon train guide, or as a military person. Students consider multiple points of view as they write and discuss information from multiple perspectives.

INTEGRATION OF KNOWLEDGE AND IDEAS

ANCHOR 7

English Language Arts Standards Reading: Informational Text ANCHOR 7

Reading Anchor 7: Integrate and evaluate content presented in diverse media and formats, including visually and quantitatively, as well as in words.

K	First	Second	Third	Fourth	Fifth
With prompting and support, describe the relationship between illustrations and the text in which they appear (e.g., what person, place, thing, or idea in the text an illustration depicts).	Use the illustrations and details in a text to describe its key ideas.	Explain how specific images (e.g., a diagram showing how a machine works) contribute to and clarify a text.	Use information gained from illustrations (e.g., maps, photographs) and the words in a text to demonstrate understanding of the text (e.g., where, when, why, and how key events occur).	Interpret information presented visually, orally, or quantitatively (e.g., in charts, graphs, diagrams, timelines, animations, or interactive elements on Web pages) and explain how the information contributes to an understanding of the text in which it appears.	Draw on information from multiple print or digital sources, demonstrating the ability to locate an answer to a question quickly or to solve a problem efficiently.

Decision Tree for
Reading: Informational Text ANCHOR 7

Do my students need focused instruction in relation to Reading Anchor 7?

Anchor 7 is aimed at helping students learn to *interpret visual information featured in text*, such as charts, graphs, and diagrams. (Refer to your grade-level standards for specific details.)

When some or all of your students could use support in this area, it is recommended that you start the process by implementing three types of instruction in sequence over the course of about a week:

Demonstration	Collaborative Engagement	Independent Application
Page 261	Page 264	Page 266

The initial demonstration requires just one session (to be repeated as needed), leaving one or two days for collaborative engagement and one or two days to begin the independent applications, which become ongoing as you choose. If you find during any phase of the instruction that some or all of your students could use more intensified support, it is recommended that you consider the lesson for intensifying the instruction.

Do my students need intensified support using images to support meaning making?

Interpreting images is an important part of reading informational text. Students who rush through text without taking time to use the illustrations or those who do not know how to interpret various kinds of illustrations can benefit from lessons focused on images. See page 263.

Demonstration

Anchor 7 requires that students *interpret the visual information featured in text*. This includes integrating the actual written text with features such as charts, graphs, photographs, animations, and interactive elements on Web pages. The present lesson may be implemented toward this goal as many times as would be beneficial, using one or more different texts each time.

1. **Choose the text.** Select a piece of literature that is familiar to the group, one with illustrations or visual features that contribute importantly to the meaning. You may wish to use a website for this lesson.

2. **Introduce the text and the concept.** Walk through the pages of the text, showing and naming the different types of illustrations it contains. Let students know that the illustrations are as important as the words themselves and that you want to work with them to be sure they are interpreting the illustrations confidently.

3. **Demonstrate and discuss the concept.** Show students how you interpret meanings of the illustrations, rereading parts of the text as it is helpful. Make your thinking processes explicit, and share your expectation that students will attend to illustrations as they are reading independently. Figure RIT 7.1 offers a starter set of prompts to support students in learning to evaluate the illustrations and integrate what the author and illustrator have created.

READING ANCHOR 7:
Prompts to Support Teacher-Led Modeling and Discussion of Text

Kindergarten

What do you notice in this illustration/image? What does this illustration help us understand?

First and Second Grades

What does this illustration/image tell us? How does it give us an even better understanding than the text alone can give?

Let's use the illustrations to talk back through the key ideas.

Third and Fourth Grades

What does this illustration/image tell us? How does it give us an even better understanding than the text alone can give?

Let's retell this text using both what we read and what we learned from the illustrations.

Fifth Grade

What if we wanted to find out _____? How could I get to that point? Let's work our way to the answer as efficiently as we can, using the text and the illustrations.

Figure RIT **7.2**

INTENSIFYING THE INSTRUCTION
Interpreting Images

Interpreting images is an important part of meaning making. It includes integrating information from the actual written text with features such as charts, graphs, photographs, animations, and interactive elements on Web pages.

1. Choose a text for modeling that contains illustrations or other visual features that are important to the meaning. Try to select a text with illustrations you believe your students will need support interpreting.

2. Walk through all of the pages of the section to be read, discussing with students the details in the display and pointing out the importance of attending to them.

3. Assign students to read short sections silently or softly. At designated points, do the following:

   - Discuss what the illustrations are for.
   - Talk students through what the illustrations mean and how to interpret them.
   - Discuss the ways the written text connects with the illustrations.

   For English Learners

   - Use the illustrations to name and discuss specific vocabulary relevant to the text.
   - Work with students to use small (one-half-by-two-inch) sticky notes to label key parts of the illustrations that will appear in the written text and to show the connection between images and the text.
   - Use transparency tape to highlight a few key words or phrases, and discuss their meanings before reading. Show the connections between the words/ phrases and the illustrations.
   - Before reading, place English learners with experienced English speakers to discuss the illustrations in the story and make predictions about the content.

4. Provide follow-up lessons for small groups as needed.

Collaborative Engagement

1. **Choose the literature and the reading context.** Gather a set of familiar texts for students to reexamine and reread with peers. Look for texts with visual or multimedia elements that are likely to capture students' interest and lead to discussion. We want the illustrations and the graphics to inspire the talk.

2. **Arrange for students to read or listen to the text.** The focus of this lesson is on browsing and rereading.

3. **Hold the meetings.** Arrange for students to come together to discuss key aspects of the illustrations. Give students key starter prompts (as in Figure RIT 7.3) to help them focus on the ideas that are critical to integrating and evaluating information from the visual display.

4. **Arrange for a follow-up discussion.** When all groups are working on the same text, organize for a whole-class discussion as a follow-up to the group activity.

READING ANCHOR 7:
Prompts to Support Student-Led Group Discussion of Text

Kindergarten

- Students sit together as they review all of the illustrations/images from the text. Each student chooses one that represents an important person, place, thing, or idea and draws a picture to help remember and describe the concepts taught.

First and Second Grades

- As a team, students review all of the illustrations/images from the text, choosing and marking one that provides helpful information about the key ideas presented by the author. They work together to describe in writing what the illustration teaches. A bulleted list may be used.

Third Grade

- Students review all of the illustrations/images from the text, discussing how the illustrator works alongside the author to provide information. Students write a short passage describing the role of each for the particular text they are reviewing.

Fourth Grade

- Students review all of the illustrations/images from the text, discussing how the illustrator works alongside the author to provide information. They use highlighting tape to show the specific language that informs the illustrations.

Fifth Grade

- Students are presented with two to four questions or problems to address together. The questions should be designed such that they challenge students to draw on information from illustrations as well as text to answer the question or solve the problems. For example:
  - What does the chart on page _____ show about population growth in the United States?
  - What does the visual show about the motion of the earth and moon around the sun?

Independent Application

Paired Reading

Paired reading typically involves two children in reading a book together and responding to its content through talk or writing. Very young children may take 10 to 15 minutes to complete the process; older children may take up to 30 minutes. To implement paired reading, provide opportunities for teams of two to browse and read through picture books together during regularly scheduled independent or paired reading times. Students can take turns reading aloud in a soft voice, or each student can have a copy of the same book to read silently at the same time. In the interest of Reading Anchor 7, use image-rich literature and encourage students to retell using the illustrations or to simply spend time talking about the information provided by the visual features in the text.

Stop-and-Chats

*Stop-and-chat*s are a forum for students to read with a specific purpose in mind and engage in conversations related to that purpose. To use stop-and-chats to support development of Reading Anchor 7, two or three students who are reading the same text work together.

1. Before they read, students turn through the pages and place a marker at an agreed-upon stopping point for discussion. Upon reaching this point, they discuss the meaning of the illustrations to the point and then place the marker at the next agreed-upon stopping point in preparation for another chat. Students generally need little prompting to talk about interesting illustrations, but to get the conversations started, you and the students can brainstorm some generic prompts, or you can offer your own. For example:

    *   What does this illustration tell us?

    *   How does this illustration connect with what the author tells us?

2. As students gain experience with stop-and-chats, provide follow-up lessons based on observations of their performance.

Illustration Studies

Illustration studies are conversations between two students designed to facilitate meaningful interpretation of the visual images in a text.

1. Work with your students to create a list of questions they might consider as they study illustrations and images with a partner. Keep the list short and manageable for the age group. For example, if you teach third grade, you might post the following:

   - What does this illustration tell us?

   - Where in the text can we find information about this illustration? What does the written part tell us?

2. Before starting a new book, students find a partner with whom to engage in an illustration study. (The partnered students need not be reading the same books for this experience to be worthwhile.) Student teams choose one to three illustrations to interpret and discuss.

3. As an option, you can have all students in the class participate through a read-aloud. Have partner-teams share observations with the class.

Creating Captions

Creating captions requires that students take a close look at an image and use concise written language to uncover its meaning for others. For example, given a diagram of the life cycle of a tadpole, students write a caption to describe each phase. Or given a chart showing the eight countries with the highest population growth rate, students create a caption to explain the trend in the most concise language possible.

Web Challenge

Place students in teams of two. Give each team a set of three or four websites to browse, focusing on a key topic that is important to your curriculum. Ask the teams to review the sites and to print one illustration that provides important information. They are to read the text that accompanies the illustration and then present the illustration to the class or a small group. (Web challenges can also be done without computers—as "text challenges.")

Outstanding Illustrator Projects

Outstanding illustrator projects are a way to draw attention to the images in a text and support students in integrating the different information presented by authors and illustrators.

1. Allow your students time to identify an outstanding informational text illustrator. Give them the choice of bringing in a book from home (send a note to facilitate this process) or browsing and choosing one from the classroom collection. The books will need to remain on display in the classroom for one to two weeks.

2. When the books have been chosen, allow students time to work on the projects. Some possibilities follow:

Kindergarten and First Grade

-   Students create a bookmark that includes a picture of something important the illustrator taught. They place the bookmark at one page that helps the reader learn about that topic. The books may be displayed in a center or shared with a partner or small group.

Second Through Fifth Grades

-   Students choose an illustration that helps them understand something important about the text. Using a half-piece of paper, they write three sentences that tell what the illustration teaches. The half-paper is placed at the chosen page. Students may share with a partner or small group, or the books may be viewed during independent reading time.

Illustration Center

Use an *illustration center* to allow your students to informally explore the informational text illustrator's craft. To prepare, work with students to create a set of challenges, or offer your own. Following are some examples:

-   Create a chart to show what the students in our class ate for breakfast today.
-   Create a diagram to show the life cycle of a butterfly.
-   Create a timeline to show the important events in Tatanka Iyotake's life.
-   Create a diagram to show what happens at a water treatment plant.

Post the possibilities on the wall near the center, make several supplies available, and allow all students the opportunity to explore the materials and activities.

English Language Arts Standards Reading: Informational Text **ANCHOR 8**

Reading Anchor 8: Delineate and evaluate the argument and specific claims in a text, including the validity of the reasoning as well as the relevance and sufficiency of the evidence.

K	First	Second	Third	Fourth	Fifth
With prompting and support, identify the reasons an author gives to support points in a text.	Identify the reasons an author gives to support points in a text.	Describe how reasons support specific points the author makes in a text.	Describe the logical connection between particular sentences and paragraphs in a text (e.g., comparison; cause-effect; first, second, third in a sequence).	Explain how an author uses reasons to support particular points in a text.	Explain how an author uses reasons and evidence to support particular points in a text, identifying which reasons and evidence support which point(s).

Decision Tree for
Reading: Informational Text ANCHOR 8

**Do my students need focused instruction
in relation to Reading Anchor 8?**

Anchor 8 requires that students *identify the reasons and evidence an author gives to support the key points made in a text.* (Refer to your grade-level standards for specific details.)

When some or all of your students could use support in this area, it is recommended that you start the process by implementing three types of instruction in sequence over the course of about a week:

Demonstration	**Collaborative Engagement**	**Independent Application**
Page 271	**Page 275**	**Page 277**

The initial demonstration requires just one session (to be repeated as needed), leaving one or two days for collaborative engagement and one or two days to begin the independent applications, which become ongoing as you choose. If you find during any phase of the instruction that some or all of your students could use more intensified support, it is recommended that you consider the lesson for intensifying the instruction.

**Do my students need intensified support with explaining
the reasons or evidence an author gives for an argument or key point?**

This is a competency that requires identifying the argument and tracking the evidence over the course of a text or section. Students who do not monitor and hold meaning across the pages of a text may benefit from intensified support in this area. See page 274.

Demonstration

Anchor 8 requires that students *identify the reasons and evidence an author gives to support the key points made in a text*. For example, after listening to *Ruby Bridges* (Bridges and Maccarone), kindergarten or first-grade students might be guided to identify the reasons for the authors' conclusion that Ruby is brave; after reading *Passage to Freedom: The Sugihara Story* (Mochizuki), fourth- and fifth-grade students might be asked to explain the author's reasons for concluding that Sugihara did something important for humanity (even though he was imprisoned for his actions). Anchor 8 prepares students for evaluating the arguments that authors make and the sufficiency of their evidence.

1. **Choose the text.** Select literature in which the author makes a key point and supplies an argument or evidence. Persuasive or opinion pieces work well because the key pieces of the argument are generally made obvious; but the text need not be limited to this genre.

2. **Introduce the text and the concept.** To get students started with evaluating an argument, let them know the key point you would like them to consider. For example, "The authors say that Ruby is brave" or "The authors say the earth is getting warmer." Then, let students know that you would like them to identify the reasons or evidence the author gives for the key point.

3. **Demonstrate and discuss the concept.** Teach students a process for evaluating arguments and demonstrate it with the text at hand. The following process may be used or adapted for most arguments:

   • Identify the point or conclusion the author is making.

   • Identify the reasons or details the author gives to support that conclusion. If creating a written evaluation, lay out the reasons or details in sequential order.

   • Evaluate whether the reasons provide adequate support for the conclusion.

Figure RIT 8.1 offers a starter set of prompts to support students in learning to identify and evaluate an author's reasons and evidence.

READING ANCHOR 8:
Prompts to Support Teacher-Led Modeling and Discussion of Text

Kindergarten and First and Second Grades

The author pointed out that _____. What reasons does the author give to support that? (Figure RIT 8.2 provides a template for recording information.)

Third, Fourth, and Fifth Grades

What are the main ideas the author wants us to consider in this section? Or, what is a key point we would want to evaluate? What reasons or details does the author give to support this point?

Let's lay out in sequence the reasons the author uses. Then we can evaluate whether we think the author has provided enough evidence. Work with students to identify the text structure the author uses to support the key points, such as providing a list of reasons/evidence or using a compare-and-contrast text structure. (Figure RIT 8.2 provides a template.)

Key Point and Evidence

Name: _____ Date: _____

Title: _____

Key Point →

Evidence →

INTENSIFYING THE INSTRUCTION
Monitoring for Evidence

Monitoring for evidence is a strategy that involves keeping track of the key points an author makes and the reasons or evidence given to support them.

1. To develop student awareness of monitoring for evidence, select a content-area text that makes a key point backed by reasons or evidence. For example: "Plants cannot live without four important ingredients" or "Population growth is a problem for the environment." Each student should have a copy of the text.

2. Work with the students to set a purpose for the reading, for example: "We are going to read through this section (book) to see if we can identify the big idea or point the author is trying to make and we are going to track the reasons given to support it."

3. Guide the students to identify the key point and begin to track the evidence or reasons the author provides. Use sticky notes or note cards to jot down the key details of evidence, and then arrange them into a visual format that helps to show the text structure. For example, the author may have listed some reasons or used a comparison or cause-effect structure. Lay out your materials to reflect the structure.

4. If your students seem to grasp the concept, allow them to take over and finish documenting the evidence either in teams of two or talking as a group.

5. Continue instruction with students who have not yet developed effective monitoring.

Collaborative Engagement

1. **Choose the literature and the reading context.** Select a piece of literature that makes an argument or key point of some sort and contains evidence to support it, for example: "Dolphins are social animals"; "Early scientists had many misconceptions about dinosaurs"; "Circus animals often suffer." Plan to either read aloud the text to the class or allow individuals to read the text independently as you provide support for those who need it.

2. **Arrange for students to read or listen to the text.** Before the reading, let students know what they will be doing afterward. (See Figure RIT 8.4.) As needed, support students in identifying the key point the author is making in a section of the text or the whole text.

3. **Hold the meetings.** Arrange for students to come together to discuss key evidence or reasons the author provides to support the key points made. Figure RIT 8.4 offers some starter prompts aimed at helping students focus on the ideas that are critical to understanding and evaluating the author's argument.

4. **Arrange for a follow-up discussion.** Students will benefit from sharing their ideas and viewing them in light of the ideas other groups have developed.

READING ANCHOR 8:
Prompts to Support Student-Led Group Discussion of Text

Kindergarten

- After working with the teacher to identify a key point in a text and to discuss the reasons or evidence given, students work together on large chart paper to draw the key reasons/evidence. They may label their drawings.

- After working with the teacher to identify a key point in a text and to discuss the reasons or evidence given, students review all of the illustrations from the text, each choosing and marking one that represents a key reason or piece of evidence. Each student draws one piece of evidence.

First and Second Grades

- After working with the teacher to identify a key point in a text and to discuss the reasons or evidence given, students work together on large chart paper to draw or write the key reasons/evidence. They may label their drawings.

- After working with the teacher to identify a key point in a text and to discuss the reasons or evidence given, students review all of the illustrations from the text, each choosing and drawing and writing about one.

Third, Fourth, and Fifth Grades

- After working with the teacher to identify a key point in a text and to discuss the reasons or evidence given, students work together on large chart paper to lay out in sequence the reasons/evidence the author uses to come to this point. Students use their work to evaluate whether they think the author has provided adequate evidence for the point made.

- After working with the teacher to identify a key point in a text and to discuss the reasons or evidence given, students work together to delineate on sticky notes the reasons/evidence the author uses to come to this point. After documenting the evidence on sticky notes, students lay out the evidence in a format that helps to show the argument (for example, in a list format, or using arrows to show cause and effect). Students use their work to evaluate whether they think the author has provided adequate evidence for the point made.

Independent Application

Tell Why

Tell why assignments are set up for students to provide a critical response to a piece of literature. After students read or listen to an informational text, present them with a key point the author made, and then assign them to read back through the text or illustrations to delineate why the author believes the statement to be true. Both the text and the key point statement (written large and posted in the classroom) should be available for reference. Students may work independently or with a partner.

To complete the assignment, students copy the key point at the top of a piece of paper, and then they either draw or write a bulleted list, focusing on presenting the reasons and evidence the author provides.

Lay It Out

Lay it out is a teacher-supported experience that involves students in using note cards or sticky notes to organize a text's ideas. The text may be one that is read aloud to the whole class, read independently, or read aloud in groups. Short pieces printed from the Internet work well.

With teacher support, students write a key point from the text on a note card. Then, working independently, they prepare additional note cards that show the reasons or evidence the author provides.

The cards may be organized in a web shape if the reasons are in no particular sequence; in columns if the author is using compare and contrast; and in a line if the author is using cause and effect. The lay it out process offers a visual representation of the structure of the text, helping to illuminate the key points of the argument.

Flap Book

Students fold two or three pieces of paper in half (long way) and staple along the fold. They cut up to the staples two times, ending up with a book containing three flapping sections. On the top of each flap, they record a key point from a text, and on each flap underneath, they describe a reason/evidence provided by the author. The flap book is used to understand how an author builds a set of key points with reasons, and is also used for rethinking or retelling.

Good Reason

After reading a text (or section) aloud to the class—or having individuals read the material independently—ask students to write down what they think is the key point. Guide them to choose a point for which the author has provided reasons or evidence. If the students' identified points vary widely, you may use this opportunity to generate a group understanding that there is often more than one key point made in a text or more than one angle from which to view an issue. Work with the class to convene on one key point to examine further. Be sure to choose one for which the author has provided evidence or reasons.

Ask students to write the key point on their papers. Then, ask the students to go back into the text and find the reasons or evidence the author gives to support it. They should write a concise statement reflecting each piece of evidence they find.

Finally, discuss what the students have identified as key evidence provided, and determine whether the class feels the author's reasoning is adequate.

Collaborative Reasoning

Collaborative reasoning (Chinn and Anderson 1998) is a teacher-guided strategy that is recommended for small-group sessions. It is designed to encourage deep and thoughtful reading, and it helps students respond in thoughtful ways to critical questions about books.

1. Select a text that lends itself to taking a position on an issue. Students read the text silently with the knowledge that they will be asked to respond to and discuss a higher-level question when they are finished reading.

2. Pose a critical question that leads students to taking a position on an issue related to the text. For example, *Bessie Coleman: Daring Stunt Pilot* (Robbins) tells the story of a woman who became America's first African American woman pilot. Throughout her life, she pays a price for various decisions she makes. A critical question could be, "Did Bessie Coleman make the right decision when she got involved in stunt flying?"

3. Students respond to the question with an initial agreement or disagreement or they may respond with "not sure."

4. Students provide supporting evidence for their initial positions using personal experience and information from the text. They may change their positions as they weigh reasons and evidence presented by peers. The teacher's role is to support the reasoning process and encourage students to lead the discussion.

Evaluate This!

To help students understand the structure of an argument, plan to have them each write their own key point with evidence and then submit the piece for peer evaluation. Demonstrate the process first, letting students know that you will be looking for them to do the following with their pieces:

- Make a key point.

- Provide two to four pieces of evidence or reasons to support the key point.

- Order the evidence in a logical sequence.

You can start with silly or simple points, such as "Mrs. K. is funny," or "Our flowers are growing." When students understand the process, they can move into content-area writing that requires more depth of thinking or research, such as with "Plants need four things to survive," or "Bats are unique mammals," or "Bessie Coleman was an American Hero."

INTEGRATION OF KNOWLEDGE AND IDEAS

ANCHOR 9

English Language Arts Standards   Reading: Informational Text ANCHOR 9

Reading Anchor 9: Analyze how two or more texts address similar themes or topics in order to build knowledge or to compare the approaches the authors take.

K	First	Second	Third	Fourth	Fifth
With prompting and support, identify basic similarities in and differences between two texts on the same topic (e.g., in illustrations, descriptions, or procedures).	Identify basic similarities in and differences between two texts on the same topic (e.g., in illustrations, descriptions, or procedures).	Compare and contrast the most important points presented by two texts on the same topic.	Compare and contrast the most important points and key details presented in two texts on the same topic.	Integrate information from two texts on the same topic in order to write or speak about the subject knowledgeably.	Integrate information from several texts on the same topic in order to write or speak about the subject knowledgeably.

Decision Tree for
Reading: Informational Text ANCHOR 9

Do my students need focused instruction in relation to Reading Anchor 9?

Anchor 9 requires that students *compare, contrast, and integrate information from different texts* to build meaning. (Refer to your grade-level standards for specific details.)

When some or all of your students could use support in this area, it is recommended that you start the process by implementing three types of instruction in sequence over the course of about a week:

Demonstration	Collaborative Engagement	Independent Application
Page 282	**Page 288**	**Page 290**

The initial demonstration requires just one session (to be repeated as needed), leaving one or two days for collaborative engagement and one or two days to begin the independent applications, which become ongoing as you choose. If you find during any phase of the instruction that some or all of your students could use more intensified support, it is recommended that you consider the lesson for intensifying the instruction.

Do my students need intensified support making connections between texts?

Making connections is so important to children's development of all kinds of knowledge that just about any student can benefit from intensified instruction in this area. However, you may find that some students do not have an efficient set of strategies in place for considering connections, and that intensifying the instruction for a short period of time can be beneficial. English learners especially may benefit, as working with two texts that have related content provides an opportunity for repeated use of vocabulary that is focused on a particular topic. See page 287.

Demonstration

Anchor 9 requires that students *compare, contrast, and integrate information across texts*. The goal is to build knowledge from multiple sources. The present lesson may be implemented toward this goal several times, using a different text set each time.

1. **Choose the text set.** A text set is a grouping of two or more texts that are related in some way. For this lesson, choose two texts focused on the same content-area topic. Allow at least two days for the lesson.

2. **Introduce the text and the concept.** Show students both texts. Let them know that you will be reading them over the course of two days and that they will be using both to learn about one topic.

3. **Demonstrate and discuss the concept.** On day one, read the first text, discussing the key content. You may focus on key elements, such as illustrations, descriptions, procedures, or key points (see your Anchor 9 grade-level standards for specifics). On day two, introduce the second text, reminding students that you will be comparing it with the first text or using it to help them add on to what they know already. In accordance with Anchor 9, if you teach kindergarten or first grade, you may wish to focus your conversation around the similarities and differences between the texts in general. If you teach second or third grade, you may wish to focus on comparing and contrasting the most important points. If you teach fourth or fifth grade, you may wish to emphasize integrating the information to build the students' knowledge base. Figure RIT 9.1 offers a starter set of prompts.

Figure RIT **9.1**

READING ANCHOR 9:
Prompts to Support Teacher-Led Modeling and Discussion

Kindergarten and First Grade

What information did we find in both books? What information did we find in just one or the other? (Figure RIT 9.2 provides a template for drawing or writing about related concepts such as illustrations, descriptions, or procedures from two books.)

Second and Third Grades

Let's think back through the important points in both texts. This is a way to build wide knowledge on a topic. (Figure RIT 9.3 provides a template for documenting information.)

Let's compare and contrast the information we got from the two different texts. (Figure RL 9.4 in Part 1 provides a template for documenting information.)

Fourth and Fifth Grades

We are going to be using different sources of information to build knowledge on this topic. Let's think through what we have learned. (Figures RIT 9.3 and RIT 9.4 provide templates for documenting information. Also see Figure RL 9.4 in Part 1.)

I Learn from Books!

Name: _____ Date: _____

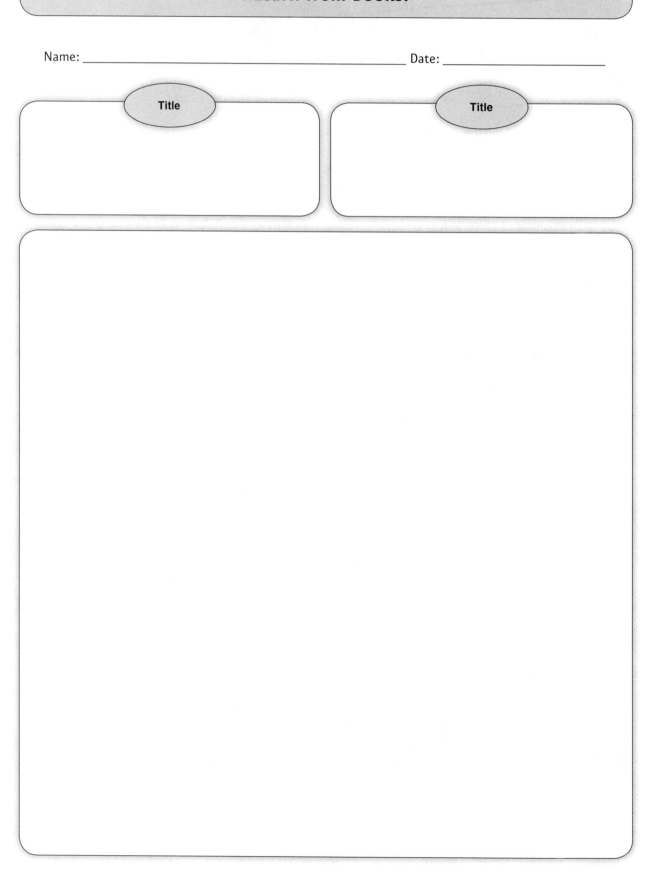

Title

Title

Important Points from Two Texts

Name: _____ Date: _____

Title 1: _____

Title 2: _____

Document the important points from each text. Draw lines to show points that are related.

Important Points from Title 1

Important Points from Title 2

Integrating Information Across Texts

Name: _____ Date: _____

Title 1: _____ Title 2: _____

Topic: _____

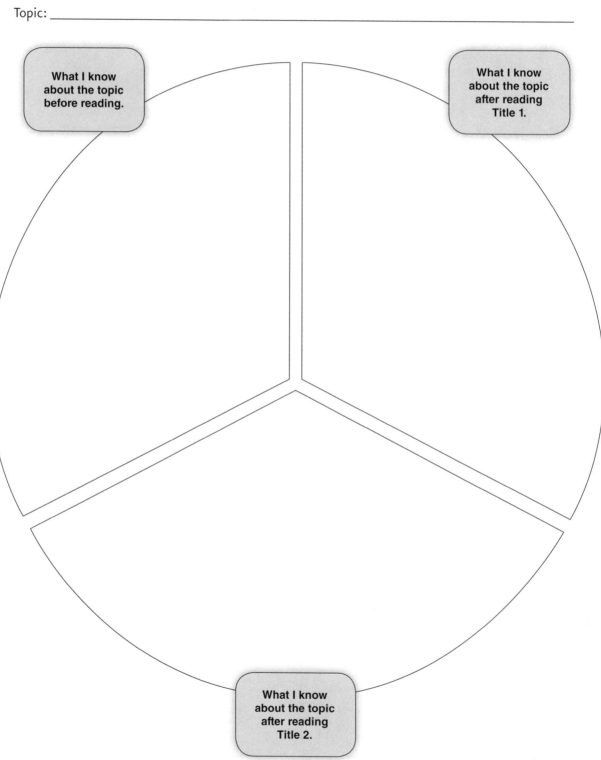

What I know about the topic before reading.

What I know about the topic after reading Title 1.

What I know about the topic after reading Title 2.

INTENSIFYING THE INSTRUCTION
Making Connections Between Texts

Making connections between texts is a way of building depth and breadth of knowledge on a topic.

1. To develop student awareness of making connections between texts, select two familiar texts that are related in some way. The texts should be important to your students' content-area learning. If you are working with a small group, give the students a large piece of chart paper. If you are working with the whole class, arrange students in groups, each with a large piece of chart paper in the middle. Each student or group needs access to a copy of the text.

2. Point out a connection between the two texts and show students how you can record it by drawing or writing on chart paper. It can help to start with a question. For example, "What are the life cycle stages of a grasshopper?" shows students that both texts provide information about the concept, but that you can gain unique information from each. Show students how you document information from both texts to help answer your question. Then, ask students to read a designated section of each text, continuing to document a response to the guiding question.

3. Ask groups or teams to share what they have learned about the topic by connecting two texts.

Collaborative Engagement

1. **Choose the literature and the reading context.** Gather a set of texts focused on one topic. Look for texts to support development of content knowledge related to your curriculum or based on student interests, a current event, or content you feel is important in general for your group.

2. **Arrange for students to read or listen to the text.** Either use texts that have been read aloud to the whole class already (ideally providing at least one copy of each per group) or arrange students in groups to individually choose and read different texts.

3. **Hold the meetings.** Students come together after the reading to gather information or compare the two texts in ways you have modeled (i.e., using a chart or Venn diagram). Give students key prompts before reading (as in Figure RIT 9.6) to help them focus on key ideas to consider in preparation for their discussions.

4. **Arrange a follow-up discussion.** When all groups are working on the same text, organize for a whole-class discussion as a follow-up to the group activity.

READING ANCHOR 9:
Prompts to Support Student-Led Group Discussion of Text

Kindergarten and First Grade

- Copy and laminate several illustrations from the texts you have been reading on a key topic and encourage students to sort them in various ways. For example, if you have read two books about gorillas, they may sort by the type of activity the gorillas are engaged in (eating, play, resting, caring for young). Students discuss the similarities and differences between the texts.

- Place two books focused on the same topic in a center (or display the books in a central area of the classroom) and ask each student to draw something similar that each author taught. For example, if the topic is gorillas, both books might show that gorillas play or that the babies stay with their mothers for a long time. Students work in proximity to one another as a way to discuss similarities across books.

- Give students ten to twelve books focused on two different topics and ask them to sort into appropriate piles based on their content. Students must tell what the books in each pile have in common and what is different. They may be asked to write or draw in response to this question.

Second and Third Grades

- Students work together to compare and contrast two texts focused on the same topic. Students should write enough detail to show both similarities and differences. Figures RIT 9.3 and RL 9.4 (from Part 1) provide templates that may be reproduced on large chart paper or given to each student for documentation.

Fourth and Fifth Grades

- Students work with their group to first consider their prior knowledge on a topic and then to purposefully add information to their prior knowledge based on the reading of two texts. At the end of the session, students prepare for presenting "some new things we learned" to the class. Figure RIT 9.4 provides a template that may be reproduced on large chart paper or given to each student for documentation.

Independent Application

Browsing Bins

Create browsing bins featuring sets of texts you want your students to compare and contrast. Label each bin according to the topic it contains. Allow students to use the bins during independent or paired reading times. To encourage accountability and reflection, you may wish to ask students to use Figure RIT 9.3, RIT 9.4, or RL 9.4 from Part 1 as a template for organizing their connections.

Graffiti Boards

Graffiti boards (Short, Harste, and Burke 1996) serve the important purpose of helping students identify and organize connections between texts. They may be used when students are reading different selections from a text set.

1. Arrange for students to sit in small groups with a large piece of paper in the middle. As students read books from the text set, they stop and write observations and reflections on the paper. Each student works alone, recording words and phrases and sketching ideas and images that come to mind.

2. After the reading session, students discuss their "graffiti" with the group as a way to build knowledge on the topic and make connections across texts. They can use arrows and lines to show connecting information.

Text Link Talks

Text link talks provide a structured opportunity for students to think together about different authors' approaches to similar themes and topics. For this lesson, you will need five or six copies each of two titles that are important to your content-area curriculum.

1. Read aloud and discuss the two related texts over the course of two days. Or you may have students read silently, providing support for individuals as needed.

2. On the third day, place students in groups, giving each group a copy of each text. Present the students with the following prompts:

    Grades K–1: Use drawing and/or writing to show what the texts have in common (or what both authors taught).

    Grades 2–3: Use a Venn diagram to show what the texts have in common and what is unique to each text.

Grades 4–5: Use information from both texts to present the class with three key concepts that are important to understand in relation to our content-area study. To help explain each concept, write one or two sentences and provide a sketch.

3. Bring the class together to compare findings and/or share information. As appropriate, follow up with a discussion regarding the groups' different interpretations, showing that texts often can be interpreted in more than one way.

What's the Connection?

To implement *what's the connection?* arrange for students to read or listen to two texts that address the same topic. After reading the first text, each student writes or draws on yellow sticky notes one to three key concepts the author taught. On the second day, after reading the second text, students do the same using pink sticky notes. Then, students work in small groups to create a group Venn diagram featuring their sticky-note observations. The notes from the first text are placed in one circle, the notes from the second text are placed in the second circle, and then students move the notes to the middle if both texts addressed the concept.

Science Writers

As *science writers*, the whole class works together to create a text that others could use to learn about an important topic, concept, or procedure relating to your content-area curriculum. Each student creates one to two pages of the text. All students are required to use at least two sources of information.

Grades K–1: After listening to two texts focused on the same topic, students use what they have learned to draw a picture of an important concept or idea. They may use labels or captions.

Grades 2–3: After reading or listening to two texts focused on the same topic, students make a key statement about the concept followed by at least three bulleted details or examples. They create an illustration to help explain the concept.

Grades 4–5: After reading at least two texts focused on the same topic, students use information from both texts to make a key statement about the concept followed by at least three paragraphs that include details or examples. They create an illustration (such as a drawing, chart, or diagram) to help explain the concept.

History Writers

As *history writers*, the whole class works together to create a text that others could use to learn about an important era or event related to your content-area curriculum. Each student creates one to two pages of the text. All students are required to use at least two sources of information.

Grades K–1: After listening to two texts focused on the same topic, students use what they have learned to draw a picture of an important person or event in history. They may use labels or captions.

Grades 2–3: After reading or listening to two texts focused on the same topic, students make a key statement about the topic followed by at least three bulleted details or examples. They create an illustration to help explain the statement.

Grades 4–5: After reading at least two texts focused on the same topic, students use information from both texts to make a key statement about the topic followed by at least three paragraphs that include details or examples. They create an illustration (such as a drawing, timeline, or map) to help explain the concept.

English Language Arts Standards Reading: Informational Text **ANCHOR 10**

Reading Anchor 10: Read and comprehend complex literary and informational texts independently and proficiently.

K	First	Second	Third	Fourth	Fifth
Actively engage in group reading activities with purpose and understanding.	With prompting and support, read informational texts appropriately for grade 1.	By the end of the year, read and comprehend informational texts, including history/social studies, science, and technical texts, in the grades 2–3 text complexity band proficiently, with scaffolding as needed at the high end of the range.	By the end of the year, read and comprehend informational texts, including history/social studies, science, and technical texts, at the high end of the grades 2–3 text complexity band independently and proficiently.	By the end of the year, read and comprehend informational texts, including history/social studies, science, and technical texts, in the grades 4–5 text complexity band proficiently, with scaffolding as needed at the high end of the range.	By the end of the year, read and comprehend informational texts, including history/social studies, science, and technical texts, at the high end of the grades 4–5 text complexity band independently and proficiently.

Recommendations for Working Toward Reading Anchor 10

The goal for Anchor 10 is that students will *read and comprehend informational texts considered to be within an appropriate range of complexity for their grade level.* Although all of the teaching strategies in this book are aimed in this direction, they become most potent when they are implemented in an environment that makes use of what is known about creating rich contexts for learning. With this in mind, the following recommendations are provided to aid you in implementing the strategies effectively. (Also see the recommendations in Part 1 for working toward Reading Anchor 10.)

- Focus from the start on reading to learn.

- Use informational text for reading instruction.

- Create opportunities for authentic reading.

- Provide materials that students will want to read.

- Provide extensive time for reading.

Focus from the start on reading to learn. It is often said that children must *learn to read* before they can *read to learn.* However, a wide body of research provides evidence to the contrary. Studies conducted in both home and school settings show that very young children can and do focus on meaning *as* they learn to read and write (Clay 1975; Dyson 1989; Goodman 1996; Harste, Burke, and Woodward 1981; Martens 1997; Rowe 2008; Wohlwend 2007). As early as age two, children demonstrate eagerness to name and ask questions about what they see in books and to use the illustrations to construct meaning. They point to signs, labels, logos, and words, hypothesizing their meaning or asking, "What does that say?" Young children are capable of focusing on print and meaning at the same time.

Even when school-aged students begin to read texts with just a sentence or a few words per page, we focus our efforts on word identification *as well as* comprehension. Making meaning is *why* children want to read and what motivates them to read more. Treating word identification as a skill set that exists separately from comprehension can narrow students' focus and confuse them in terms of the ultimate goal of reading, which is to experience a thoughtful, meaningful encounter with text (Applegate, Applegate, and Modla 2009).

Use informational text for reading instruction. In K–5 classrooms, we should not feel compelled to use only narrative text for reading instruction. Research evidence shows that informational text offers meaningful opportunities for supporting many aspects of early reading, including phonological awareness, word identification, and a variety of comprehension strategies (Duke 2004). In fact, because informational text "requires greater effort to process and understand, students need more—not fewer—print experiences" with this material (Brozo and Flynt 2008).

Create opportunities for authentic reading. To grow as readers, K–5 students need to be reading with purpose and engagement (Guthrie and Wigfield 2000). If we want students to engage, we must do more than simply assigning them to read, or assigning them to read and answer a set of questions. Probably the most powerful way to work toward engagement is to create opportunities for *authentic* reading.

Authentic reading serves a true purpose rather than being an event constructed just to teach reading skills. When students read authentically, they do so to satisfy genuine curiosities, answer real questions, inform their discussions, and inform their writing. A recent study of second- and third-grade classrooms showed that students who participate in more authentic informational reading show stronger growth in comprehension than children who experience more traditional instruction (Duke et al. 2006).

To create authentic situations for reading, Duke (2004) and Duke et al. (2006) recommend the following:

- Offer hands-on experiences or demonstrations that lead to curiosities and the passion to know more.

- Respond to spontaneous inquiries by making it possible for students to read and find out about the topic at hand.

- Read about a topic with the class and then ask for questions students would like to pursue.

- Work with students to identify real-life or curricular problems to solve.

- Arrange for students to read to inform their writing. (Having a real audience for their writing will lead them to read more strategically and with greater interest and purpose.)

Provide materials that students will want to read. Research in the field of reading shows a strong connection between engagement and achievement (Braunger and Lewis 2006; Guthrie and Wigfield 2000). When students are interested in what they are reading, they process the text more deeply, show deeper levels of learning, and are more willing to put forth high effort to comprehend the material (Guthrie and Davis 2003; Taboada, Tonks, Wigfield, and Guthrie 2009). They are also likely to read more (Allington 2012).

However, too often, texts that truly engage students are scarce or not available in school settings. Often, textbooks are the major or only tool used for science and social studies reading. Even if trade books are available, they are often not sufficient in quantity or quality for effectively supporting curricular goals. With this in mind, it is recommended that we work to create new school literacy practices that include the following: collecting trade books with a tighter focus on school curriculum but that still allow for choice; using graphic novels, magazines, and online material that will engage young readers; and creating new ways of considering and interpreting text through activities such as blogging, clip art, photographic or film montages, and literary "remixing," in which students use multimodal cultural artifacts (music, art, written language, oral language) to form new interpretations (Brozo and Flynt 2008; Gainer and Lapp 2010; Knobel and Lankshear 2008; Zawilinski 2009).

Provide extensive time for reading informational text. To develop as readers, students need to read. To develop reading strategies for content-area learning, students need to read informational text. Numerous studies have shown that the more children read and listen to a text read aloud, the more their vocabulary and associated conceptual knowledge grow—and, of course, their literacy knowledge (Jitendra et al. 2004; Walsh 2008; Cunningham and Allington 2011). Yet, one recent study of first-grade classrooms showed that students were spending on average 3.6 minutes per day engaged with informational text (Duke 2000).

It makes sense that if we want students to get good at reading informational text, we need to offer them time to read it. A widely recommended solution to finding time for reading informational text is to integrate our literacy instruction across content areas, teaching content reading strategies as part of content-area instruction. "The answer is to view every subject you teach as an opportunity to add reading and writing" (Cunningham and Allington 2011).

Instructional Strategies for Reading: Foundational Skills

The Common Core Reading: Foundational Skills standards are designed to guide instruction related to print concepts, phonological awareness, word recognition, and fluency. The four standards outlined in Table C provide overarching goals for K–5 students, and the more specific sets of standards outlined at the beginning of each section in Part 3 define the specific competencies students are expected to master by each year's end. The first two standards, Print Concepts and Phonological Awareness, are primarily intended for kindergarten and first grade, but if you teach grades beyond these levels you may find that some of your students could still benefit from work in these areas.

In general, students are expected to work with their grade-level standards, using increasingly complex text as they move through the K–5 years. This is with the understanding that some students will need extra support mastering certain competencies from earlier grades before they can be expected to demonstrate full competency with their own grade-level standards. In turn, others will be ready to explore concepts and text beyond those recommended for the grade range.

Each section in Part 3 is focused on one of the four foundational skill areas: print concepts, phonological awareness, word recognition, and fluency. In each section, you will find practices and activities for supporting student development through a sequenced process of demonstration, collaborative engagement, and independent application. Each section begins with a decision tree to help you determine whether to pursue the lessons for the anchor at hand.

Table C

Category	Foundational Skills for Reading K–5	Page
Print Concepts	1. Demonstrate understanding of the organization and basic features of print.	**299**
Phonological Awareness	2. Demonstrate understanding of spoken words, syllables, and sounds (phonemes).	**320**
Phonics and Word Recognition	3. Know and apply grade-level phonics and word analysis skills in decoding words.	**340**
Fluency	4. Kindergarten: Read emergent-reader texts with purpose and understanding. Grades 1-5: Read with sufficient accuracy and fluency to support comprehension.	**356**

READING: FOUNDATIONAL SKILLS

English Language Arts Standards Reading: Foundational Skills

Print Concepts: Demonstrate understanding of the organization and basic features of print.

Kindergarten	First Grade
a. Follow words from left to right, top to bottom, and page by page. b. Recognize that spoken words are represented in written language by specific sequences of letters. c. Understand that words are separated by spaces in print. d. Recognize and name all upper- and lowercase letters of the alphabet.	a. Recognize the distinguishing features of a sentence (e.g., first-word capitalization, ending punctuation).

Decision Tree for **Reading: Foundational Skills**
PRINT CONCEPTS

Do my students need focused instruction in relation to Print Concepts?

The Print Concepts standard is aimed at helping students develop knowledge about the *basic features and organization of print, including directionality, concept of word, concept of sentence, and letter recognition.* (Refer to your grade-level standards for specific details.)

When some or all of your students could use support in this area, it is recommended that you provide scaffolding, first emphasizing demonstration, and then encouraging exploration of the concepts through collaborative engagement and independent application. All three types of instruction can be implemented on the same day, with demonstrations occurring during whole-class or small-group time, and opportunities for collaborative engagement and independent application occurring during center or independent work time.

Demonstration   **Collaborative Engagement**   **Independent Application**
Page 302   **Page 307**   **Page 312**

Observation is a key to determining which lessons to use and how to focus these lessons. If you find during any phase of the instruction that some of your students could use intensified support, it is recommended that you implement the lessons with smaller groups (no more than three students), arrange extra time to meet with these groups, and specifically tailor the lessons to the group's needs based on assessments you have conducted.

Print Concepts: Instructional Strategies

Demonstration	Grade-Level Standards				
	K				1
	a	b	c	d	a
Shared Reading	✓	✓	✓	✓	✓
Interactive Writing	✓	✓	✓	✓	✓
Structured Writing	✓	✓	✓	✓	✓
Word Study		✓		✓	

Collaborative Engagement	Grade-Level Standards				
	K				1
	a	b	c	d	a
Partner Reading	✓	✓	✓	✓	✓
Partner Writing	✓	✓	✓	✓	✓
Choral Reading	✓	✓	✓		✓
Scrambled Rhymes	✓	✓	✓		✓
Alphabet Mat Activities		✓		✓	

Independent Application	Grade-Level Standards				
	K				1
	a	b	c	d	a
Independent Reading	✓	✓	✓	✓	✓
Independent Writing	✓	✓	✓	✓	✓
Bookmaking Center	✓	✓	✓	✓	✓
Literature Response	✓	✓	✓	✓	✓
Alphabet Book Center	✓	✓	✓	✓	✓
Big Book Center	✓	✓	✓	✓	✓
Interactive Writing Center	✓	✓	✓	✓	✓
Environmental Print Center		✓	✓	✓	
Letter and Word Play Center		✓		✓	
Hands on Letters		✓		✓	
Word Collage Center		✓	✓		
Reading Our Writing	✓	✓	✓	✓	✓

Demonstration

The Print Concepts standard is aimed at helping students develop knowledge about the *basic features and organization of print, including directionality, the concept of a word, letter recognition,* and *the concept of a sentence.* This standard is considered to be primarily relevant for kindergarten and first-grade students, keeping in mind that some students enter kindergarten with print concepts already in place, and others exit first grade still needing support in this area. The four lessons in the demonstration section support student development of print concepts through shared reading, interactive writing, structured writing, and word study. The lessons may be implemented as many times as needed based on demonstrated student needs.

Shared Reading with an Emphasis on Print Concepts: Grades K–1

Shared reading is a teacher-led instructional technique that involves the teacher and students reading high-quality literature together while discussing various concepts related to print. The focus of the present lesson is on early print concepts. The procedures may be implemented with the whole class or small groups, depending on student needs.

> **BOOKS FOR SHARED READING**
>
> *Brown Bear, Brown Bear, What Do You See?*, Bill Martin Jr.
>
> *Does a Kangaroo Have a Mother, Too?*, Eric Carle
>
> *Hattie and the Fox*, Mem Fox
>
> *Have You Seen My Cat?*, Eric Carle
>
> *I Went Walking*, Sue Williams
>
> *Mary Engelbreit's Mother Goose*, Mary Engelbreit
>
> *Moo, Baa, La La La!*, Sandra Boynton
>
> *Mouse Mess*, Linnea Asplind Riley
>
> *Mrs. Wishy Washy*, Joy Cowley
>
> *Rosie's Walk*, Pat Hutchins
>
> *Silly Sally*, Audrey Wood
>
> *Time for Bed*, Mem Fox
>
> *To Market, to Market*, Anne Miranda
>
> *The Very Busy Spider*, Eric Carle

1. Select a big book or rhyme that is written at an appropriate level for students to read with teacher support. If working with a small group, provide each child with a copy of the text. The sidebar features recommended books for shared reading lessons.

2. Preview the cover and illustrations with students, highlighting any vocabulary or content that will support meaning making.

3. Read the text *to* the students as they follow along. Briefly discuss the content. If working with English learners, support meaning making by using gestures, referring to the illustrations, and extending the explanation as appropriate.

4. Read the text *with* the students, emphasizing selected print concepts. Choose from the following concepts based on demonstrated student need:

   - **Concept of directionality.** Use a pointer to show left-to-right, top-to-bottom progression. Tell the children what you are doing with the pointer and why. After you have modeled, ask volunteers to use the pointer to demonstrate directionality as you read together.

- **Concept of word.** Use a pointer to show how sequences of spoken words match sequences of written words. Pause during the reading to name words and ask volunteers to use the pointer to show their location on the page. Help volunteers use Wikki Stix or highlighting tape to mark words.

- **Concept of letter and sound.** Pause to discuss interesting words. Ask students to locate each word that is discussed and to tell how they found the word on the page. Use the opportunity to teach letters and sounds.

- **Concept of sentence.** Pause to point out how the author uses capitalization and punctuation to form sentences. Read chosen sentences aloud, using the intonation suggested by the punctuation.

5. Follow up with small groups or intervention groups as needed. Follow-up should involve continuing the lesson with different books and different concepts until the students demonstrate competency.

Interactive Writing with an Emphasis on Print Concepts: Grades K–1

Interactive writing involves the teacher acting as scribe while discussing and demonstrating various print concepts. The procedures may be implemented with small groups or the whole class, depending on student needs.

1. Select a purpose for writing that will be meaningful to the participating students. For example, you may write a note to a person the class knows, a list of things to gather for a class project, or a sentence about something the class has observed or experienced.

2. Use chart paper or a whiteboard to write, emphasizing selected print concepts. Your emphasis will depend on what you have observed through your assessments.

- **Concept of directionality.** As you write, point out where to begin writing and point out the left-to-right, top-to-bottom progression. After you have written, ask volunteers to use the pointer to demonstrate directionality as you read your text together.

- **Concept of word.** As you write, emphasize what a word looks like and how it is spaced. Reread your writing to show how sequences of spoken words match sequences of written words.

Pause during the rereading to name words and ask volunteers to use the pointer to show their location on the page. Help volunteers use highlighting tape to mark key words. Have students count the number of words in the phrases you are working with.

- **Concept of letter and sound.** Emphasize letter names and formation as you write. Allow students to write some of the letters for you and support them when they are unsure of how to form the letters. More advanced students will be appropriately challenged if you encourage them to consider letter–sound relationships as part of the writing. Less advanced students will also benefit from this process.

- **Concept of sentence.** As you write, pause to point out how you are using punctuation. Read chosen sentences aloud with expression, using the intonation suggested by the punctuation.

- **Concept of organization.** As you write, emphasize how you organize the text. (A list is organized differently than a note or sentence.)

- **Concept of function.** Throughout the demonstration process, emphasize the concept that written language can serve a variety of functions, such as remembering things, communicating with others, telling stories, and providing information.

3. As a possible extension, provide an individual photocopy of the material that has been created for participating students to read and reread. Allow students to use highlighting tape or highlighters to mark letters, words, or punctuation. You may also provide the copy on strips so that students can cut up the words and put them back together again. Also, provide opportunities for students to do their own writing in relation to what you have demonstrated, either through work in a center or an assignment for small groups. The writing assignment need not be formal. For example, "We have written a note together, now you write a note by yourself."

Structured Writing: Grades K–1

Structured writing involves teacher guidance as students use individual whiteboards or paper and clipboards to explore print concepts. The following structured writing experiences may be implemented in the interest of supporting print concept development:

- Choose a set of four to six words related to some topic of importance to the curriculum. Write the words, one at a time, having the students read and copy each. After writing all of the words, have the students read their lists to a partner. Then, in random order, name one word at a time for the students to erase or cross off. (As an alternative, you may name one letter at a time.)

- One word at a time, write a sentence related to some topic of importance to the curriculum. Have the students read and copy each word. After writing the sentence, have the students read it to a partner, pointing to each word. Then in random order, name one word at a time for the students to erase or cross off.

- One word at a time, write a series of rhyming words. Have the students read and copy each. After writing all of the words, have the students read their lists to a partner. Then, in random order, name one word at a time for the students to erase or cross off.

Word Study with an Emphasis on Print Concepts: Kindergarten

The word study lesson uses familiar words to support children's development of letter knowledge and concept of word. Depending on need, it may be implemented with the whole class or with individuals/small groups of students.

1. Prepare a set of word cards. Choose from a high-frequency word list appropriate for your grade level or choose words that are part of a theme your class is studying, such as: *chicken, pig, cow, crop, barn, harvest, farm*. Make two or three cards for each word so that you can use them to team up the students. For example, working with a class of twenty-seven, you might use nine different words (make three cards each). You can use the same set of cards for several lessons.

2. Hand out the cards to the children (two different words per child if working with a small group, one if working with the whole class). Using a few cards, think aloud about how looking at the letters could help you read the words. For example, "We're going to be using our farm cards. Here's a card with a word that starts with *P*.

This might be *pig.*" Move your finger from left to right across the letters and read the word aloud.

3. After students have their cards, ask them to find the other students with the same word. In teams, students attempt to read the word and then point to and name each letter. Provide support as needed. Then give them a challenge: Have each team show their word to the rest of the group and tell about it. They can be encouraged to name the letters, tell the sounds the letters make, tell a rhyming word, or tell another word with the same sound. Offer many possibilities that are reflective of your students' current knowledge.

4. Place the cards in a word study center and encourage students to sort them and read them to one another, continuing with the challenge process you have demonstrated. Also, you may wish to hang the set of cards to be visible from the writing table, encouraging students to use the cards in their writing as appropriate.

Collaborative Engagement

Partner Reading: Grades K–1

Partner reading provides a rich opportunity for peers to exchange knowledge and understandings about print. To prepare, take a quick trip around the classroom to ensure that you have enough comfortable places for all of the partners to sit. Plan to let teams choose their favorite areas, but be prepared to help them spread out and get comfortable the first few times they meet. Plan for 10 to 15 minutes at first, and then allow more time as the year progresses.

1. On two or three tables, lay out enough books for each pair, along with a few additional books to ensure that all students will have a choice. If some of the books are hardcover, stand them on end to enhance the visual appeal of the display. Make it a point to help students find books they *want* to pick up and read. You may wish to keep a bin of books to be used expressly for partner reading. Over time, add books that you have used for guided reading and whole-class instruction. Include easy reads and books with outstanding illustrations.

2. Select two children who have different strengths and needs in their reading or language development to serve as models. (It is recommended that you use such a mix when the aim of partner reading is to develop basic print concepts.) Bring the whole class together and ask the two children to show how to go to the book display and choose a text together.

3. Let students know that when they read together you would like them to engage in a process of previewing, reading, and rethinking. To help students remember what to do, you can create a poster with the steps, referring to it as needed. Ask the two students to preview the book by looking at the cover and title and turning through the first few pages to see how the text is set up. The next step is to either take turns to read every other page, or work together to turn through and talk about the illustrations. Finally, ask the students to rethink. This involves collaboratively articulating a response to "What is this book about?" or "What did the author teach?" If desired, you can add a challenge step: ask them to go back and name words they know or discuss words that presented a challenge.

As you observe partners reading, take note of how many teams are actually reading versus browsing and talking through the text. When children *can* read connected narrative, we want them to do so during partner reading—at least most of the time.

Partner Writing: Grades K–1

Partner writing involves two students working together. To support early print concept knowledge, start the process by inviting students to draw something in relation to the curriculum (as in drawing what floats and what sinks in the science center) or something they have experienced together (such as a recent thunderstorm or a flood in the bathroom) and then having them use words, phrases, or sentences to label what they have drawn. Model all processes before setting students off in teams.

It is recommended that you pair students who have more developed print concepts with those who are just beginning. This allows the students with further-developed skills to articulate and firm up key concepts, while allowing the students who are just beginning to benefit from working with the skill set of a more knowledgeable partner.

As you observe your students, take note of the print concepts they are demonstrating (directionality, word, sentence, letter) and scaffold accordingly.

Choral Reading: Grades K–1

Choral reading involves students in reading familiar text aloud together. This type of reading can be arranged as a small-group or center experience.

To implement, make available either a large copy or individual copies of several books/rhymes you have read together. Students may read through a stack of six to eight texts in one sitting, so be sure to have a large supply available. Choose texts with a memorable pattern such as *Brown Bear, Brown Bear, What Do You See?* (Bill Martin Jr.), *Silly Sally* (Audrey Wood), and *Mrs. Wishy Washy* (Joy Cowley). Be explicit with your expectations. For example, if you want students to read four texts, make that clear and have the texts ready to go. If you want them to focus on the concept of word, give them a pointer and ask that they take turns using it while reading, helping one another to match the pointing to what is actually being read (one-to-one correspondence).

Scrambled Rhymes: Grades K–1

After reading short rhymes or songs with the class, copy the sentences onto a page and cut them into strips for groups to place in order before reading again together. You may wish to laminate the strips for durability and use a different color of paper for each rhyme so that students can easily work with several in one session. For example, for one 10-minute session, each participating group might use *Little Miss Muffet, Humpty Dumpty, Row, Row,*

Row Your Boat, and *Twinkle, Twinkle Little Star*. Working with scrambled rhymes encourages students to work with the concepts of word, sentence, and directionality.

Alphabet Mat Activities: Kindergarten

Alphabet mat activities are designed as a way for students to explore concepts of letters and sounds. They are generally implemented with small groups and some teacher supervision, but may also be designated for centers. To get started, prepare for each student a laminated mat and a bag of laminated letter tiles and pictures (see Figure RFS 1.1 and RFS 1.2). For some activities, students use their own mats, and they share mats for others. Students may engage in the following experiences:

- Students point to each letter while singing the alphabet song or saying the alphabet. The goal is to maintain one-to-one correspondence.

- Students work together to place lowercase letters along the mat to match with the uppercase letters.

- Working with a partner, each student takes thirteen random letters, lining them up so that all are visible. Moving *A* to *Z*, the students place the letters on the mat in alphabetical order.

- Students work together to name each picture and tell what sound that they hear at the beginning of that word.

- Students work together to place pictures along the mat based on their first sound. For example, the pig picture is matched with letter *P*.

- Students work together to say a sound that each letter on the mat makes.

- Students work together to say a word beginning with each letter on the mat.

- Teams choose six to eight letters on the mat and find the matching picture. For each chosen picture, they write the word.

Use your assessments to identify the specific letters and sounds students need to work with. The experience should be challenging but achievable for all who participate.

Uppercase Alphabet Mat

A	B	C	D	E	F	G
H	I	J	K	L	M	N
O	P	Q	R	S	T	U
V	W	X	Y	Z		

Lowercase Alphabet and Pictures for Alphabet Map

a	b	c	d	e	f	g
h	i	j	k	l	m	n
o	p	q	r	s	t	u
v	w	x	y	z		

PRINT CONCEPTS

Independent Application
Independent Reading: Grades K–1

The field has long known that *independent reading* correlates positively with vocabulary, comprehension, and fluency—and, ultimately, higher school achievement (Anderson, Fielding, and Wilson 1988; Krashen 1993; Krashen 2009). Children who develop a habit of independent reading end up reading more and as a consequence getting better. With knowledge of this research, many teachers have moved from using a "seatwork" time first thing in the morning to implementing a high-quality reading time in which students choose their own books and read them for a set amount of time. Interaction is encouraged, but with clear expectations that the reading and the books will remain the focus of the conversations.

To implement independent reading with young children, have an appropriate set of materials always ready for use. You can have bins of books on the students' tables or you may keep each child stocked with a set of three or four books to pull out at any time. Ready availability prevents students from spending too much time selecting material. Try to work toward 15 to 20 minutes of independent reading three to five times per week. Make yourself available to monitor what is happening and initiate brief over-the-shoulder conferences to support individual students. This is easiest to do if students develop the habit of using whispers to communicate with one another. You and the children need to be able to focus and to hear each other talk.

Holding students accountable by having them write or orally share a thought about what they have read has been found to help keep students on task, as has conferencing with students about what they have read (Reutzel, Jones, and Newman 2010). Conferencing can be as simple as moving about the classroom and spending no more than a minute per student, listening to the student read, talking about the illustrations, or talking about the content in general. You can also use this time to do more in-depth kidwatching, focusing more intensely on documenting information about students' print concept knowledge. Figure RFS 1.3 provides a form for documenting student knowledge.

Independent Reading Conference

Name: _____ Date: _____

Print Concept	Competency	Date Observed
Directionality		
Show me where you read. Use your finger to show me how you read.	____ Moves left to right. ____ Uses return sweep. ____ Moves top to bottom.	
Concept of Word and Sentence		
Show me a word. What is this word? How did you know that? Show me a sentence. Do you know what the first word in a sentence needs? Show me a period. Show me a question mark.	____ Frames a word. ____ Demonstrates understanding of letter–sound relationships. ____ Frames a sentence. ____ Understands first-word capitalization. ____ Recognizes a period. ____ Recognizes a question mark.	
Letter Recognition		
Show me the letter ____. (Randomly name the letters of the alphabet on the pages).	A a B b C c D d E e F f G g H h I i J j K k L l M m N n O o P p Q q R r S s T t U u V v W w X x Y y Z z	

Independent Writing: Grades K–1

Right from the start of kindergarten, students need opportunities for independent writing, as this facilitates their development of key print concepts and shows them that the act of writing can be meaningful even for young children. In kindergarten and first-grade classrooms, the environment for writing is social, with students sharing their knowledge and thought processes as they work on their own pieces.

To get students started, choose a genre such as personal narrative or description. Make it a habit to model your own writing, keeping the content short and manageable. You can start by drawing a picture and labeling it or writing a sentence that describes it. You could write or draw about your morning, your lunch, your weekend; write about a topic from your science or social studies curriculum; write about your family members, your friends, your pets, your interests, your joys, your observations, and your fears. Encourage your students to do the same. Don't worry if they attempt to mimic your topics at first. As they discover the power of writing and as you offer continued encouragement their confidence and initiative will grow.

By observing your students while they are writing, you can informally assess their print concept knowledge. For example, is the student using left-to-right directionality? Does the writing show a concept of word and/or sentence? What letter knowledge does the student demonstrate? Informal observations can be useful in understanding student needs and providing well-tailored individual or group instruction. You can also document progress more systematically by using a form such as that featured in Figure RFS 1.4.

Independent Writing Conference

Name: _____ Date: _____

Print Concept	Competency	Date Observed
Directionality		
Show me how you write.	____ Moves left to right. ____ Uses return sweep. ____ Moves top to bottom.	
Concept of Word and Sentence		
Tell me about what you have written. What is this word? How did you know how to write it? Show me a word. Show me a sentence.	____ Demonstrates concept of word. ____ Demonstrates concept of sentence. ____ Uses first-word capitalization. ____ Uses punctuation. ____ Demonstrates understanding of letter–sound relationships	
Letter Recognition		
Show me the letters you have used ____.	A a B b C c D d E e F f G g H h I i J j K k L l M m N n O o P p Q q R r S s T t U u V v W w X x Y y Z z	

Literature Response: Grades K–1

Read a book to the whole class before center, small-group, or independent work time. Ask students to respond to the piece in writing. Working in a collaborative environment will provide opportunities for sharing knowledge about key print concepts. You can ask students to draw first and then label the picture with words or a sentence. To get ideas flowing, you may use a simple prompt such as:

- Record one important part.

- What part did you like?

- Write three important words from the text and create an illustration for each.

- Which character was most interesting?

- What did the author teach?

Bookmaking Center: Grades K–1

Provide materials for students to create their own books. To support their development of print concepts, show them how to fold or staple two pieces of paper to form a book. Show them where to put the title, and remind them to set up the pages to be read from left to right. Bookmaking centers provide a good opportunity to help students see the many functions of books. You may encourage students to write their books about topics from your content area curriculum (such as insects, friendship, or numbers); topics from their lives (such as their families, their favorite animals, or things they like to do); or personal narratives (about something they have recently experienced at school or home). If you have students who draw but are hesitant to include writing, you can start by encouraging them to label their illustrations.

Alphabet Book Center: Grades K–1

Make it a regular practice to read alphabet books to your students, discussing their various forms and features. When they understand the general format (an *A* to *Z* progression), set up a center containing several alphabet books. Encourage the students to enjoy, read aloud, and talk about the books. Alphabet books are useful for supporting student development of early print concepts. Their familiar format provides a scaffold for identifying letters and words, and for examining left-to-right directionality.

As part of the center, you can make small alphabet books for students by cutting three sheets of paper into nine sections each and using a strong stapler to fasten them into a little book. (This leaves one extra page for the cover.) Students can write one letter per page and add illustrations or clip art of their choosing—or you can preprint the letters for them. The students will enjoy reading and decorating these little books. Arranging students to work on this project during center or small-group time provides a rich opportunity for sharing knowledge and supporting one another in learning.

Big Book Center: Grades K–1

To provide ongoing support for print concept development, a *big book center* can be maintained throughout the year. Set up an easel or a reading area on a rug, and include big books, poster-sized rhymes, and a pointer. Encourage students to read the displayed text to one another and to read it chorally.

Interactive Writing Center: Grades K–1

An *interactive writing center* can be maintained throughout the year. Just place writing utensils at the easel, make available your whiteboard or large chart paper, and encourage students to write together and teach one another about important things they know. If you find that students are drawing, but doing little actual writing on the board, let them know that you want them to use the center to teach one another about *writing*, much as you do during interactive writing sessions (see above). If students do not smoothly take turns acting as teacher or scribe, you may have them set a timer (each "teacher" gets 5 minutes) or you may decide to provide additional materials so that more than one student can act as teacher at any given time.

Environmental Print Center: Kindergarten

An *environmental print center* is an opportunity to connect home with school literacies. The center is designed to support children's concept of word, including attention to the letters and sounds. To prepare, invite students to bring in two or three pieces of disposable print from home, such as restaurant and store logos, packaging from foods and household products, and logos related to games and toys. Prepare two copies of each item. Then, instruct partners or teams to do the following during center or other instructional time:

* Read each word.

* Match the pairs.

* Match a hand-printed version of the word with the colorful logo version.

* Make the words with magnetic letters or letter tiles.

- Copy five to eight of the words on note cards and then read them without the colorful context.

- Choose a word and draw a picture to show where it appears in the environment.

Letter and Word Play Center: Kindergarten

Letter and word play centers offer children the opportunity to study, talk, and share information about letters and words in a collaborative and purposeful context. To implement, have available a set of magnetic letters or letter tiles for the children to use. On different days, assign activities such as the following. You can differentiate by assigning different activities to different students.

- Name as many letters as you can. Sort into piles of letters you can and cannot name. Select at least one letter from the unknown pile and find out its name. Write it on a sticky note and take it home.

- Make your names. (Because names are often a whole-class focus of study in the kindergarten classroom, students can benefit from exploring them collaboratively with peers. Many students begin to recognize others' names early on and can use these to generalize and gain new understandings about letters and sounds. English learners can especially benefit, as they may be using a new symbol system, and names are something that will appear again and again and will be useful for their daily writing and communication.)

- Make words. (Allow English learners to work in both languages.)

- Make words from the word wall.

- Make three-letter or four-letter words.

- Put the letters in alphabetical order.

- Put the letters in alphabetical order and then copy them on paper. (This experience may be especially useful for English learners whose first language has a symbol system different than the one used for English, such as Chinese or Arabic; Meier 2004).

- Make color words, number words, or words from a unit of study. (Post a list.)

- Sort the letters into uppercase and lowercase piles.

- Match uppercase and lowercase letters.

- Separate the consonants and vowels.

Hands on Letters: Kindergarten

Hands on letters is a student-centered experience that offers a multimodal, nonthreatening way to experiment with forming letters. Depending on need, it may be implemented in centers, in small groups, or with the whole class.

1. Have available a set of trays containing either Play-Doh or sand.

2. Show the students how to use the material to form letters. As you are demonstrating, encourage students to suggest words for you to form. Show how you can copy different words from around the room, including from books.

3. Set up a center for children to use the material to form letters and words, or arrange for the whole class to participate in this activity as they sit together in groups.

4. If you are working with small groups, use an assessment to inform the specific letters or words students should practice.

Word Collage Center: Kindergarten

Set up a center or small group to work on a word collage. Show students how to identify a word by the spaces that surround it. Have students cut out a variety of words from old magazines or newspapers, and when the collage is complete, work together to read them. (You can ask that all of the words start with the same letter or sound.) This experience supports students in developing the concept of word as well as exploring letter–sound relationships.

Reading Our Writing: Grades K–1

To support authentic exploration of print concepts, keep a photocopy of the interactive writing you do with students (see above). Have available a folder of pieces that have been created together. Assign small groups to read the pieces together, or make the folder available at a center for individuals or partners to read informally.

PHONOLOGICAL AWARENESS

GRADE-LEVEL STANDARDS

English Language Arts Standards Reading: Foundational Skills

Phonological Awareness: Demonstrate understanding of spoken words, syllables, and sounds (phonemes).

Kindergarten	First Grade
a. Recognize and produce rhyming words. b. Count, pronounce, blend, and segment syllables in spoken words. c. Blend and segment onsets and rimes of single-syllable spoken words. d. Isolate and pronounce the initial, medial vowel, and final sounds (phonemes) in three-phoneme (consonant-vowel-consonant, or CVC) words. (This does not include CVCs ending with /l/, /r/, or /x/.) e. Add or substitute individual sounds (phonemes) in simple, one-syllable words to make new words.	a. Distinguish long from short vowel sounds in spoken single-syllable words. b. Orally produce single-syllable words by blending sounds (phonemes) including consonant blends. c. Isolate and produce initial, medial vowel, and final sounds (phonemes) in spoken single-syllable words. d. Segment spoken single-syllable words into their complete sequence of individual sounds (phonemes).

Decision Tree for **Reading: Foundational Skills**
PHONOLOGICAL AWARENESS

Do my students need focused instruction in relation to Phonological Awareness?

The Phonological Awareness standard is aimed at supporting students in learning to analyze *spoken words and their syllables and sounds*. (Refer to your grade-level standards for specific details.)

When some or all of your students could use support in this area, it is recommended that you provide scaffolding, first emphasizing *demonstration* and then moving to *collaborative engagement* and *independent application*. All three types of instruction can be implemented over the course of a week, with demonstrations occurring daily (whether with the class or groups) and opportunities for collaborative engagement and independent application occurring throughout the week during center or independent work time.

Demonstration	**Collaborative Engagement**	**Independent Application**
Page 323	**Page 336**	**Page 338**

Observation is a key to determining which students will benefit from which types of support. You may find that you have students who have already mastered phonological awareness and need little support in this area. If you find during any phase of the instruction that some of your students could use intensified support, it is recommended that you implement the lessons with smaller groups (no more than three students), arrange extra time to meet with these groups, and specifically tailor the lessons to the group's needs based on assessments you have conducted.

Phonological Awareness: Instructional Strategies

Demonstration	Grade-Level Standards								
	K					1			
	a	b	c	d	e	a	b	c	d
Immersion in Verse	✓	✓			✓		✓	✓	
Interactive Writing			✓	✓		✓		✓	✓
Word Analysis: Ten Brief Lessons									
Thumbs Up or Down	✓				✓	✓			
Move the Syllables		✓							
Move the Parts			✓						
Move the Sounds				✓				✓	✓
Move the Letters			✓	✓	✓		✓	✓	✓
Solve the Mystery	✓		✓		✓				
Scaffolded Spelling	✓		✓		✓		✓	✓	✓
Today We Play			✓	✓				✓	
Tell the Sound				✓				✓	
Apart and Together				✓			✓	✓	✓

Collaborative Engagement	Grade-Level Standards								
	K					1			
	a	b	c	d	e	a	b	c	d
Pass the Basket	✓			✓				✓	
Move the Blocks		✓		✓				✓	✓
Sort the Objects				✓				✓	
Match the Sounds	✓			✓				✓	
Word Machines			✓	✓	✓				
Word Makers						✓	✓		
Letter Play				✓	✓	✓	✓	✓	✓
Picture Sorts						✓		✓	

Independent Application	Grade-Level Standards								
	K					1			
	a	b	c	d	e	a	b	c	d
Poetry and Rhyme Center	✓	✓					✓		
Listening Center	✓	✓					✓		
Recording Center	✓	✓							
Interactive Writing Center	✓	✓	✓	✓	✓	✓	✓	✓	✓
Scaffolded Writing			✓	✓	✓	✓		✓	✓
Search for Sounds				✓				✓	
Search for Syllables		✓				✓			

Demonstration

The phonological awareness standard is aimed at supporting students in learning to *analyze spoken words and their syllables and sounds*. A student with strong phonological awareness can do the following within an oral language environment:

COMPETENCY	EXAMPLE
Recognize and produce rhyming words	*cat* rhymes with *bat*
Blend syllables	/cat/ /fish/ into *catfish*
Blend onsets with rimes	/c/ /at/ into *cat*
Blend phonemes	/f/ /i/ /sh/ into *fish*
Segment words into syllables	*catfish* into /cat/ /fish/
Segment onsets from rimes	*fish* into /f/ /ish/
Segment phonemes	*fish* into /f/ /i/ /sh/
Substitute sounds to make new words	*cat* into *bat*

One major reason that phonological awareness is considered important is that when children know how to blend and segment orally, they can use this knowledge to write and read words. For example, if students learn to orally blend the sounds /c/ /a/ /t/ into *cat*, they will have developed a useful competency for beginning reading. They can look at the word *cat* and (presuming they know the sounds that the three letters make) blend them together to read the word. Following this same principle, if students learn to orally segment the spoken word *cat* into /c/ /a/ /t/, they will have developed a useful competency for writing. However, the relationship between phonological awareness (oral concepts) and phonics knowledge (written concepts) is not linear, but *reciprocal*. One does not directly precede the other, and we know that working with words in print facilitates phonological awareness (National Reading Panel 2000; Stanovich 1986).

For this reason, you will find that many of the teaching strategies below integrate oral with written analysis of words. Three types of demonstration lessons are presented in this section: immersion in verse, interactive writing, and word study. As described, these are typically recommended for use with kindergarten and first-grade students, but may be used with older students who still need support with phonological awareness. They should be implemented as needed, based on demonstrated student needs.

Immersion in Verse: Grades K–1

Immersion in verse involves students in listening to, chorally reading, and playing around with poetry, rhymed text, lyrics, and tongue twisters. To implement, set aside 10 to 15 minutes daily for students to relish in their favorite pieces and discuss the special words, syllables, and sounds they contain. If you are working with English learners, provide opportunities for students and/or their family members to share children's verse from their native languages, as phonemic awareness extends across languages. Each lesson requires at least one written poem or rhyme. The following activities are recommended:

- Have students listen to the text several times, chiming in on familiar parts or chorally reading the text with you.

- Help students identify the rhyming words.

- Pause before the rhyming words and have students fill in the blanks.

- Help students identify the alliterative words (same initial sounds are repeated).

- Discuss with students what makes each piece appealing or fun to say. For example, after listening to tongue twisters such as *Peter Piper picked a peck of pickled peppers*, discuss the alliteration. After listening to nursery rhymes, discuss the creativity of the rhyming words.

- Tap or clap along with poems and rhymes to help students notice and attend to syllables or beats. You can give each student an object that clicks or makes a sound (a drum, rattle, clacker, maraca, or tambourine) as a way of helping to make the syllables stand out.

- Help students count or clap syllables in words or in lines of print.

- Substitute the first sound of each word in a poem with a target sound. (*Twinkle, twinkle, little star* becomes *Binkle, binkle, bittle bar*.)

- Write the words that rhyme or alliterate and point out their visual similarities and differences.

- Provide an individual copy of the studied material for small groups to reread.

- Send home individual photocopies of the studied material so that children can share it with family members.

Repeat the rhymes and language study activities often so that the material becomes part of a growing repertoire of known verses. Knowing rhymes *orally* helps children to make connections between spoken and written language when they see the rhymes in *print*. This provides a strong foothold for beginning to read.

Interactive Writing: Grades K–1

Interactive writing is a teacher-led instructional technique that involves modeling and making explicit a planned set of key concepts. In the present lesson, the focus is on teaching about how words are made up of individual sounds and parts. The lesson integrates phonological awareness and phonics.

1. Select a purpose for writing that will be meaningful to the participating students. For example, you may write a note to someone the group knows, create a list of items to gather for a project, or write a sentence to record something the group has read about, observed, or experienced. Use chart paper or a whiteboard.

2. As the students observe, demonstrate how to stretch (segment) words and listen for the sounds and parts. Be aware that in other languages, some letters correspond with different sounds than in English. For example, the letter *i* usually makes the /ee/ sound in Spanish. Also, keep in mind that students may not have experience working with an alphabetic writing system at all. For example, in Japanese and Korean, each symbol represents a syllable, but in Chinese, each character represents a morpheme—or unit of meaning.

3. As a follow-up to interactive writing, provide opportunities for students to do their own writing, encouraging them to listen for the sounds and parts in words. For students who are unsure of what to write, encourage drawing first and then labeling what they have drawn. For students who are unsure about stretching words, do the stretching for them at first, making the sounds obvious.

Word Analysis: Ten Brief Lessons: Grades K–1

In a review of studies, the National Reading Panel (2000) found that just 5 to 18 hours of teaching focused on phonemic awareness can yield very large effects. This section contains ten short, interactive lessons focused on fostering phonological awareness. The lessons may be used with needs-based groups or adapted for the whole class.

✱ Thumbs Up or Thumbs Down: Grades K–1

Competency: Listening for Rhymes and Phonemes

Write a target word on a whiteboard. Read the word aloud and tell students that you are going to say words that rhyme and do not rhyme with the word. Show students how to use a "thumbs up" when you say a word that rhymes and a "thumbs down" when you say a word that does not rhyme. Then, write a few more words, helping students to listen for rhymes and use thumbs up when they hear one. Finally, reverse roles and ask students to challenge *you* with some words: write a target word that the students suggest and ask the students to tell you some more words that rhyme or do not rhyme. Use the thumbs-up or thumbs-down gesture to respond. You may also use this lesson format to analyze beginning, middle, and ending sounds.

✳ Move the Syllables: Kindergarten

Competency: Counting, Segmenting, and Blending Syllables

Provide each student with four blocks. Show the students how to line up the blocks in a row. Let the students know that you will be saying some words, and they should move a block down for each syllable in the word. For example, show that *butterfly* would require moving down three blocks and *caterpillar* would require four. After demonstrating, present students with several additional words and then allow them to suggest the words. To reverse the experience, you can also present students with already-segmented syllables (*but-ter-fly*) and have them blend them into words.

✳ Move the Parts: Kindergarten

Competency: Blending and Segmenting Onsets and Rimes

Have available six to eight printed onsets and one rime that can be moved around. (See Figures RFS 2.1 and RFS 2.2.) Tell the students that you will be working together to blend word parts. Show the first parts (onsets) to be blended into the one rime. Ask the students to read each onset and then blend it into the rime (as in *d-ime* and *ch-ime*). Using a catchy rhyming chant will help the students carry on the wordplay throughout the day. For example:

Blend *d* with *ime*.	Blend *ch* with *ime*.
And out rolls *dime*.	And out rolls *chime*.

As a follow-up activity, you can provide teams or groups with their own onset—rime sets to work through. Encourage them to use the chant you have demonstrated. To differentiate, you can give beginners several onsets and one rime. More advanced students can work with a mix of onsets and rimes. As students work, support them in both blending and segmenting the onsets and rimes to build fluency in working with words.

Common Onsets

b	c	d	f	g
h	j	k	l	m
n	p	qu	r	s
t	v	w	x	y
z	br	cr	dr	fr
gr	pr	tr	wr	bl
cl	fl	gl	pl	sl
sc	sk	sm	sn	sp
st	sw	ch	sh	th
wh	tw			

PHONOLOGICAL AWARENESS

Thirty-seven Common Rimes

ack	ail	ain	ake	ale
ame	an	ank	ap	ash
at	ate	aw	ay	eat
ell	est	ice	ick	ide
ight	ill	in	ine	ing
ink	ip	it	ock	oke
op	ot	ore	uck	ug
ump	unk			

From Wylie and Durrell (1970)

❊ Move the Sound: Grades K-1

Competency: Segmenting Words into Phonemes

Copy and laminate several sound cards (see Figure RFS 2.3), or make your own. The cards should contain a picture of a one-syllable word at the top, a box for each sound (phoneme) in the middle, and a blank space for markers at the bottom. Choose pictures of familiar, one-syllable words with a consonant-vowel-consonant (CVC) pattern (as in *can* and *cup*).

1. Model how to orally segment words into their phonemes, pushing a marker into one of the boxes for each phoneme articulated. For example: "*Bag.* /b/ /a/ /g/."

2. Give each student a sound box card. Orally stretch the words from the cards as students push the markers into the boxes.

3. Switch roles: You push the markers as students stretch the words.

4. Finally, help students stretch and push independently. (McCarthy 2008/2009)

❊ Move the Letters: Grades K–1

Competency: Segmenting and Blending Phonemes

Give each participating student a sound box mat (see Figure RFS 2.4) and a small set of letter cards or tiles (see below). Say a one-syllable vowel-consonant or CVC word such as *in* or *pin*, helping students to segment the word into its individual phonemes as they push the corresponding letter into each box. Then, encourage students to run a finger under the letters as they blend the sounds to read the word. The sidebar contains sequenced sets of words to be used for segmenting and blending.

WORDS	LETTERS NEEDED
fin, bin, tin, win, pin, fan, ban, tan, pan, can	A B C F I N P T W
bat, cat, fat, hat, mat, rut, but, cut, hut, mut	A B C F H M R T U
cap, gap, lap, map, nap, rap, sap, tap, yap, zap	A G L M N P R S T Y Z
bay, pay, lay, day, hay, may, gay, ray, say, way	A B D G H L M P R S W Y
dip, hip, lip, rip, sip, tip, zip, hop, mop, top	D H I L M O P R S T Z
bug, dug, hug, mug, rug, tug, big, dig, pig, wig	B D H I G M P R T U W
bun, fun, gun, nun, run, sun, rub, pub, sub, tub	B F G N P R S T U
bog, dog, fog, hog, jog, log, cob, job, mob, sob	B C D F G H J L M O S

Sound Boxes with Pictures

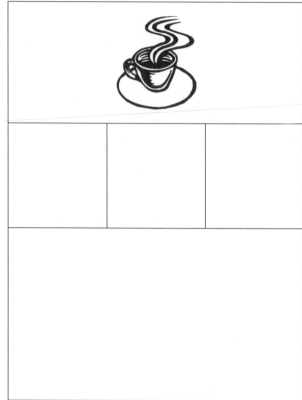

Sound Boxes with Pictures

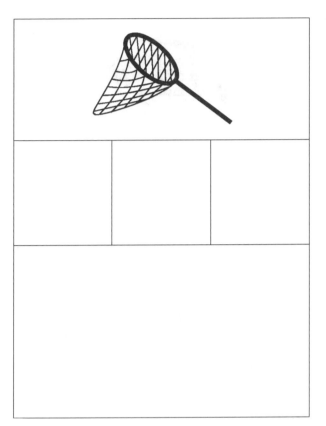

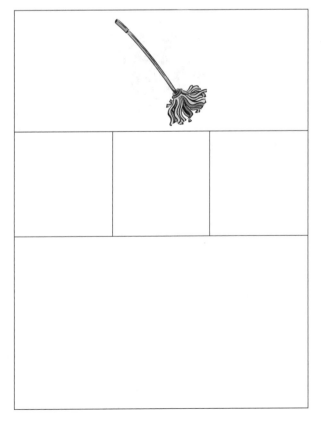

Sound Boxes with Pictures

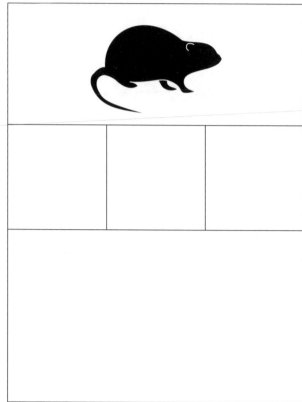

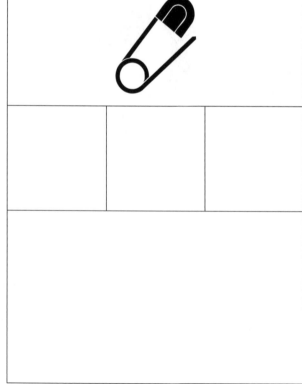

Sound Boxes

❋ **Solve the Mystery: Kindergarten**

Competency: Rhyming and Blending

Gather several small objects and place them in a box. Reach into the box and ask students to guess what you are holding based on clues you give. You can start with simple clues and then increase the complexity. For example:

- It rhymes with *hen*.

- It starts with the sound /p/ and rhymes with *hen*.

- It starts with the letter *P* and rhymes with *hen*.

❋ **Scaffolded Spelling: Kindergarten**

Competency: Segmenting, Substituting, and Blending Phonemes

Scaffolded spelling (Manyak 2008) supports students in learning to listen for the sounds in words. The experience integrates the study of phonological awareness and phonics.

1. Choose three to five words that include letters and sounds the students know or have been taught. You can choose words that are similarly spelled (*bed*, *fed*, *led*, *red*). Have available small whiteboards or half-sheets of paper for each student.

2. Saying one word at a time, encourage students to use a hand to "stretch the word like bubble gum" while articulating each phoneme. Then, ask them to stretch the word again, stopping after each sound to think about and write the letter or letters that make that sound.

3. After the words are written, read them with the children two times.

4. Continue the scaffolding process until students consistently stretch words and record appropriate sounds independently.

❋ **Today We Play: Grades K–1**

Competency: Isolating Initial Phonemes

Tell the students that today is going to be an unusual day because they can only play with things starting with a special sound. (Be sure they know you are pretending.) Name the sound and ask students to provide suggestions as you record on a whiteboard the objects they may play with today. As another option, fill a basket with objects representing different beginning sounds and show students each object, asking if it would be okay to play with that object today based on the sound you have chosen.

＊ Tell the Sound: Grades K–1

Competency: Isolating Initial, Medial, and Final Phonemes

Say two words or show two pictures that have the same beginning sound. Coach students to tell the sound that both words have at the beginning. Continue with several word pairs. If you use pictures, students can then use them to do their own sorting as a follow-up activity. The task is to sort the words into matching pairs. You may also use this strategy to support analysis of medial sounds, ending sounds, and rimes.

＊ Apart and Together: Grades K–1

Competency: Blending and Segmenting Phonemes

First, present students with words segmented into their constituent phonemes and ask, "What am I saying?" For example, when you say /f/ /a/ /n/, students say *fan*. Then, give each student a picture of a one-syllable word. Challenge students to cover their pictures so that they are not visible to others and break the word into its constituent sounds, such as breaking *dog* into /d/ /o/ /g/. The other students in the group blend the sounds to form the word.

Collaborative Engagement

Pass the Basket: Grades K–1

Competency: Rhyming, Isolating Sounds

Pass the basket may be implemented as a small-group or center activity. Fill a basket with small objects or pictures. Going around the table, students pull an object from the basket, name it, and say a word that rhymes. They continue until the basket is empty. Students then categorize the objects by rhyme (as in *cat, rat, bat, hat*; *pen, hen*; *lock, clock, rock, sock*). To increase difficulty, students may pass the basket with the requirement that they generate and sort words with the same beginning, middle, or ending sound.

Move the Blocks: Grades K–1

Competency: Segmenting and Blending Syllables and Phonemes

Place students in groups and provide each student with four blocks. All students line up the blocks in a row and then they take turns saying words, with everyone moving a block down for each syllable. For example, *penguin* would require moving down two blocks and *pineapple* would require three. To differentiate or increase the difficulty, you can set up students to segment into phonemes, which is more challenging than segmenting into syllables. Ask students to choose words with just one syllable. For example, *pin* and *pine* have three phonemes, so three blocks would be moved down.

Sort the Objects: Grades K–1

Competency: Isolating Phonemes

Sort the objects may be implemented with small groups or in centers. Prepare three or four buckets to be used as containers for teams to sort objects. (Or you can use pictures.) The names of the objects should start with just three or four different sounds. Tape a target letter or a target picture to each bucket and have students sort the objects by beginning sound. After working with a partner or group to sort the objects, students may write the names of the objects from one or more of the buckets.

Match the Sounds: Grades K–1

Competency: Rhyming, Isolating Sounds

Students work in teams to match anywhere from twelve to twenty-four pictures into rhyming pairs. To differentiate or increase the difficulty, students may match pictures according to their beginning, middle, or ending sounds.

Use professionally published cards, printed clip art from your word processor, or images from Google.com (click Images).

Word Machines: Kindergarten

Competency: Blending and Segmenting Onsets and Rimes;
Isolating Phonemes; Adding and Substituting Sounds
Tell students they are going to be *word machines*. Give partners a written word and ask that they substitute or add sounds to make as many new words as possible. For example, if you give them *fan*, they can make words such as *fun*, *run*, *bun*, and *buns*. Partners work together to write the words and then read the entire list when they have finished.

Word Makers: Grade 1

Competency: Blending Phonemes; Distinguishing Long from Short Vowels
Give partnered students small ziplock bags with cutout three- to four-letter words. Include about six to eight words per bag, with each word on a different color of paper. Students sort by color and then work with the letters until they have made all the words. To differentiate, students are given different words ranging from simple to complex.

Letter Play: Grades K–1

Competency: Isolate, Blend, Segment, and Substitute/Add Sounds
Letter play integrates phonological awareness and phonics. To implement, give partners or groups of students a set of letter tiles and a set of pictures. Students use the tiles to make a word representing each picture. To differentiate, you can give students different pictures. For example, one group might work with CVC words, and another might have a combination of long and short vowels to work with. After the words are made, students read the entire list.

Picture Sorts: Grade 1

Competency: Distinguishing Long from Short Vowels; Isolating Phonemes
Grouped students are given a set of pictures featuring objects with names that have long and short vowels. (Other vowel sounds may be used as well.) The students separate the pictures into columns. For example, the columns might be labeled *long*, *short*, and *other*.

Independent Application

Poetry and Rhyme Center: Grades K–1

Competency: Rhyming Words; Segmenting into Syllables; Tracking Print
A *poetry and rhyme center* can be maintained throughout the year as an extension to the immersion in verse lessons (see previous description). Set up an easel or a comfortable area on a rug. Use the center as a holding place for the big books and poster-sized rhymes you have read with your students. To support collaborative exploration of key concepts, encourage students to read the displayed poems and rhymes to one another and to chant them chorally. Give them a pointer and small wands or clackers to tap out the beats together.

Listening Center: Grades K–1

Competency: Rhyming Words; Segmenting into Syllables; Tracking Print
Set up a *listening center* in which students can listen to rhymes and poems as they doodle and draw pictures to represent what they are hearing. To support their collaborative development of phonological awareness, give them small wands, clickers, or clackers to follow the beat together, and provide copies of the material so they can follow along with the print.

Recording Center: Kindergarten

Competency: Rhyming Words; Segmenting into Syllables
Set up a *recording center* for students to record themselves repeating familiar verses that rhyme and to listen to others' creations. Require that teams practice before recording, working to clearly enunciate. The recordings they create can become part of the materials used in a listening center.

Interactive Writing Center: Grades K–1

Competency: All
An *interactive writing center* can be maintained throughout the year. Place writing utensils in the center and make available your whiteboard, chalkboard, or large chart paper. Encourage students to write and study words together as you have done through interactive writing and scaffolded writing (next).

Scaffolded Writing: Grades K–1

Competency: Isolating, Substituting, Blending, and Segmenting Onsets, Rimes, and Phonemes

For *scaffolded writing*, students sit in small groups. All of the students in the class can write at the same time, supporting one another as you move about the room working with individual students or groups needing support. Make it a point to provide support with stretching words and listening for their sounds and carefully rereading words to see if they look as they should. Show students how thinking about one word (*cat*) can help them spell other words (*rat* and *bat*).

Search for Sounds: Grades K–1

Competency: Isolating Phonemes

Show students how to design a collage using cutout pictures. Give students working in centers or small groups old magazines and encourage them to cut out pictures of objects beginning with a certain sound and use them to create a collage. Discuss the students' findings when the whole class meets together.

Search for Syllables: Grades K–1

Competency: Syllables; Short and Long Vowels

Show students how to design a collage using cutout pictures. Give students working in centers or small groups old magazines and encourage them to cut out pictures of objects whose names have two, three, or four syllables. You may also assign students to find pictures of objects whose name has a single syllable with a long vowel or a single syllable with a short vowel.

English Language Arts Standards Reading: Foundational Skills

Phonics and Word Recognition: Know and apply grade-level phonics and word analysis skills in decoding words.

Kindergarten	First	Second	Third	Fourth	Fifth
a. Demonstrate basic knowledge of one-to-one letter–sound correspondences by producing the primary or many of the most frequent sounds for each consonant. b. Associate the long and short sounds with common spellings (graphemes) for the five major vowels. c. Read common high-frequency words by sight (e.g., *the, of, to, you, she, my, is, are, do, does*). d. Distinguish between similarly spelled words by identifying the sounds of the letters that differ.	a. Know the spelling–sound correspondences for common consonant digraphs. b. Decode regularly spelled one-syllable words. c. Know final *e* and common vowel team conventions for representing long vowel sounds. d. Use knowledge that every syllable must have a vowel sound to determine the number of syllables in a printed word. e. Decode two-syllable words following basic patterns by breaking the words into syllables. f. Read words with inflectional endings. g. Recognize and read grade-appropriate irregularly spelled words.	a. Distinguish long and short vowels when reading regularly spelled one-syllable words. b. Know spelling–sound correspondences for additional common vowel teams. c. Decode regularly spelled two-syllable words with long vowels. d. Decode words with common prefixes and suffixes. e. Identify words with inconsistent but common spelling–sound correspondences. f. Recognize and read grade-appropriate irregularly spelled words.	a. Identify and know the meaning of the most common prefixes and derivational suffixes. b. Decode words with common Latin suffixes. c. Decode multisyllabic words. d. Read grade-appropriate irregularly spelled words.	a. Use combined knowledge of all letter–sound correspondences, syllabication patterns, and morphology (e.g., roots and affixes) to read accurately unfamiliar multisyllabic words in context and out of context.	a. Use combined knowledge of all letter–sound correspondences, syllabication patterns, and morphology (e.g., roots and affixes) to read accurately unfamiliar multisyllabic words in context and out of context.

Decision Tree for **Reading: Foundational Skills**
PHONICS AND WORD RECOGNITION

What types of instruction do my students need in relation to phonics and word recognition?

The Phonics and Word Recognition standard is aimed at students learning to *recognize and identify written words*. (Refer to your grade-level standards for specific details.)

When some or all of your students could use support in this area, it is recommended that you provide scaffolding, first emphasizing demonstration, and then moving to collaborative engagement and independent application. All three types of instruction can be implemented over the course of a week, with demonstrations occurring every day (whether with the class or groups) and opportunities for collaborative engagement and independent application occurring throughout the week.

Demonstration
Page 343

Collaborative Engagement
Page 350

Independent Application
Page 354

Observation is a key to determining which types of lesson to implement and which students will benefit from continued or more intensive support. If you find during any phase of the instruction that some of your students could use intensified support, it is recommended that you implement the lessons with smaller groups (no more than three students), arrange extra time to meet with these groups, and specifically tailor the lessons to group needs based on assessments you have conducted.

Instructional Strategies for Phonics and Word Recognition

Demonstration

Demonstration	K				1							2						3				4	5
	a	b	c	d	a	b	c	d	e	f	g	a	b	c	d	e	f	a	b	c	d	a	a
Environmental Print Study	✓	✓																					
First Reads	✓	✓	✓	✓																			
Mine to Learn			✓								✓												
Drawing and Labeling	✓	✓			✓	✓	✓		✓		✓	✓	✓	✓		✓	✓						
Word Building	✓	✓		✓	✓	✓	✓			✓		✓	✓				✓						
Word and Part Study	✓	✓		✓	✓	✓	✓	✓	✓	✓	✓	✓	✓	✓	✓	✓	✓	✓	✓	✓	✓	✓	✓
Retrospective Miscue Analysis: Words					✓	✓	✓	✓	✓	✓	✓	✓	✓	✓	✓	✓	✓	✓	✓	✓	✓	✓	✓
Spelling In Parts							✓	✓	✓	✓			✓	✓	✓	✓	✓	✓	✓	✓	✓	✓	✓
Tricky Passages							✓	✓	✓	✓			✓	✓	✓	✓	✓	✓	✓	✓	✓	✓	✓
Parts Analysis														✓	✓		✓	✓	✓	✓	✓	✓	✓
Morphological Analysis																		✓				✓	✓

Collaborative Engagement

Collaborative Engagement	K				1							2						3				4	5
	a	b	c	d	a	b	c	d	e	f	g	a	b	c	d	e	f	a	b	c	d	a	a
Word Concentration			✓								✓												
Scrambled Words			✓			✓					✓												
Word Sorts	✓	✓		✓	✓	✓	✓	✓	✓	✓		✓	✓	✓	✓	✓		✓	✓	✓			
Partner Reading	✓	✓	✓	✓	✓	✓	✓	✓	✓	✓	✓	✓	✓	✓	✓	✓	✓	✓	✓	✓	✓	✓	✓
Partner Writing	✓	✓	✓	✓	✓	✓	✓	✓	✓	✓	✓	✓	✓	✓	✓	✓	✓	✓	✓	✓	✓	✓	✓
Word Hunts	✓	✓	✓	✓	✓	✓	✓	✓	✓	✓	✓	✓	✓	✓	✓	✓	✓	✓	✓	✓	✓	✓	✓
Making Big Words							✓	✓	✓	✓			✓	✓	✓	✓	✓	✓	✓	✓	✓	✓	✓

Independent Application

Independent Application	K				1							2						3				4	5
	a	b	c	d	a	b	c	d	e	f	g	a	b	c	d	e	f	a	b	c	d	a	a
Writing Center	✓	✓	✓	✓	✓	✓																	
Scaffolded Writing	✓	✓	✓	✓	✓	✓	✓	✓	✓	✓	✓	✓	✓	✓	✓	✓	✓	✓	✓	✓	✓	✓	✓
Scaffolded Rereading	✓	✓	✓		✓	✓	✓	✓	✓	✓	✓	✓	✓	✓	✓	✓	✓	✓	✓	✓	✓	✓	✓
Word Recording								✓		✓			✓	✓		✓	✓			✓	✓	✓	✓

Demonstration

The Phonics and Word Recognition standard is aimed at supporting students as they learn to recognize and identify written words. The competencies developed under this standard range from knowing basic letter–sound correspondences to decoding unfamiliar multisyllabic words. The twelve lessons in the demonstration section support student development of phonics knowledge and word analysis skill through various forms of word study, reading, and writing. (Note: While the focus here is on *word-level* knowledge, the focus in the Fluency section (starting on page 356) is on reading *connected text*.)

Environmental Print Study: Kindergarten

An important part of early literacy is coming to understand that words can be predicted and identified by looking at their letters. *Environmental print studies* are teacher-guided experiences designed to build this foundational understanding. The studies generally begin with the whole class and then move to teams and centers.

1. Collect a set of environmental print items that will be familiar to your students (such as restaurant or store logos, food packaging, toy and game logos, and street signs). Make a book that features three or four logos per page. Prepare a photocopy of the book for each participating child.

2. Read the original color copy of the book with your students. (Students should be able to read most pages to you.) Point to the words from left to right. Talk about their letters and the sounds. Point out to students that they can read many words in the environment, and they should look for these and read them whenever they can.

3. Show the students the book you have photocopied for them. Place each student with a partner to read the book, or place a few books in a center and allow students to browse and read them.

4. As a follow-up, have students make the words from the book with magnetic letters or letter tiles. This will help them begin to rely less on context and more on the letters themselves.

First Reads: Kindergarten

Collect a set of books that children can negotiate successfully as their *first reads*. Typically, these books have just a few words per page, or they follow a highly repetitive pattern that students can pick up and follow easily. Students need not be able to recognize all letters of the alphabet or know all sounds to participate. Read the book aloud to a small group and then have students reread it to you as they point to each word. Provide support with words as needed.

Mine to Learn: Grades K–1

Mine to learn is an approach to word learning that makes use of varied modalities. It can be used to teach high-frequency words as well as word parts or families. The activity is implemented with small groups and can be embedded into guided reading lessons.

1. Choose three words each student needs to practice for fluency. Students should be able to claim the words, "These are *mine* to learn." Use a reading assessment or high-frequency word inventory to help identify the words.

2. Students observe as you say the chosen words while writing them with a crayon or other writing utensil that provides texture.

3. Students say the words while tracing them with a finger

4. Students write the words from memory.

5. The textured words from step 2 are kept in a file for practice. (Put in a ziplock bag or use a key ring to bind.) The words may be taken home for review.

Drawing and Labeling: Grades K–2

Drawing and labeling is a lesson designed to support students in developing various aspects of their word knowledge. It is specifically useful in working with English learners.

1. Allow students 5 to 10 minutes to use colored markers to draw, sketch, or doodle. You need not be working with the group at this time. Let the students know that this creation will be a *shared* piece, as you will be writing some words on their papers after they have finished drawing—or you can use sticky notes (half-inch-by-two-inch) to record the words if you wish.

2. Ask each child to tell something about his or her drawing, supporting and extending the use of oral language. Work with the child to decide what might be appropriate to label. For example, if the child has drawn a rainbow, you might label it with *rainbow* or you might write the color names and ask that the child draw arrows to each color. If the child has drawn a bicycle, you might label *wheels*, *handle bars*, and *seat* or *black wheels*, *red handle bars*, and *black seat*.

   As another option, you can support the students in doing the spelling rather than doing the writing for them. Be sure to emphasize that you are helping with the adult (conventional) way to spell the words *only* for this lesson, and that you will want them to spell on their own when working independently. This will prevent them from feeling that they need to rely on you for all spellings.

3. You can send these drawings home for students to read with their families, or use them for follow-up instruction. Students can read the labels, and you can work together to add more words as appropriate. If you have used sticky notes, you can pull off the notes and ask that the student place them back where they belong before adding new labels. Or you can ask that the student copy any sticky-note words you have written for them onto the paper.

Word Building: Grades K–2

Word building is a teacher-led experience designed to support children's exploration of letter–sound relationships and word patterns. The experience is highly adaptable to meet different levels of knowledge.

1. Start by showing students on a whiteboard how you can build words by starting with a core word and then changing a letter. For example, starting with *in*, you can make *an* or *on*.

2. After demonstrating the process with a few words, allow children to form their own words using individual whiteboards or letter tiles. Start by naming a series of two-letter words for the students to build and progress from there. For example, students might be instructed to build these words: *it, at, cat, bat, fat, that, rat, rated, rates, fit, bit, bite, kite, kites*.

3. Consistently elevate the complexity of the words to the point that what you are asking children to do is challenging but achievable. Work on parts that reflect demonstrated needs.

Word and Part Study: Grades K–5

Word and part study is a practice designed to support children's development of knowledge about words and patterns ranging from simple to complex and regular to irregular. The lesson may be implemented throughout the year, in small groups, or with the whole class and can be embedded into guided reading sessions.

1. Have available a large whiteboard or sheet of chart paper for recording words. Place students in teams of two. Each team will need a small whiteboard and a marker.

2. Select a focus word to get the study started. It is recommended that you select words or parts that have presented difficulty to the participating students in their reading, words/parts that students are using frequently in their writing but spelling incorrectly, or multisyllabic words in general. A spelling inventory or reading assessment can help you make selections based on demonstrated needs.

3. Write the focus word on the chart paper and read it aloud or ask students what they notice. Depending on whether you are studying word parts or high-frequency words, support students in answering questions such as the following:

To Study Words and Parts

- What are some words that rhyme with this word?

- What are some words that start the same?

- What are some words with parts (rimes) that look like this?

- Have you seen other words that look like this?

- What are some words with the same vowel sound?

- What are some words with the same prefix or suffix?

- How would you break this word into syllables?

After the whole group generates a few ideas, ask the partners to write as many words as they can with the onset, rime, prefix, suffix, root, or number of syllables you are exploring.

To Study High-Frequency Words

- What is this word? Have you seen it before?

- Does it look like other words you know?

- Count the number of letters.

- Talk about the sounds the letters make.

- Name (or write) words with similar onsets.

- Name (or write) words with similar rimes/parts that look similar.

For each study, tell students to look closely at the word because you are going to cover it and ask them to spell it. Ask each partner to write the word and then check the spelling. Place the studied words on a word wall or have students place them in a personal word bank (which could be constructed with a key ring and hole-punched note cards). Check your students' knowledge the next day, asking them to write the studied words from memory. Encourage them to use the word wall to support their writing.

Retrospective Miscue Analysis: Words: Grades 1–5

Retrospective miscue analysis (RMA; Goodman and Marek 1996) is an individual or small-group instructional tool that begins with supported reading and is followed by analysis that helps students to become consciously aware of their reading knowledge and strategies. RMA can be used as a way for students to explore the words that are presenting a challenge for them and to identify any patterns of error in relation to these words.

1. Listen to readers and document their miscues on a typewritten copy of the text. You can set aside varying levels of this text to be used exclusively for this purpose.

2. Show the students the documented miscues. Work with the students to look for patterns of error and to highlight any words they do not easily read during the analysis.

3. Support the students in solving the words and then have them read the words again, within the context of their sentences or the whole text.

Spelling in Parts: Grades 1–5

Spelling in parts (Powell and Aram 2008) is a strategy that helps students learn to break tricky multisyllabic words into chunks to read them. The lesson is designed for small-group settings.

1. Have available a short list of multisyllabic words from the texts the students have been reading.

2. Looking at one word, the teacher reads it then students repeat the word slowly, clapping once for each syllable. (Check to see that the

division is reasonable; this can be done without teaching the specific rules for dividing words into syllables.)

3. Students say the syllables one at a time, writing the spelling of each on a whiteboard or paper. With teacher guidance, they circle and discuss syllables that have difficult spelling patterns.

4. Students cover or erase the word and write it independently, saying each syllable before writing it.

Tricky Passages: Grades 1–5

Tricky passage lessons (Manning, Chumley, and Underbakke 2006) are designed to support students in reading multisyllabic words in context. The lessons may be implemented with individuals or small groups.

1. Select a passage containing numerous multisyllabic words. Discuss the importance of these words, having students highlight them or cover them with colored tape to consider their prevalence.

2. Think aloud about the strategies you use to read and understand multisyllabic words (break into syllables, look for known chunks, cover chunks to see if meaningful parts can be found, use context to make a prediction).

3. Have the students read the passage silently, trying out the strategies. Ask them to mark any unknown multisyllabic words. Then, have them take turns reading sections of the passage aloud. They should help one another, sharing the strategies they used and working together to decode any unknown words.

Parts Analysis: Grades 2–5

Parts analysis activities support students who could benefit from strategies for decoding multisyllabic words. The lesson is generally implemented with a small group.

1. Collect three to five multisyllabic words that have presented difficulty for the students. You will be working with one word at a time.

2. Have students copy the challenging words.

   • Examples: *expansion, continuous*

3. Have students use a slash mark to separate prefixes and suffixes/endings from the base word/middle part of the word.

   • Examples: ex / pan / sion, con / tinu / ous

Then, have students divide the base word into pronounceable parts by inserting a slash mark as needed (con / tin / u / ous). Encourage flexibility. For example, if a long vowel sound doesn't work for a word part, try another vowel sound, playing with the parts until a known word has been constructed.

Morphological Analysis: Grades 3–5

Morphological analysis is designed to support students in looking for meaning-based units in unfamiliar words they encounter. Specifically, students are taught to look for recognizable prefixes and suffixes and to take note of root words. A list of common prefixes and suffixes recommended for elementary-level instruction appears below. It is recommended for this age group that prefixes are identified and examined for meaning and the suffixes are identified primarily for removal, so that the *root* can aid in determining meaning (White, Sowell, and Yanagihara 1989). Morphological analysis can be especially useful to English learners, because it provides an explicit focus on word meanings.

To implement, select a focus word from the text to be read. Provide a list of four to six words with the same prefix (*rerun, redo, repaint, rework, reform, reappear*). Discuss the meanings of the words and work together to construct a definition of the prefix. Discuss how to use morphological analysis to help figure out the meaning of unknown words while reading.

Prefixes and Suffixes for Elementary Instruction		
Prefix	**Meaning**	**Example**
un	not	unsolved
dis	not	dishonest
in	not	inefficient
im	not	improbable
ir	not	irresponsible
non	not	nonsense
re	again or back	rearrange
en, em	(forms verb)	enrage
over	too much	overdo
mis	wrong	misunderstand
Suffixes: s, es, ed, ing, ly, er/or, ion/tion/ation/ition, ible/able, al/ial, y, ness		

Based on White, Sowell, and Yanagihara (1989)

Collaborative Engagement

Word Concentration: Grades K–1

Word concentration is a game that may be played as a center or small-group activity. The game can be designed to offer students practice reading high-frequency words or word parts. It is especially well suited for early readers developing their visual memory for frequently used words, such as *the*, *what*, *my*, *when*, *that*, and *me*.

1. Prepare twenty-four cards (twelve written words to match twelve identical written words, or twelve pictures to match twelve words).

2. Show students how to lay the cards out so the words cannot be seen. Students take turns turning over two at a time to find matches. They are encouraged to help each other read the words.

Scrambled Words: Grades K–1

Scrambled words involves groups of students in reordering mixed-up words from familiar rhymes and then reading them aloud together. To prepare, each sentence from a rhyme is put on a sentence strip of a different color and then cut apart for students to put back together. This experience provides an opportunity to use familiar text as a frame for decoding words.

Word Sorts: Grades K–5

Word sorts involve teams or groups in using prepared cards to study words. Care should be taken to determine the types of sorts that will be most beneficial. High-frequency word assessments, spelling inventories, and reading assessments can help you make selections based on students' demonstrated needs. For each sort, students need a stack of prepared word cards along with some blank cards.

Onsets: Sort word cards by onsets (for example, *l-*, *tr-*, *ch-*). Read the words. Write some words to add to the stack.

Rimes/rhymes: Sort the word cards by rimes or rhymes (for example, *cone*, *bone*, and *stone* or *bear*, *care*, and *hair* are categorized together). Read the words. Write some words to add to the stacks.

Multisyllabic words: Sort the word cards by affixes or endings. Read the words. Write some words to add to the stack.

Number of syllables: Sort the word cards into stacks according to the number of syllables they contain. Read each pile. Write a word to add to each stack.

Number of letters: Sort the word cards into stacks according to the number of letters they contain. Read each pile. Write a word to add to each stack.

Vowel sounds: Sort the word cards into stacks according to the sound that their vowels make. Write a word to add to each stack.

Partner Reading: Grades K–5

Reading with a partner provides a close-up demonstration of how print works (Braunger and Lewis 2006). To support students in developing their word-level knowledge through partner reading, ask partners to take turns reading pages or sections of a text. If a partner gets stuck on a word, the *reader* should first try to solve it, but it's okay for the partner to provide a hint or name the word rather than interrupting the reading at that point. Words that are *told* are marked with highlighting tape or an erasable marker. After reading, the students go back and talk about the *told* words and how they might be solved.

Partner Writing: Grades K–5

Partner writing involves teams of two in writing and editing a short piece together. Students are assigned to compose a draft. After preparing the draft, they read through for conventions as well as ideas, making revisions and editing as appropriate. The draft is then shared with another partner team, and feedback is exchanged. Finally, the drafts are polished and the piece is shared with an appropriate audience. Writing a short, manageable piece in a collaborative environment and having an audience for the final piece will encourage attention to detail, including spelling conventions. The sidebar shows some doable genre ideas for partner writing.

> ### PARTNER WRITING
>
> - how to be a good _____ (brother, dancer, driver, student, friend)
> - list of favorite _____ (books, games, places to go, singers, things to do)
> - list of things we can do to _____ (improve our school, make someone's day, protect wildlife, save the planet)
> - recipe
> - note to the class or someone in the school
> - cartoon
> - joke
> - poem
> - map
> - script to perform
> - instructions for a favorite game or activity

Word Hunts: Grades K–5

Word hunts involve students in moving through the classroom or looking through a set of familiar books, hunting for words, talking about their makeup, and recording them on clipboards. To implement, assign a word hunt (see next page for examples). Give a time limit and then send the students off in teams.

You can differentiate by sending students on different types of word hunts. For example, some students might be required to find five words that begin with *B* (relatively simple), and others might be required to find five words with more than eight letters (relatively complex). A spelling inventory and samples of student writing can be used to develop hunts that will be challenging but achievable for each team. Assign as many different hunts as would be beneficial to your students.

- Find five words that you can read.

- Find five words that start with ___.

- Find five words with the vowel sound ___.

- Find five words to take home and read to a family member.

- Find two words that rhyme with *fox*.

- Find five words with only one or two letters.

- Find a word beginning with each letter of the alphabet.

- Find five words that you would like to remember how to spell.

- Find five words written in a language other than English.

- Find three words that start like *quack*.

- Find three words that end with *ing*.

- Find five words that end with *ed*.

- Find five words in their plural form.

- Find five past-tense words.

- Find three compound words.

- Find five contractions.

- Find three words with more than eight letters.

- Find five words with three syllables.

- Find five first names.

- Find the two shortest and two longest last names in our class.

- Find three words that have a spelling pattern like *grape*, *game*, *have*, and *tape*.

- Find three words that start with vowels.

Making Big Words: Grades 1–5

Making big words supports students in developing familiarity with common word parts and in learning to deal flexibly with parts by trying more than one way if the first attempt does not work.

1. Have available multisyllabic words on strips of paper, cut apart by syllable. Choose the words from the content area texts or other literature your students are reading.

2. Give each team three to five cut-up words (all mixed together). The students put the syllables together until they have formed a complete set of multisyllabic words. Show students how to be flexible when reading parts. For example, if the short vowel sound doesn't work, try another vowel sound. If the stress doesn't work in one part of the word, try another. To vary the difficulty, less experienced students can be given two-syllable words to work with at first. If different groups are using the same words, have them compare their findings.

Independent Application

Writing Center: Grades K–1

A tremendous amount of word knowledge is gained as young students spend time in a writing center or just writing together. Although you can expressly ask students to focus on certain topics, often it is enough to simply say, "You can write during this time" and to provide inviting materials. For English learners, you may find it helpful to encourage writing in the native language. Encouraging writing in both languages promotes bilingual development and provides rich ground for exploring similarities and differences between the two languages. Include materials such as the following in the writing center:

- pencils, markers, and crayons

- paper with and without lines

- stapled-together booklets

- small whiteboards or chalkboards

- familiar books

- posters showing frequently used words

- note cards, hole punchers, and key rings for collecting words

- bilingual books and books written in your students' first languages

- alphabet strips with the vowels marked in a different color

- strips with characters or scripts representing students' first language (such as Chinese or Hindi characters or scripts)

Scaffolded Writing: Grades K–5

In *scaffolded writing*, students write as the teacher observes and moves around the room providing support. The teacher support can focus on developing word knowledge and knowledge of phonics as needed, but the students' focus should be kept on meaningful content. After they have written for meaning, they can go back to look for spellings to correct and can even work in teams to do so. As students write, they are encouraged to talk, share ideas, and help one another. Helping with words becomes a natural part of this process. To make the writing feel manageable for students who are just getting started or who are hesitant or lacking confidence, you may assign them to start by drawing and labeling what they have drawn.

Scaffolded Rereading: Grades K–5

Each student is given a passage or book to read. The text should be challenging but achievable. On the first read, the teacher documents miscues and provides support (as during guided reading groups). The student then rereads independently or with a peer, and also takes the piece home for practice. The teacher then documents miscues *after* the practice, showing students their progress and developing competency.

Word Recording: Grades 1–5

Word recording typically takes place during silent or independent reading. Students place a sticky note on the cover of the book they are reading. When they come to a word they are unable to solve, they record it on the sticky note, including the page number. After reading, the students meet with the teacher, and the collected words are used for strategy instruction. As an alternative to meeting with the teacher, students can meet with a partner or small group to discuss the words.

GRADE-LEVEL STANDARDS

English Language Arts Standards Reading: Foundational Skills

Fluency: Read with sufficient accuracy and fluency to support comprehension.*

*Note: In kindergarten children are expected to demonstrate increasing awareness and competence in the areas that follow.

Kindergarten	First	Second	Third	Fourth	Fifth
a. Read emergent-reader texts with purpose and understanding.	a. Read on-level text with purpose and understanding. b. Read on-level text orally with accuracy, appropriate rate, and expression on successive readings. c. Use context to confirm or self-correct word recognition and understanding, rereading as necessary.	a. Read on-level text with purpose and understanding. b. Read on-level text orally with accuracy, appropriate rate, and expression on successive readings. c. Use context to confirm or self-correct word recognition and understanding, rereading as necessary.	a. Read on-level text with purpose and understanding. b. Read on-level prose and poetry orally with accuracy, appropriate rate, and expression on successive readings. c. Use context to confirm or self-correct word recognition and understanding, rereading as necessary.	a. Read on-level text with purpose and understanding. b. Read on-level prose and poetry orally with accuracy, appropriate rate, and expression on successive readings. c. Use context to confirm or self-correct word recognition and understanding, rereading as necessary.	a. Read on-level text with purpose and understanding. b. Read on-level prose and poetry orally with accuracy, appropriate rate, and expression on successive readings. c. Use context to confirm or self-correct word recognition and understanding, rereading as necessary.

Decision Tree for **Reading: Foundational Skills**
FLUENCY

What types of instruction do my students need in relation to fluency?

The Fluency standard is aimed at supporting students as they learn to *decode text with purpose and understanding*. (Refer to your grade-level standards for specific details.)

When some or all of your students could use support in this area, it is recommended that you provide scaffolding emphasizing demonstration, collaborative engagement, and independent application. All three types of instruction can be implemented throughout the week.

Demonstration
Page 359

Collaborative Engagement
Page 365

Independent Application
Page 368

Observation is a key to determining which students will benefit from more intensive support with fluency. If you find during any phase of the instruction that some of your students could use intensified support, it is recommended that you implement the lessons with smaller groups (no more than three students), arrange extra time to meet with these groups, and specifically tailor the lessons to group needs based on assessments you have conducted.

Instructional Strategies for Fluency

Demonstration

Demonstration	Grade-Level Standards															
	K	1			2			3			4			5		
	a	a	b	c	a	b	c	a	b	c	a	b	c	a	b	c
Supported Reading for Fluency	✓	✓	✓	✓	✓	✓	✓	✓	✓	✓	✓	✓	✓	✓	✓	✓
Fluency Development	✓	✓	✓		✓	✓		✓	✓		✓	✓		✓	✓	
Echo Reading	✓	✓	✓		✓	✓		✓	✓		✓	✓		✓	✓	
Language Transcription	✓	✓	✓		✓	✓		✓	✓		✓	✓		✓	✓	
Retrospective Miscue Analysis				✓			✓			✓			✓			✓

Collaborative Engagement

Collaborative Engagement	Grade-Level Standards															
	K	1			2			3			4			5		
	a	a	b	c	a	b	c	a	b	c	a	b	c	a	b	c
Partner Reading	✓	✓	✓	✓	✓	✓	✓	✓	✓	✓	✓	✓	✓	✓	✓	✓
Performance Reading	✓	✓	✓		✓	✓		✓	✓		✓	✓		✓	✓	
Best Passages	✓	✓	✓		✓	✓		✓	✓		✓	✓		✓	✓	
Reader's Theatre	✓	✓	✓		✓	✓		✓	✓		✓	✓		✓	✓	
Primed Reading	✓	✓	✓	✓	✓	✓	✓	✓	✓	✓	✓	✓	✓	✓	✓	✓

Independent Application

Independent Application	Grade-Level Standards															
	K	1			2			3			4			5		
	a	a	b	c	a	b	c	a	b	c	a	b	c	a	b	c
Independent Reading	✓	✓	✓	✓	✓	✓	✓	✓	✓	✓	✓	✓	✓	✓	✓	✓
Listening Center	✓	✓	✓	✓	✓	✓	✓	✓	✓	✓	✓	✓	✓	✓	✓	✓
Repeated Reading	✓	✓	✓	✓	✓	✓	✓	✓	✓	✓	✓	✓	✓	✓	✓	✓
Poetry Podcasts	✓	✓	✓	✓	✓	✓	✓	✓	✓	✓	✓	✓	✓	✓	✓	✓
Reading at Home	✓	✓	✓	✓	✓	✓	✓	✓	✓	✓	✓	✓	✓	✓	✓	✓

Demonstration

The Fluency standard is aimed at supporting students in learning to *decode with purpose and understanding*. To become fluent, readers need three central competencies: a large store of automatically recognized words, effective strategies for analyzing unfamiliar words, and the understanding that the purpose of reading is to make meaning (Nathan and Stanovich 1991). The five lessons in the demonstration section are designed to support K–5 students working toward the integration of these competencies.

Supported Reading: Grades K–5

Supported reading is a time to work with your students in small groups, observing and providing individualized instruction. The students' focus is on reading fiction and informational text with purpose and enjoyment. Your focus is on supporting their comprehension as well as their developing fluency.

1. Decide how to group your students. Flexible, changing groups are recommended and can be based on the following criteria.

    Text level. Grouping students who are reading texts of similar difficulty helps ensure that the material they read together is challenging but achievable for all. Students can discuss tricky or interesting words, phrases, and concepts from the book.

    Interest. Grouping by interest creates a motivation to read and to persevere through difficulties.

    Area of need. Grouping by area of need helps you home in on specific competencies. For example, you may have students with whom you want to work on high-frequency words, decoding multisyllabic words, or using context to confirm and self-correct while reading.

    Checking in. You may wish to form groups just because you haven't met with particular students for a while and you want to catch up with them and see how they are doing.

2. Choose the literature. For the most part, text used for fluency instruction should be slightly challenging: not too easy and definitely not too hard. Working with students having a slight challenge will give you opportunities to help them develop strategies for analyzing unfamiliar words but will allow them to read with enough flow to keep meaning making in place. Using short texts that can be read in one or two sessions allows for quality instruction in relation to the *whole* piece. Along with building fluency, we want to also be sure students are building meaning across the pages of a *whole* text. You can use the same texts for fluency instruction as you use for comprehension-related instruction (as described in Parts 1 and 2 of this book.)

3. Provide a meaningful introduction to the text. Rather than opening up a lengthy conversation involving extensive student input, the teacher does the introducing. A good introduction is concise, overviews the story elements (fiction) or the structure (nonfiction), and provides background information that will ease entry into the text (Calkins 2001).

4. Support each member of the group to read the text. Students read at their own paces, silently or with a soft voice. (Taking turns reading is not recommended as it minimizes the time each student spends actively reading.) Listen to each student read short segments of text, taking notes to inform future instruction (Figure RFS 4.1 may be useful).

5. Do periodic checks for comprehension by asking students to retell or answer pointed questions aimed at both literal and inferential understanding. If students are not comprehending sufficiently, support them in rereading for meaning.

Notes: Supported Reading Groups

Student	Ideas for Instruction
Name Text/Level	
Name Text/Level	
Name Text/Level	
Name Text/Level	
Name Text/Level	

Fluency Development Lesson: Grades K–5

The *fluency development* lesson (Rasinski, Padak, Linek, and Sturtevant 1994) involves a teacher-led demonstration of fluent reading followed by choral reading and independent practice. This lesson can be especially useful for students showing slow progress with fluency.

1. Read aloud a short text as students silently follow along on their own selections.

2. Discuss the selection and your expressiveness during reading.

3. Chorally read the text several times with students.

4. Have students move into prearranged pairs and take turns reading the selection with expression.

5. Arrange for individuals to perform for some audience. If working in a small group, the audience could be the other members of the group.

6. Work with the students to choose some critical words from the piece and use them for word study.

7. Send home a copy of the text for practice with family members.

8. The passage from the previous day is then reread during the following session, and the words chosen for study are reread, grouped, and sorted as appropriate.

9. The lesson routine begins again with step one.

Echo Reading: Grades K–5

Echo reading is a teacher-led strategy designed to support fluency. It may be used with the whole class or small groups and can be nested into the work of guided reading/intervention groups. Echo reading can be especially useful for early readers and for students showing slow progress with fluency.

1. The teacher reads a section of a passage using appropriate phrasing and prosody. Depending on student needs, the section could be as short as a sentence or as long as a paragraph. (Several sections are read during one session.)

2. After the teacher completes the section, the students use their own copies of the passage to echo the teacher's reading. Students developing one-to-one correspondence should point to each word.

Language Transcription: Grades K–5

Language transcription involves students in describing an experience, observing as you take dictation (by hand or on a word processor), and then reading and rereading what has been written. This strategy is especially valuable for developing word knowledge and building fluency and is widely recommended for use with English learners and older students who are reading below grade level and having difficulty finding reading material of interest.

1. Provide a prompt that leads the student(s) to talk about a familiar experience. Depending on your purposes, the piece may range from about one to six sentences. You can add to the piece on subsequent days. (After each day, the child or group reads what has been created so far.) The following prompts may be useful:

   Let's write about . . .

   - something that has happened to you
   - something you know a lot about
   - something you do often
   - something you did when you were little
   - something you like to do
   - something you don't like to do
   - a special place
   - a special person
   - a special object
   - how to do or make something
   - something you have just learned about

2. After discussing the experience, indicate that you will now write the experience as it is dictated to you. Encourage a logical sequence using student language, but helping with revision of language if the written result will lack clarity for the participating students. As you write, emphasize how to stretch words to listen for their sounds and how you can use known word parts to spell new words.

3. After taking dictation, provide a neat copy to each participating student. You can use the piece for reading instruction in subsequent sessions. Have the students reread until fluency is achieved.

Retrospective Miscue Analysis: Three Cue Systems: Grades 1–5

RMA (Goodman and Marek 1996) is a small-group instructional strategy that helps students to focus on making sense as they process text. RMA is especially useful for students who make low-quality miscues without self-correcting or who tend to focus on decoding more than on meaning making. RMA lessons can be nested into your guided/supported reading sessions.

1. Select a text that your students will find challenging to decode. Prepare a copy of the material for yourself to be used for taking notes and documenting miscues.

2. Introduce the text as you regularly do for supported reading (see previous description on p. 347), and have each student silently or quietly read the text as you move from student to student taking notes and documenting miscues.

3. Choose one or two sections of the text that contain several documented miscues. Request student permission to share miscues.

4. Discuss the miscues using the starter questions below (adapted from Goodman and Marek 1996). During initial RMA sessions, be prepared to rephrase and modify questions and to provide a lot of prompting and guidance.

RMA Questions

- Why do you think you made this miscue?
- Did it affect your understanding?
- Does the word you said look like the word in the text? How could you get a little closer?
- Do you know what the word in the text means?
- Did you correct the miscue? Should you have noticed that something was off and done something about it? What could you do next time?

CODING SYSTEM FOR DOCUMENTING MISCUES

If you have a copy of the text to use for documentation, mark miscues on the text. If you do not have a copy of the text, use a check to denote each word that is read correctly, and document all miscues. Be sure to document punctuation miscues.

Substitutions: Write the substitution just above the substituted word.

Omissions: Cross off the omission, including omissions of punctuation.

Insertions: Write the insertion just above where it occurred, and use a caret to show its placement.

Repetitions: If the reader repeats or self-corrects any section of the text, underline the whole repeated/corrected segment.

Corrections: Mark the corrections with a C.

Collaborative Engagement

Partner Reading: Grades K–5

It is important that children have opportunities to read together. *Partner reading* provides an opportunity to talk and a close-up demonstration of how print works (Braunger and Lewis 2006).

1. Reserve a short period of the school day for partner reading—or if you teach young children you may use partner reading as a center activity. To get ready, take a quick trip around the classroom to ensure that you have enough comfortable reading places for all of the partners. You may wish to place a bright note card at each location so that children can quickly find a place to sit.

2. Decide how to partner the students. Research suggests that permitting children to choose their own partners yields more effective results than choosing for them. It makes sense that children who are comfortable together are going to take more risks, talk more, and engage more deeply. However, if children frequently choose partners with similar skill, consider sometimes suggesting alternatives because mixed-level pairs seem to yield the most effective collaboration (Meisinger et al. 2004). When a beginning reader is paired with one who is more developed, the effects are positive for both (Griffin 2002).

3. Provide access to well-chosen text that students will be able to read with meaning. To build fluency, students need *accessible* text. Early on, you will want to monitor the book-choosing process closely. You may wish to keep a bin of books to be used expressly for partner reading. Or create two or three bins (easier, midrange, and more difficult) and let each child know which to "usually" choose from. Over time, add books that you have used for guided reading and whole-class instruction. As another option, provide each student with a personal bag of choices.

4. Let students know how long they will have for reading, and provide instructions regarding how to proceed. Taking turns reading every other page as the partner follows along has shown more positive results than choral reading and entire-story reading by one child (Dudley-Marling and Paugh 2004; Meisinger et al. 2004).

5. Observe your students to determine where support is needed. Take note of which teams are actually reading versus browsing and talking through the text. When children *can* read connected narrative, we want them to do so during partner reading—at least most of the time. This will build their fluency and help them develop and broaden their range of strategies.

Performance Reading: Grades K–5

Performance reading builds fluency by setting up students to read and reread. To implement, work with each of your students to choose an engaging, short passage of one to three hundred words to perform. The passages should be selected from texts the students have read with your support and found appropriately challenging. The passages may be from fiction or informational text.

Working with a partner, students practice reading the chosen passages with appropriate intonation, phrasing, and expression. Then they perform for the class or a small group. You may wish to initially implement performance reading with all students in the class and then continue with students who need extra support building fluency.

Best Passages: Grades K–5

Best passages are student-chosen favorite passages to read aloud for an audience. Students working in small groups are assigned a book from which they collaboratively choose one *best passage* for reading aloud. Each student practices reading the passage silently, seeking support from group members as needed, and then each reads it aloud for the group with amazing expression. Best passage reading is recommended for students who need extra support developing fluency.

Reader's Theatre: Grades K–5

Reader's theatre is a dramatic experience that can be used to enhance students' engagement with literature as well as their reading fluency. The process is taught to the whole class and then implemented with small groups.

1. Either choose a professionally published script (see a list on the next page) or work with students to write a short script of their own that is based on a book they have read. When younger students write their own scripts, you or an adult volunteer can take dictation to facilitate the process, showing the students how to use a narrator as

well as direct quotations from the characters. To differentiate, you can vary the difficulty of the parts or modify a published script to match the needs of each reader. Be sure that English learners understand the content and adjust their parts as necessary to match their current facility with the language. In addition, English learners may benefit from adding props and gestures for additional support (Rea and Mercuri 2006).

2. Set up group time for students to read the material over and over for fluency (intonation, phrasing, and expression) rather than memorization.

3. The script is performed for the class or another available audience.

RECOMMENDED WEBSITES FOR READER'S THEATRE SCRIPTS

www.teachingheart.net/readerstheater.htm

www.readinga-z.com/book/scripts.php

http://pbskids.org/zoom/activities/playhouse/

http://suzyred.com/readerstheater.html

Primed Reading: Grades K–5

Primed reading involves students in listening to a text read aloud by the teacher and then rereading the text or part of it with a partner.

1. As part of your small-group instruction, read aloud a text or passage that you know will be appropriately challenging for the participating students. Demonstrate how you solve potentially difficult words and use context to confirm or self-correct. This reading *primes* the students for reading the material on their own.

2. Pair each student with a partner and ask that each child reread the text/part aloud to the other, supporting one another to use context or closely examine word parts.

3. Finally (usually the next time the small group meets), allow volunteers to take turns reading the text/part with high expression as the others follow along.

Independent Application

Independent Reading: Grades K–5

Independent reading correlates positively with reading achievement. The more time students spend reading, the more fluent they become (Anderson, Fielding, and Wilson 1988). Independent reading works best when it is closely monitored and scheduled on a regular basis. The goals are for students to deeply engage and to read extensively. To organize beneficial sessions, you can do the following:

- Gather a collection of books on topics you know will interest your students. Let them choose. Capturing their interest will support their motivation and give them the impetus to push through any difficult material they may encounter.

- See that each student finds text that is accessible. Having books that can be decoded with relative ease helps readers to firm up their word knowledge and develop their fluency (Allington 2006).

- When considering text levels, keep in mind that along with difficulty, the particular student's motivations and the context for reading will have an impact on the degree of success (Glasswell and Ford 2011). Avoid letting *level* dictate what students may choose.

- Monitor to see that students are engaged. Observing during independent reading can involve quick over-the-shoulder conferences in which you listen to children reading short sections of text or talk with them about content. You can use Figure RFS 4.1 to document your observations.

Listening Center: Grades K–5

Research shows that listening to a text while following along with the print enhances comprehension and supports children's development of the skills and strategies that make fluency possible (Opitz and Rasinski 1998). To prepare a *listening center*, set up a group area that includes audio recordings of picture books, the matching text, and headphones. Storyline Online (www.storylineonline.net) is an excellent website to use for a listening center, as it features professional actors reading high-quality picture books and also includes streaming video and subtitles.

To introduce the listening center, select one of the listening/reading experiences listed below. Show the students what is expected and use this center throughout the year, introducing new experiences over time.

- Listen and follow along with the printed text.

- Listen and then draw something you learned or found interesting.

- As you listen, draw pictures related to the text. Afterward, share what you have drawn.

- Listen to the beginning of a story and draw how you think it will end.

- Listen and then retell the piece with your group or partner.

- Follow along with the printed text. Then read the text aloud with a partner, taking turns reading every other page.

- Choose one of the texts and read it aloud into a recorder. Listen to the recording.

- Choose one of the texts and practice reading it aloud into the recorder. Listen to the recording, thinking about how to read more expressively. Record yourself again.

Repeated Reading: Grades K–5

Repeated reading is widely recognized as a helpful way to support fluency, including for English learners. To implement this practice, arrange for repeated reading of familiar texts to occur any time throughout the day. Independent reading time is a good time to support repeated reading. Students may read texts that have been used for instruction or texts you have read aloud. To work toward motivation and extended reading, allow children to choose their favorites.

Poetry Podcasts: Grades K–5

Each student audio records a favorite poem for peers to listen to, creating a class audio anthology. (Video may also be used.) Before recording, provide class time for students to practice in teams and allow students to take home a copy of the poem for additional practice. Make available a collective hard copy of all poems and keep it near the listening center so that students may follow along if they wish.

Reading at Home: Grades K–5

Reading at home is a form of homework that can be enjoyable for students and highly facilitative of their developing fluency. Figure RFS 4.2 provides a form for family-teacher communication regarding reading at home.

Reading at Home

Name: _____ Date: _____

Please work with your child to read *five times* over the course of the week and weekend. Use the chart below to record the important aspects of literacy your child exhibited. Encouraging all of these over time will support your child's development as a reader.

Book Titles ➡ If the child is reading a chapter book, record the page numbers.					
My child listened to someone read.					
My child read the book independently.					
My child read the book (or parts) more than one time.					
My child discussed the book.					
My child retold parts (or all) in his/her own words.					
My child asked questions.					
My child talked about some of the words.					
My child seemed to enjoy the experience.					

Allington, R. 2001. *What Really Matters for Struggling Readers: Designing Research-Based Programs.* New York: Longman.

———. 2002. "What I've Learned About Effective Reading Instruction from a Decade of Studying Exemplary Elementary Classroom Teachers." *Phi Delta Kappan* 83 (10): 740–47.

———. 2006. *What Really Matters for Struggling Readers: Designing Research-Based Programs,* 2d ed. New York: Longman.

———. 2009. *What Really Matters in Response to Intervention: Research-Based Designs.* Boston: Allyn & Bacon.

———. 2012. *What Really Matters for Struggling Readers: Designing Research-Based Programs,* 3d ed. New York: Longman.

Anderson, R. C., L. G. Fielding, and P. T. Wilson. 1988. "Growth in Reading and How Children Spend Their Time Outside of School." *Reading Research Quarterly* 23: 285–304.

Applegate, A., and M. Applegate. 2010/2011. "A Study of Thoughtful Literacy and the Motivation to Read." *The Reading Teacher* 64 (4): 226–34.

Applegate, M., A. Applegate, and V. Modla. 2009. "'She's My Best Reader; She Just Can't Comprehend': Studying the Relationship Between Fluency and Comprehending." *The Reading Teacher* 62 (6): 512–21.

Bang, M. 2000. *Picture This: How Pictures Work.* New York: Seastar.

Boulware-Gooden, R., S. Carreker, A. Thornhill, and R. Joshi. 2007. "Instruction of Metacognitive Strategies Enhances Reading Comprehension and Vocabulary Achievement of Third-Grade Students." *The Reading Teacher* 61 (1): 70–73, 75–77.

Braunger, J., and J. Lewis. 2006. *Building a Knowledge Base in Reading.* Urbana, IL: National Council of Teachers of English.

Brown, T. 2010–2011. "Learning to Read: The Unofficial Scripts of Succeeders and Strugglers." *The Reading Teacher* 64 (4): 267–71.

Brozo, W., and E. Flynt. 2008. "Motivating Students to Read in the Content Classroom: Six Evidence-Based Principles." *The Reading Teacher* 62 (2): 172–74. Retrieved May 5, 2011, from Research Library (Document ID: 1575025311).

Burke, J. 1998. "103 Things to Do Before/During/After Reading." *Reading Rockets.* Available at www.readingrockets.org/article/82/. Accessed 11/21/11.

Caldwell, J., and L. Leslie. 2009. *Intervention Strategies to Follow Informal Reading Inventory Assessment: So What Do I Do Now?* Boston: Pearson.

Calkins, L. 2001. *The Art of Teaching Reading.* New York: Longman.

Chinn, C., and R. Anderson. 1998. "The Structure of Discussions that Promote Reasoning." *Teachers College Record* 100 (2): 315–68.

Clay, M. 1975. *What Did I Write?* Auckland, NZ: Heinemann.

———. 1991. *Becoming Literate: The Construction of Inner Control.* Portsmouth, NH: Heinemann.

Cunningham, P., and R. Allington. 2011. *Classrooms That Work: They Can All Read and Write.* Boston: Allyn & Bacon.

Dalton, B., and D. Grisham. 2011. "eVoc Strategies: 10 Ways to Use Technology to Build Vocabulary." *The Reading Teacher* 64 (5): 306–17.

Dudley-Marling, C., and P. Paugh. 2004. *A Classroom Teacher's Guide to Struggling Readers*. Portsmouth, NH: Heinemann.

Duke, N. 2000. "3.6 Minutes per Day: The Scarcity of Informational Texts in First Grade." *Reading Research Quarterly* 35: 202–24.

———. 2004. "The Case for Informational Text." *Educational Leadership* 61 (6): 40–44.

Duke, N., V. Purcell-Gates, L. Hall, and C. Tower. 2006. "Authentic Literacy Activities for Developing Comprehension and Writing." *The Reading Teacher* 60 (4): 344–52.

Dymock, S., and T. Nicholson. 2010. "'High 5!' Strategies to Enhance Comprehension of Expository Text." *The Reading Teacher* 64 (3): 166–78.

Dyson, A. 1989. *Multiple Worlds of Child Writers*. New York: Teachers College Press.

Echevarria, J. 2006. "Helping English Language Learners Succeed." *Principal Leadership (Middle School Edition)* 6 (6): 16–21.

Fountas, I., and G. Pinnell. 2006. *Leveled Books: Matching Texts to Readers for Effective Teaching*. Portsmouth, NH: Heinemann.

Gainer, J., and D. Lapp. 2010. *Literacy Remix: Bridging Adolescents' In and Out of School Literacies*. Newark, DE: International Reading Association.

Gersten, R., S. Baker, T, Shanahan, S. Linan-Thompson, P. Collins, and R. Scarcella. 2007. "Effective Literacy and English Language Instruction for English Learners in the Elementary Classroom: A Practice Guide." Washington, DC: National Center for Education Evaluation and Regional Assistance, Institute of Education Sciences, U.S. Department of Education.

Glasswell, K., and M. Ford. 2011. "Let's Start Leveling About Leveling." *Language Arts* 88 (3): 208–16.

Goodman, Y. 1996. *Notes from a Kidwatcher*. Portsmouth, NH: Heinemann.

Goodman, Y., and A. Marek. 1996. *Retrospective Miscue Analysis*. Katonah, NY: Richard C. Owen.

Goodman, Y., D. Watson, and C. Burke. 2005. *Reading Strategies: Focus on Comprehension*, 2d ed. Katonah, NY: Richard C. Owen.

Graves, M., and S. Watts-Taffe. 2008. "For the Love of Words: Fostering Word Consciousness in Young Readers." *The Reading Teacher* 62 (3): 185–93.

Griffin, M. 2002. "Why Don't You Use Your Finger? Paired Reading in First Grade." *The Reading Teacher* 55: 766–74.

Guthrie, J., and M. Davis. 2003. "Motivating Struggling Readers in Middle School Through an Engagement Model of Classroom Practice." *Reading & Writing Quarterly* 19 (1): 59–85.

Guthrie, J., and A. Wigfield. 2000. "Engagement and Motivation in Reading." In *Handbook of Reading Research*, Vol. 3, edited by M. Kamil, P. Mosenthal, P. Pearson, and R. Barr, 403–22. New York: Erlbaum.

Harste, J., C. Burke, and V. Woodward. 1981. *Children, Their Language and World: Initial Encounters with Print*. (Project NIE-G-79-0132). National Institute of Education.

Harvey, S., and A. Goudvis. 2000. *Strategies That Work: Teaching Comprehension to Enhance Understanding*. Portland, ME: Stenhouse.

Hiebert, E., S. J. Samuels, and T. Rasinski. In press. "Comprehension-Based Silent Reading Rates: What Do We Know? What Do We Need to Know?" *Literacy Research and Instruction*. Available at http://textproject.org/assets/library/papers/Hiebert-Samuels-RasinskiComprehension-Based-Silent-Reading-Rates-PREPRINT.pdf. Accessed 12/14/11.

Jitendra, A., L. Edwards, G. Sachs, and L. Jacobson. 2004. "What Research Says About Vocabulary Instruction for Students with Learning Disabilities." *Exceptional Children* 70 (3): 299–322.

Keene, E. 2008. *To Understand: New Horizons in Reading Comprehension*. Portsmouth, NH: Heinemann.

Keene, E., and S. Zimmermann. 2007. *Mosaic of Thought: Teaching Comprehension in a Reader's Workshop*, 2d ed. Portsmouth, NH: Heinemann.

Knobel, M., and C. Lankshear. 2008. "Remix: The Art and Craft of Endless Hybridization." *Journal of Adolescent and Adult Literacy* 51 (1): 22–33.

Kohl, H. 1999. *A Grain of Poetry: How to Read Contemporary Poems and Make Them a Part of Your Life*. New York: HarperFlamingo.

Krashen, S. 1993. *The Power of Reading: Insights from the Research*. Englewood, CO: Libraries Unlimited.

———. 2009. "Anything But Reading." *Knowledge Quest* 37 (5): 18–25.

Leu, D. J. Jr., C. K. Kinzer, J. Coiro, and D. W. Cammack. 2004. "Toward a Theory of New Literacies Emerging from the Internet and Other Information and Communication Technologies." In *Theoretical Models and Processes of Reading*, 5th ed., edited by R. B. Ruddell and N. Unrau, 1570–613. Newark, DE: International Reading Association.

Manning, M., S. Chumley, and C. Underbakke. 2006. *Scientific Reading Assessment: Targeted Intervention and Follow-Up Lessons*. Portsmouth, NH: Heinemann.

Manyak, P. 2008. "Phonemes in Use: Multiple Activities for a Critical Process." *The Reading Teacher* 6 (18): 659–62.

Martens, P. 1997. *I Already Know How to Read: A Child's View of Literacy*. Portsmouth, NH: Heinemann.

McCarthy, P. 2008/2009. "Using Sound Boxes Systematically to Develop Phonemic Awareness." *The Reading Teacher* 62 (4): 346–49.

Meier, D. 2004. *The Young Child's Memory for Words: Developing First and Second Language and Literacy*. New York: Teachers College Press.

Meisinger, E., P. Schwanenflugel, B. Bradley, and S. Stahl. 2004. "Interaction Quality During Partner Reading." *Journal of Literacy Research* 36: 111–40.

Mesmer, H., and S. Cuming. 2009. "Text-Reader Matching: Matching the Needs of Struggling Readers." In *Finding the Right Texts: What Works for Beginning and Struggling Readers*, edited by E. Hiebert and M. Sailors, 149–76. New York: Guilford.

Mohr, K. 2006. "Children's Choices for Recreational Reading: A Three-Part Investigation of Selection Preferences, Rationales, and Processes." *Journal of Literacy Research* 38: 81–104.

Nagy, W., R. Anderson, and P. Herman. 1987. "Learning Word Meanings from Context During Normal Reading." *American Educational Research Journal* 24: 237–70.

Nathan, R., and K. Stanovich. 1991. "The Causes and Consequences of Differences in Reading Fluency." *Theory into Practice* 30: 176–84.

National Governors Association Center for Best Practices and Council of Chief State School Officers. 2010. Common Core State Standards. Available at www.corestandards.org/ Accessed 11/21/11.

National Reading Panel. 2000. *Teaching Children to Read: An Evidenced-Based Assessment of the Scientific Research Literature on Reading and Its Implications for Reading Instruction*. Washington, DC: National Institute of Child Health and Human Development.

Norton, D. 2011. *Through the Eyes of a Child*. Boston: Allyn & Bacon.

Opitz, M., and T. Rasinski. 1998. *Good-Bye Round Robin: 25 Effective Oral Reading Strategies*. Portsmouth, NH: Heinemann.

Powell, D., and R. Aram. 2008. "Spelling in Parts: A Strategy for Spelling and Decoding Polysyllabic Words." *The Reading Teacher* 61 (7): 567–70.

Rasinski, T., N. Padak, W. Linek, and E. Sturtevant. 1994. "Effects of Fluency Development on Urban Second-Grade Readers". *Journal of Educational Research* 87: 158–65.

Rea, D., and S. Mercuri. 2006. *Research-Based Strategies for English Language Learners*. Portsmouth, NH: Heinemann.

Reutzel, D., C. D. Jones, and T. H. Newman. 2010. "Scaffolded Silent Reading: Improving the Conditions of Silent Reading Practice in Classrooms." In *Revisiting Silent Reading*, edited by E. H. Hiebert and D. Reutzel, 129–50. Newark, DE: International Reading Association.

Rowe, D. 2008. "Social Contracts for Writing: Negotiating Shared Understandings About Text in the Preschool Years." *Reading Research Quarterly* 43 (1): 66–95.

Santori, D. 2011. "'Search for the Answers' or 'Talk About the Story'? School-Based Literacy Participation Structures." *Language Arts* 88 (3): 198–207.

Scott, J., and W. Nagy. 2004. "Developing Word Consciousness." In *Vocabulary Instruction: Theory to Practice*, edited by F. Baumann and E. Kame'enui, 210–17. New York: Guilford.

Short, D., and I. Echevarria. 2005. "Teacher Skills to Support English Language Learners." *Educational Leadership* 62: 8–13.

Short, K., J. Harste, and C. Burke. 1996. *Creating Classrooms for Authors and Inquirers.* Portsmouth, NH: Heinemann.

Strickland, K. 2005. *What's After Assessment?* Portsmouth, NH: Heinemann.

Taboada, A., S. Tonks, A. Wigfield, and J. Guthrie. 2009. "Effects of Motivational and Cognitive Variables on Reading Comprehension." *Read Writ* 22: 85–106.

Tompkins, G. 2001. "Video: Guidelines for Reading Comprehension Instruction." Upper Saddle River, NJ: Merrill.

———. 2011. *Literacy in the Early Grades.* Boston: Allyn & Bacon.

Stanovich, K. 1986. "Matthew Effects in Reading: Some Consequences of Individual Differences in the Acquisition of Literacy." *Reading Research Quarterly* 21: 360–407.

Valencia, S., and M. Buly. 2005. "Behind Test Scores: What Struggling Readers Really Need." In *Reading Assessment: Principles and Practices for Elementary Teachers*, 2d ed., edited by S. Barrentine and S. Stokes, 134–46. Newark, DE: International Reading Association.

Vygotsky, L. 1978. *Mind in Society: The Development of Higher Psychological Processes*, edited by M. Cole, V. John-Steiner, S. Scribner, and E. Souberman. Cambridge, MA: Harvard University Press.

Wade, S., and E. Moje. 2001. "The Role of Text in Classroom Learning: Beginning an Online Dialogue." *Reading Online 5* (4). Available at www.readingonline.org/articles/art_index.asp?HREF=/articles/handbook/wade/index.html. Accessed 12/14/11.

Walsh, B. A. 2008. "Quantity, Quality, Children's Characteristics, and Vocabulary Learning." *Childhood Education* 84 (3): 163–64.

White, T., J. Sowell, and A. Yanagihara. 1989. "Teaching Elementary Students to Use Word-Part Clues." *The Reading Teacher* 42: 302–309.

Wohlwend, K. E. 2007. "Playing to Read and Reading to Play: A Mediated Discourse Analysis of Early Literacy Apprenticeship." In *57th Yearbook of the National Reading Conference*, edited by D. W. Rowe, R. Jiménez, D. Compton, D. K. Dickinson, Y. Kim, K. M. Leander, and V. J. Risko, 377–93. Oak Creek, WI: National Reading Conference.

Wong, H., and R. Wong. 2010. *Developing and Retaining Effective Teachers and Principals.* Available at www.effectiveteaching.com/pdf/DevelopingandRetaining.pdf. Accessed 12/14/11.

Wylie, R., and D. Durrell. 1970. "Teaching Vowels Through Phonograms." *Elementary English* 47: 787–91.

Yopp, R., and H. Yopp, H. 2003. "Ten Important Words: Identifying the Big Ideas in Informational Text." *Journal of Content Area Reading* 2: 7–13.

———. 2007. "Ten Important Words Plus: A Strategy for Building Word Knowledge." *The Reading Teacher* 61 (2): 157–60.

Zawilinski, L. 2009. "HOT Blogging: A Framework for Blogging to Promote Higher Order Thinking." *Reading Teacher* 62 (8): 650–61.